2

The Saddled Cow

The Saddled Cow

East Germany's Life and Legacy

Anne McElvoy

faber and faber

LONDON · BOSTON

First published in 1992
by Faber and Faber Limited
3 Queen Square London WC1N 3AU

Photoset by Parker Typesetting Service, Leicester
Printed in England by Clays Ltd, St Ives plc

A CIP record for this book is available from the British Library

ISBN 0-571-16591-5

For my mother and father

One of the prisoners ventured the view that Germany after the war would surrender so completely to communism that it would become a communist state and then seek to assume control of the world. Stalin's reply was spontaneous. 'Communism fits Germany as a saddle fits a cow,' he said.

Stanislav Mikolajczyk, head of the Polish government in exile,
recalling a conversation with Stalin, 1944

Our tables will be decked with the best nature has to offer: with meat and milk products of the highest quality, rare vegetables and the finest fruits – early raspberries and tomatoes in and out of season, grapes in winter ... Socialist society will within a few decades be not only prosperous, but wealthy, and will guarantee a life in which no sensible wish will go unfulfilled.

Walter Ulbricht, *Our World of Tomorrow*, 1961

The winning side pleased the Gods, the losing side pleased Cato.

Lucan *Pharasalia*

Contents

Acknowledgements

My deepest gratitude is due to those East Germans who became my friends when it was not without risk for them to meet and correspond with me, and whose spirit encouraged me to explore their country in both its geographical and spiritual nooks and crannies. They are too numerous to list, but Matthias Müller in East Berlin and Burkhardt Kolbmüller in Leipzig deserve special thanks for their hospitality and patience with my questions over many years.

Professor Jürgen Kuczynski has always kept his door open to me. My respect too for his not objecting too vociferously to my interpretation of his life, although he heartily disagrees with it. Günter Schabowski engaged in time-consuming reconstructions and satisfied my curiosity for tales of life in the Politburo. Professor Wolfgang Leonhard assisted with recollections of the Moscow period and the early years.

My thanks to the Committee for the Dissolution of the State Security Service for allowing me access to its records and guiding me through the labyrinth of the Stasi's obsessive filing system, and also to the archives of East German television. The Deutschlandarchiv in Cologne has been unstinting in its assistance to East German researchers for many years and deserves recognition for the splendid service it has provided.

Cornelia Rudat kept a semblance of order in *The Times* Berlin office while this was in progress, and complied without demur with the most abstruse of research requests. Thanks also to Jörg Sohst for much help and to Reiner Oschmann for his enthusiasm and co-operation from the beginning.

I am indebted to Simon Jenkins, editor of *The Times*, and Martin Ivens, foreign editor, without whose support and flexibility the project would have been impossible. Daniel Johnson read most of the text and supplied invaluable corrections and wise advice.

Thanks are due to Suhrkamp for permission to quote from Bertolt

Brecht. The translations are those of John Willett and Ralph Mannheim, from Bertolt Brecht's *Poems*, published in English by Methuen.

Natasha Fairweather was a splendid agent. Susanne McDadd and Julian Loose at Faber and Faber were the gentlest of bullies in keeping my nose to the keyboard and in supplying sound advice on my first venture between hard covers.

To Philip for comfort, commas and much more, thank you.

Introduction

When I arrived in East Germany for my first extensive stay in 1986, I was escorted through Berlin's divided Friedrichstrasse station by a man from the People's Solidarity League. He enjoyed his job, he said, because it meant that he got to the West once every few months to pick up visiting 'guests of the state'. What he meant by the west was a waiting-room on the other side of the tracks. He had long stopped imagining what lay beyond the station other than the poverty, homelessness and violence described by the East's media. He had no desire to go any further.

To cross the border from West to East in those days was like a foray into Germany's forgotten attic. The station was as the war had left it, the air heavy with diesel fumes and the sour, metallic smell of antiquated heavy industry. Billboards urged East Germans to 'travel with the Soviet railway system' but then again, they had precious little choice of travelling with anyone else's.

The Wall looked unbreachable, the government of Erich Honecker unassailable. There was still a stubborn pride in the achievements of the country which contrasted with the stoical resignation one encountered in Poland, Czechoslovakia and Hungary. In the course of the year, I was to witness the first cracks in the monolith as the reforms of Mikhail Gorbachev began to catch the imagination of the people and awaken their appetite for change.

My first lecture at Humboldt University introduced me to an ideology and a vocabulary which was a mirror image of the one I knew from West Germany. The 'Wall of Shame' became 'the anti-fascist protective barrier', the 'communist dictatorship' the 'political expression of the will of the working people'. The country's ideology chief, Kurt Hager, faced with the Soviet reforms, commented that, just because your neighbour had changed his wallpaper, there was no need to start tearing off your own.

Now there is nothing left to redecorate. The house that Walter Ulbricht built and Erich Honecker maintained has fallen down, and with it the dreams and delusions of its architects. The Wall has disappeared so completely that the Berlin Senate has had to declare the few sections left standing a protected monument. For 16 million people, not only their state but their entire realm of experience came to an end when the 'other Germany' which had existed for forty years collapsed unceremoniously in two months.

Forty years: longer than the Weimar Republic and the Third Reich added together. Long enough for an entire generation to be born into half a country masquerading as a state. Long enough to be deemed stable by the West and calculated by strategists as a solid fixture on the map. Few doubted that one day there would be a united Germany again, it was just that no one could envisage what it would take to achieve the reunion. The optimists spoke of convergence, the pessimists of war. Only the outlandish few believed that it would simply collapse, politically exhausted and economically rotten, into the arms of the West without even a struggle. I cannot claim to have been one of them, which made the experience of charting the decline and fall of the state in 1989, the emergence of the united Germany in 1990 and the teething troubles of unity, in my role as *The Times*'s Berlin correspondent, all the more exhilarating.

East Germany no longer exists, but the unified Germany will take a long time to cope with the legacy of division and the vestiges of the old order. Like two sides of a long-separated family, both Germanies are having to get to know each other once again. The joy of rediscovery is over. Acceptance of each other's customs, foibles and attitudes will be a lengthy task, the dimensions of which have been greatly underestimated by both parties.

To understand the new Germany, it is essential to explore the old. To dwell, as Cato under Caesar, on the story of the losing side and the reasons for its defeat should help us interpret not only Germany's recent past but also its present, as it becomes accustomed to its role as uncertain giant in the heart of Europe.

There were many shortages in East Germany, but no lack of eccentric, gifted and ludicrous characters who shaped its fate. For this reason I have based much of this account on studying and, where possible, interviewing the people who were instrumental in or affected by events there. Some were the victims of dictatorship, some its perpetrators: many were both at once.

The Saddled Cow makes no pretence to the exhaustiveness of academic history, but attempts to cover the key periods in the country's development and those aspects of life behind the Wall which have absorbed me over many years, be they major political chapters or individual fates. It is shamelessly subjective and selective, but aims to provide as wide a picture as possible of what this strange, unloved country was like, from its beginnings in the chaos of the defeat of fascism, to its end in the unification of Germany and beyond, as its people come to terms with life in the West.

The complicated nature of Germany's recent history is well expressed by the names applied to it. Generally, I have used East and West Germany to refer to the two states which existed from their respective foundations in 1949 until 3 October 1990. Thereafter I have called them east or west Germany to distinguish what are still very different societies with their own preoccupations and problems. In quotations, or where it was necessary for clarity, I have used the official titles of the two former countries as the Federal Republic of Germany (FRG) and the German Democratic Republic (GDR).

I

Arisen from Ruins

It should look democratic, but we must have everything in hand.

Walter Ulbricht, May 1945

The German Democratic Republic was a child of chaos, sired by National Socialism, mothered by Stalinism and destined for a short but eventful life.

Five months after the founding of the Federal Republic, the political parties of the Soviet Zone gathered on 7 October 1949 in Goering's cavernous former air ministry amid the rubble in the heart of Berlin. With the cry '*Es lebe Deutschland*' the socialist German state, in effect a Soviet satellite, was born. It could scarcely have been a more poorly-chosen slogan: the transition of the Soviet Zone to a separate state effectively ended strivings to maintain a single Germany.

For the communists who made up the majority of the revellers, this day was the fulfilment of hopes cherished throughout the years spent in exile, in the underground or in Nazi prisons and concentration camps. Together with the Social Democrats – who had merged with them three years earlier to form the Socialist Unity Party – and the token Christian Democrats and Liberals, they streamed from the building in a procession intended to display the unity of forces behind the new German state.

The elderly communist Wilhelm Pieck, the state's new President, was driven standing in an open car through Berlin, triumphant if a touch unsteady on his feet. Thousands of young people in the blue and yellow uniform of the mass Free German Youth movement held a torchlight procession through the darkened streets and enjoined the new state to strive 'towards a new dawn'.

While Stalin sent a telegram greeting the day as 'a turning-point in the history of Europe', the West German *Wochenschau* newsreel commented

I

that the celebrations were ominously reminiscent of the not too distant past. Other western countries simply ignored the event completely. As the foundation had been a rushed affair, the country did not have its own anthem until a month later. A competition was held, and was won by the poet Johannes R. Becher, later to become the country's first minister of culture, with music by Hanns Eisler:

> Auferstanden aus Ruinen
> Und der Zukunft zugewandt
> Lass uns dir zum Guten dienen
> Deutschland einig Vaterland.
> (Arisen from ruins
> Our faces turned towards the future
> Let us serve you for the good
> Germany, one fatherland.)

Germany had its first socialist state, the frontier of Soviet communism pushed to its most westerly limit. Five years earlier Stalin had dismissed the notion of a communist Germany, telling the exiled Polish leader Stanislav Mikolajczyk in 1944, 'Communism fits Germany like a saddle fits a cow'. Now the reluctant beast was firmly under the yoke.

With the creation of a Soviet satellite on German soil, the intricate history of Russian-German relations had taken a new and unexpected turn. Stalin's intentions after the defeat of Hitler were increased co-operation with the Western powers, a neutral Germany which he hoped might eventually incline towards Bolshevism, and a favourable economic deal on reparations from the defeated power. These goals appealed to the Soviet dictator, who feared a revival of German might and influence and wanted to isolate the country while it was still sapped of confidence by defeat to prevent it joining the Western Alliance later.

The pragmatic Stalin had no objections to Germany remaining capi-talist, as long as he could prevent it joining hands with America, giving the USA influence over the heart of Europe. Closer to home, he also needed funds to revive the exhausted Soviet Union and hoped to use the industrial Ruhr heartland to provide them. All of these aims presumed that Germany would remain united.

In May 1949, the integration of the British, American and French zones was sealed with the foundation of the Federal Republic of Germany, the result of a change of heart by the Western Allies, particularly the Americans, about the practicability of co-operating with Stalin and the hardening of the fronts between capitalism and communism, most visibly in Berlin. The ill-conceived Soviet attempt to erase 'the anomaly' of West Berlin by force, in the blockade which began in June 1948, had strengthened its resolve not to be subsumed into Moscow's sphere of influence.

The airlift which saved the city changed the nature of the relationship between West Germany and the USA. Victors became protectors. The blockade was a major tactical mistake by the Soviets as it focused the attentions and sympathies of the western world on the plight of the city. When the ruling mayor, Ernst Reuter, stood up before the Brandenburg Gate in June 1948 and thundered, 'Ye peoples of the earth, look upon this city', his message struck home to the governments of Washington, London and Paris. West Berlin was to be preserved at any cost.

The foundation of the German Democratic Republic followed close on the heels of the Federal Republic's inception. Wilhelm Pieck's role as president was largely symbolic. The real power broker was the Socialist Unity Party's leader Walter Ulbricht, a calculating *apparatchik* primed for power in Soviet exile and already showing dictatorial tendencies. The gentler Otto Grotewohl, who had joined the party from the ranks of the Social Democrats, was appointed prime minister as a concession to the old SPD members.

The accession to the Soviet family of the smaller, poorer part of Germany was not the outcome Stalin had hoped for, but it had its compensations. It provided a victory for the Soviet Union in the centuries-old battle for supremacy of ideas and military might between Russia and Germany. The triumph over Hitler's Germany had only latterly become identified as the defeat of fascism, whose pernicious nature was understood belatedly in Moscow. Stalin, after all, had not entered the war with Germany to liberate the concentration camps and restore human rights, but because he was forced to do so by Hitler's attack. The Red Army was in no doubt, when the Red Flag was placed atop the Brandenburg Gate in May 1945, that it was Germany that had been conquered, not merely Hitler.

East Germany was a strange synthesis of the love-hate German-Russo relationship which had pertained since the eighteenth century. It was the fatal attraction of great rivals which led Stalin to remark that Hitlers came and went, but Germany and the German people remained. The two countries had a long-established mutual interest in good relations. Bismarck's coalition with Russia had been the guarantee of German unity in 1871. Many German historians saw the lapse of the German-Russian alliance when Bismarck fell from power in 1890 as the mistake which had unleashed misfortune on the country. The post-1850 *Osto-rientierung* (eastern orientation) pertained across the political spectrum, with even the Russian Bolsheviks initially attaching greater significance to a German Revolution than their own. Dostoevsky had the measure of it when he wrote that Germany counted on Russia 'not as a temporary, but as an eternal ally'. In the years leading up to the Bolshevik Revolution, 60 per cent of all German investment exports went to Russia.

The convergence of interests and bilateral deals which have marked Russo-German relations can be charted back to before the Napoleonic wars. Catherine the Great was a German, Queen Luise of Prussia had attempted to gain Alexander I's support against Napoleon after Prussia's heavy defeat in 1806. At Tauroggen in 1812, units of the Prussian army under the leadership of General Yorck, sensing that Napoleon's fortunes were waning, made an agreement against the King's orders with the enemy Tsar. In 1918, the Bolsheviks concluded a separate peace accord with Germany before the end of the war when Trotsky signed the Treaty of Brest–Litovsk, an unhappy agreement which, while it saved the Russians from further losses in the east, conceded a large part of western Russia to Germany and freed the Germans to pursue their objectives on the western front.

Brest–Litovsk led the West to the view that the Bolsheviks were little more than German agents and cemented the view of Russia as a treacherous ally. It was an impression which deepened when, four years later, the Treaty of Rapallo was signed without prior announcement at an international economic conference in Genoa. Superficially, it declared no more than the establishment of diplomatic relations and favoured-nation trading status between Germany and Bolshevik Russia. In fact, it also formalized German-Russian military co-operation, by which the Reichswehr could circumvent the military restrictions prescribed by the Treaty of Versailles.

In 1939 followed the notorious Hitler-Stalin pact; and latterly, under more propitious global circumstances, came the meeting between Helmut Kohl and Mikhail Gorbachev in Shelesnovodsk in the Caucasus in July 1990, to approve NATO membership for a united Germany. All these agreements have a single factor in common: they were contracted by the two sides without reference to their respective allies and are as such examples of the German tradition of *Alleingang* – going it alone – and the Russian tendency to tie its interest to a single mighty partner.

But while both sides perceived the need for co-operation, the relationship was continually plagued by misunderstanding. For Russia, which had never had a middle class of political significance until the emergence of Lenin and his followers in the last years of the Tsar, the dominance of bourgeois thinking in Germany was anathema to the governing nobles. In his between-the-wars novel, *The Magic Mountain*, Thomas Mann returned to the theme of alienation between the two cultures in the encounter of the exotic Russian Madame Chauchat with her middle-class German admirer Hans Castorp. Hans asks her if she considers the Germans pedantic and gets the damning, bi-lingual reply, 'Mais c'est vrai. You are a little bourgeois. Vous aimez l'ordre mieux que la liberté, toute l'Europe le sait.'

Perhaps Mme Chauchat's diagnosis explains why, after the fall of Hitler, eastern Germany was swallowed into the Soviet bloc with relatively little resistance from its own citizens and uncomfortable acceptance in western Germany. Despite its protests, West Germany's priority was to live in prosperity rather than unity, while East Germany grudgingly accepted a revolution by command. As Mme Chauchat would undoubtedly have remarked, what could one expect? Order was to be more highly valued than liberty in the Germany of the immediate post-war period.

If the German Democratic Republic lurched to its feet in 1949, its prehistory was a lengthy affair. The abortive socialist republic declared by Karl Liebknecht from the balcony of the Berlin Stadtschloss in the chaos of November 1918 and the short-lived 'soviet republics' of Bremen and Munich had kindled the dream on the left of a socialist Germany. But by the mid-thirties, following Hitler's ascent to power, the emigration of German communists was in full flow. The most politically motivated were dispatched by the Party to the Soviet Union, although rumours of the purges meant that Jews were often sent elsewhere. Its more liberal intellectuals chose Britain, France or, until the 1939 occupation of Prague, Czechoslovakia. A handful of the more adventurous comrades, mainly journalists and film-makers, went to America. Even for non-Jews, the Soviet Union was anything but a cosy haven from persecution. Stalin's xenophobia and paranoia about plots against him, combined with traditional misunderstanding and distrust of the Germans, made the new arrivals natural targets of suspicion.

Wolfgang Leonhard is one of only two surviving members of the original Ulbricht Group, the first German exiles to return to the Soviet Zone on 30 April 1945 under Walter Ulbricht's stewardship, and entrusted by Moscow with setting up political structures in the East. As a thirteen-year-old, he had fled with his communist mother Susanne to

5

Moscow. Now he is one of Germany's most respected Soviet experts and a former Professor of History at Yale. When we arranged to meet in Mainz to discuss his life, he gave instructions which included the fact that the train from the airport would take twenty-eight minutes. I could not suppress the observation that it was very German to know exactly how long a train journey took. 'Yes,' he sighed, 'The terrible exactitude of the German and the Stalinist are impossible to root out of oneself. We were doubly inculcated.'

He was fourteen when he looked at the six-page *Pravda* of 12 June 1937. Five of the pages were taken up with the account of an alleged Red Army conspiracy under the headline 'Spies, Contemptible Mercenaries of Fascism, Traitors to the Fatherland: Shoot Them!' His own mother, a stalwart of the old German communist movement, had been arrested shortly before. By 1937 the purges had reached the Karl Liebknecht school for the children of German emigrants. The atmosphere at the school is nowhere better described than in his autobiography *The Revolution Dismisses Its Children*:

Once during a lesson in government studies when the teacher, exuding the compulsory enthusiasm, was speaking of the democratic character of the constitution and the unity of morality and politics among the Soviet people, he wanted to crown his exegesis with Stalin's well-known saying: 'Those who try to attack our country will receive such a devastating rebuff that they will lose any future desires to poke their swines' noses into our Soviet garden.' Here, of all places, he mixed up his words and pronounced, 'they will lose any future desire to poke their Soviet noses into our swines' garden'. A few seconds later, the teacher realized his mistake, turned chalk white and his whole body trembled ... We knew that this meant the end for him, that he would have to report what had happened to the Party. A few days later he disappeared. We never saw or heard of him again.

Those who showed promise there were selected for the Comintern school based in Ufa, in the remote autonomous republic of Bashkirya. Intended to school young communists for positions of leadership or opposition in their own countries, it provided the harshest training in underground methods and the most undiluted indoctrination on offer anywhere in the world. The young communists were given pseudonyms and ordered never to reveal their real names. Alcohol and relations with the opposite sex were banned.

'Whenever there was any sign of that sort of thing a lecturer would produce a deterrent example of an underground operation which had failed because someone had fallen in love,' Leonhard recalls. The days were punctuated by exercises in 'self-criticism', based on denunciation by one's classmates. Those who failed to satisfy the criteria were dropped by the Party and turfed out of the school, left to fend for themselves in wartime Russia. Leonhard remembers encountering a former Comintern pupil roaming the streets of Ufa in rags after being expelled from the school. The man asked him to smuggle a slice of bread out of the dining-room for him.

Life in this most repressive of boarding-school regimes was governed by rules which were neither explained nor questioned. The young people led a monastic life of unrelenting puritanism, relieved by occasional stiff attempts at recreation and relaxation which, as Leonhard recalls them, sound even worse than the daily regime. On New Year's Eve 1942, the young men and women were called together for a rare celebration. It began with the unpromising declaration, 'I think we can now begin our sociable evening. The comrades may sit at the tables', and consisted of tea and stifled conversation. 'The extraordinary conditions in which we lived did not allow for friendship or cosiness. Distrust and fear were second nature to us,' says Leonhard. 'It was only later that I realized that this evening was not an isolated occurrence. Other "sociable evenings" with highly-placed functionaries – particularly those who had spent many years in the Soviet Union – were much the same.'

The school's single aim was to strip its pupils of all sensibilities, bar an unwavering commitment to the cause of Soviet communism. It has been said that few left it with their personality intact, and those who did were probably considered failures. Certainly it – and its successor institution, the Party School in which the next generation of politicians were trained – turned out a certain type of character which one came to recognize among older East German functionaries. All students left with a deep knowledge of Marx and Lenin, much more rigorous than the catechism-inspired parroting encouraged in other Party schools. Intended as the intellectual armoury its graduates would need to promote and defend communism outside the protected atmosphere of Stalin's Soviet Union, it was, however, channelled towards certain pre-ordained conclusions by an uncanny blend of superstitious faith in the fathers of the ideology and 'scientific' proofs of the historical inevitability of communism.

The roots of this generation's political education are also the roots of their adult personalities. Scarcely any conversation I held about Stalin and his influence, no matter how critically it began, ended without a

7

mitigating comment. One old functionary broke down in tears when I asked him how he had reacted to the discovery of Stalin's crimes:

However much I read of his atrocities, however much I appreciate that what has happened here was a consequence of his ideology, I cannot forget that millions of Soviet soldiers fell with the name 'Stalin' on their lips. It is our conundrum. As humanists we should hate him, but as communists we cannot stop loving him. He was the father of our religion. You can stop going to church but you can't root the religion out of your heart. You die with it.

Their personalities also developed several similar traits: a tendency to seriousness and a dislike of flippancy, an implacable calm in the face of difficult or emotional issues and an unbreakable bond to the Soviet Union as a cross between ersatz parent and super-ego. These are characteristics I found in two very different graduates of the Comintern, Wolfgang Leonhard and his contemporary, Markus Wolf, later the renowned head of East German espionage. For all the years, experience, and political convictions which were to separate them, these two men still bear the indelible marks of their education. Leonhard, although resident in the Federal Republic since 1950 – a year after he abandoned East Germany for a brief stint in Tito's Yugoslavia – and a convert to western democracy, still defines the dominant interest in his life as the fate of the Soviet Union and Eastern Europe. 'I have lived all these years in the West, but my intellectual and emotional energies remain devoted to the East.'

Those Germans schooled in Soviet institutions found their comrades returning from Western exile suspiciously gregarious. The early years of East Germany's history were to present a struggle between the children of the Eastern and Western emigrations, between dogma and flexibility.

By 1953, few Western emigrants would be left in positions of power. Kurt Hager, latterly ideology chief and long-time member of the Central Committee, had spent his exile in Britain and France but managed to survive the purge by hiding his occasional flashes of progressiveness in a thicket of harsh orthodoxy. The writers who bore the brunt of his unpredictable moods used to greet his sunnier periods with the remark, 'See what you can get away with: Hager's in a Western mood at the moment.'

The late Robert Havemann, an eminent scientist who was imprisoned alongside Erich Honecker in Brandenburg jail during the war as an anti-fascist, and later became one of the most celebrated (and hounded) opponents of his fellow-inmate's regime, tells in his diaries of a particularly stormy meeting at the Academy of Sciences. Hager, unable to quench the academics' criticisms, symbolically threw the keys to his office on to the table and invited those who wished to challenge the Politburo's authority to take them. 'Quick,' came a voice from the back, 'grab them before he changes his mind again.' No one could screw up enough courage to take the challenge, however, and Hager survived in the Politburo until 1989.

The German communists who set up the GDR had found their purpose in the fight against fascism: their brightest chapter in a history beset by error, miscalculation and intrigue. Their country's descent into Nazism remained the motor for a belief which, once set in motion, could not be halted, whatever the revelations of persecution committed in its name. They treated the Third Reich as an original sin, to be expunged by building socialism on German soil as payment of the debt they believed due to the Soviet Union. The satellite relationship common throughout the Eastern bloc had particular resonance in East Germany which, more than forty years after the defeat of Nazism, continued to define itself as the anti-fascist state, as if the Brownshirts were still snapping at its heels.

On 16 May 1943 the Comintern was dissolved and with it the school. Stalin had recognized that, far from promoting revolution, the membership of the various national communist parties in the International hindered their access to labour movements and thus limited their chances of widening their appeal to the working classes.

The British and American Parties had indicated that being released from the Comintern would facilitate their work – in America because political organizations whose headquarters were based abroad were not permitted; in Britain because the hoped-for entry of communists into the Labour Party was hindered by their party's Comintern membership. With the dissolution, the students prepared for a return to their home countries. The senior functionaries – at any rate those who had survived the random purges – returned from rural evacuation to Moscow's Hotel Lux, a seedy *fin de siècle* building which was the headquarters of the *émigré* German communists. They promptly established the National Committee for a Free Germany to prepare for their return under the leadership of the KPD chief Wilhelm Pieck and his deputy Walter Ulbricht. The other members of the committee were soldiers and officers, prisoners of war who were graduates of the Soviet re-education schools and had embraced communism, and ten leading *émigrés* including Johannes R. Becher (the first minister for culture in the GDR and author of its anthem), and the writers Friedrich Wolf (father of Markus), Willi Bredel and Erich Weinert. Ulbricht lost no time in converting the

9

National Committee for a Free Germany into his power base. The genial and conciliatory Pieck, whose reputation remained rather brighter than the rest of the Communist Party leadership despite his failure to constrain the dictatorial Ulbricht, concentrated on building bridges with the converted officers, and on the thorny political and ideological question of how the communists were to rebuild Nazified Germany after the war. Ulbricht, whose grimly subservient manner and devotion to Stalin had gained him steady preferment over Pieck throughout their time in the Soviet Union, took over the apparatus and decided cadre matters. By the last months of the war, he had assumed the task of translating the Soviet Union's *Deutschlandpolitik* into guidelines for the returning communists.

As Hitler's imminent defeat would be the result not of an uprising against the National Socialists but of the Allies' military victory, both Stalin and the Western Allies presumed that the German people could not be trusted with political independence without a thorough re-education. A lengthy occupation of the country was considered unavoidable. Moscow also feared that the Nazis would try to undermine harmony between the Allies. It was therefore – so ran the thinking at this time in Moscow – the task of the communists to help create and sustain a broad anti-fascist front and not to threaten the unity of the Allies. The suggestion from several *émigré* communists that a socialist system should be introduced immediately after the Nazi defeat was dismissed by Ulbricht as 'sectarian'. Their task on returning to the shattered Germany, he said, was not to install a dictatorship of the proletariat but to complete the 1848 revolution, to slay the beast of German imperialism for good.

If Stalinism had a German face, it was the bearded, pinched visage of Walter Ulbricht. It is no exaggeration to say that the ghost of his countenance hovered above East Germany until the fall of the regime. He epitomized the bureaucratic, intolerant narrow-mindedness which was to be the basic tone of the republic to its end.

Ulbricht was the embodiment of the revolutionary as functionary, a parody of the type of bureaucrat who thrived under Stalinism. He was not a Robespierre, with his revolutionary vision, but a St Juste: an ancillary in the grip of an unwavering devotion which suspended morality and mercy to achieve its fulfilment. Opinions of him do not vary greatly between communists and anti-communists, friends and foes. All describe him as an efficient organizer with an awesome memory for names, skilled in the minutiae of cadre formation, cold, humourless and hostile to intellectuals. The painter Otto Nagel was later to provide a neatly double-edged tribute to him on the occasion of his seventieth birthday when he described the task of accompanying him to an exhibition: 'Just when I was warming to my theme, he would interrupt sharply with a question. "Yes, but what does it all do for the working class? How does this art help our working people in their struggle?"'

Another artist, Bernhard Heisig, fell out of favour when he produced a painting of the Paris Commune showing some of the Communards lounging or sleeping. Ulbricht was outraged. 'The Communards did not sleep. They ... they, er, stormed,' he declared and added his inevitable conclusion: 'Artistic representation must always proceed from ideology.'

Ulbricht had joined the KPD as a young man in his native Leipzig, where he had been brought up in poverty as a cobbler's son. He later described himself as a carpenter by trade, although acquaintances from his youth recall him working as a bouncer in a notoriously rough pub in the red-light district, a chapter he later suppressed. He rose through the party ranks and became its leader after the arrest and incarceration of the more popular Ernst 'Teddy' Thälmann, following the Nazi accession to power in 1933. Motivated almost exclusively by the Leninist component in his professed Marxism-Leninism, he even cultivated his pointed beard in honour of his hero, whom he used to boast he had met as a young man (he had, in fact, merely been present at a meeting addressed by Lenin).

He followed every change of course ordained by Moscow without the slightest sign of resentment and without – as far as one can gather from those close to him – devoting any inner resources to seeking explanations.

The Hitler-Stalin pact of August 1939 had unleashed widespread confusion and distress among German *émigrés* in the Soviet Union. Ulbricht countered this by turning the KPD's anti-fascist offensive throughout the thirties on its head, and condemning 'primitive anti-fascism'. The *émigrés* were told that only propaganda for Stalin was now acceptable, anti-fascist or anti-Hitler pronouncements were promptly forbidden. The old lash of Party discipline, combined with the distinctly unscientific adoration of Stalin amid the rank and file, ensured that the volte-face was accepted.

He also defended the change as essential to the realization of Stalin's foreign policy goal: the division of Europe between himself and Hitler. So, he ordered, the main thrust of the Party's propaganda was to be against British imperialism. 'The revolutionary workers and progressive powers in Germany do not want to exchange the current regime for national and social oppression through English imperialism and the

English-orientated circles of German capital.'

Heinrich Mann, the author and brother of Thomas, had observed Ulbricht's facility to pirouette on an ideological pinhead as early as 1937 when he told a colleague: 'I can't sit down at the same table with a man who suddenly announces that the table at which we're sitting isn't really a table at all, but a duck pond, and then wants to force me to believe him.'

Throughout the emigration and after the return of the *émigrés* to Germany, Ulbricht tried, as his biographer Carola Stern would later define it, to be

more Soviet than the Soviets, more Catholic than the Pope . . . He began to see his compatriots with Soviet eyes, to hate them as the Soviets did. But Ulbricht's hatred was more complex. He must have hated the Germans more than ever the Russians did. The old communist's dream of representing a victorious Sovietized Germany, achieved by revolutions, had ended. Ulbricht despised the Hitler-Volk but he had nothing else with which to prepare the ground for a Bolshevik state on German soil.

His leadership was to be characterized by an obedience to the Russians which bordered on servile obsession. His favourite slogan, which became the unofficial national motto of the GDR, was 'To learn from the Soviet Union is to learn victory'. (This was neatly re-applied in May 1989 by an anonymous band of *perestroika*-inspired protestors after the sham election. They distributed leaflets reading 'To learn from the Soviet Union is to learn to hold elections'.) He distrusted those communists who had not spent the Nazi period in the Soviet Union. The groundwork for the purges of Western *émigrés* in the fifties was laid by his suspicion that those who had gone West had been infected with bourgeois morality. In his dealings with them, he repeated the attitudes shown towards the German *émigrés* in the Soviet Union. Stalin's cold-blooded purges of the communists who had fled to the Soviet haven were based on the premise that Germans were by nature more prone to treachery than Soviet citizens because of the political background from which they came: never mind the detail that they were fleeing persecution in their own country. Xenophobia was an underlying political motive for both men. Ulbricht refined this vice by managing to be xenophobic about his own countrymen as well.

He was equally suspicious of those communists who had remained in Germany to fight in the underground under the Nazis. Leonhard recalls his own disappointment at Ulbricht's *froideur* when he saw his old comrades again after twelve years of separation. They were visiting communists in the proletarian Berlin district of Neukölln, engaged in a discussion about the future of Germany after National Socialism. 'We knocked and entered. The comrades' faces were filled with surprise and joy but Ulbricht remained stern and factual. Even his greeting was cool. He introduced us and the discussion continued – albeit now under the leadership of Ulbricht.'

One of Ulbricht's first orders was the dissolution of the spontaneous anti-Nazi committees which had sprung up throughout the Eastern Zone, the umbrella groups of opponents to the regime who had enthusiastically seized their first opportunity to organize openly since Hitler's accession to power. He announced that these were merely covers for former Nazis and dispatched his Group to close them down.

Within days of his arrival, he set about the construction of local councils, the administrative base of the city. Communists were not to be installed as mayors except in proletarian districts where the KPD had held sway before the war, while Social Democrats were generally to carry out the representative functions, with bourgeois candidates assigned to well-heeled areas. For the up-market Berlin suburb of Zehlendorf, for instance, he recommended 'a doctor, or someone with a title', and added – pure Ulbricht this – 'someone we can work with, of course'. The posts of deputy mayor (who would be less burdened with representative work and thus a more powerful policy instrument), education and personnel were to go to the communists. So was the office responsible for establishing and supervising the police.

The training Ulbricht had received in the Soviet Union in the building of cadres was coming into its own. He relied on his Group, who had received a similar training in the Comintern and in the National Committee for a Free Germany, to work quickly and decisively at a time when all other political forces in Berlin were in a shambles. Out of chaos were to emerge local administrations which presented a gratifying mixture of anti-fascist political forces with which the Western Allies, who were to enter the city some weeks later, could not quarrel.

The sharing of power meant that the communists appeared generous and conciliatory, and ensured that they alone could not be blamed for mistakes and unpopular decisions. At the same time the communists had strung themselves throughout the new apparatus in prime positions. When, after one directive-issuing meeting, a flurry of hands was raised with questions about how to approach the delicate task of administrative reconstruction, Ulbricht dismissed the gathering with the words: 'It must look democratic, but we must have everything in hand.' It was to become the motto of the next four years, as the non-communists were to discover to their cost.

By May 1945, four parties had been formed in Berlin: the Communist KPD, the Social Democrats, the Christian Democrats, and the Liberal Party (LDPD). The Soviet authorities who engineered this feat of political organization stressed the need to establish broad-based coalitions with the so-called 'bourgeois parties'. This was not as easy as they hoped. Outside Berlin, where food supplies were even poorer than in the capital and infrastructures barely functioning, the foundation of the parties, intended to convince the populace of their new masters' democratic credentials, was barely noticed. Homeless and often hungry, most people were more concerned with the quest for potatoes than parties.

Leonhard recalls the panic in June 1945, reported by a comrade from Brandenburg, the mainly rural region surrounding Berlin, when it turned out that, apart from the Communists, no other anti-fascist party had emerged. The local Soviet commandant called in the Party secretary to berate him for his tardiness in not seeing to the establishment of the requisite Christian Democrat, Social Democrat and Liberal parties and promptly bade him found all three himself.

'But I can't do that, Comrade Commandant,' said the unfortunate functionary, 'I am the local secretary of the Communist party. I can't go round founding other parties as well.'

'Do you know any Social Democrats then?' asked the impatient commandant.

'Yes, Comrade Commandant, but they've all joined the Communist Party.'

'*Nichevo*,' ('It doesn't matter') said the Russian. 'They'll have to resign and found the SPD like it says in this directive from Berlin.'

Nevertheless, the founding document of the communists came as an initial relief to those who feared that the Soviets intended to use the German party to impose the dictatorship of the proletariat on the shattered country. It read:

We are of the opinion that the path of imposing the Soviet system upon Germany would be false as it does not correspond to the current development and conditions in Germany. Rather we believe that the decisive interests of the German people in Germany's current situation prescribe another way: the establishment of an anti-fascist, democratic regime, a parliamentary, democratic republic with all democratic rights and freedoms for the people.

If the word 'regime' seemed a little out of place, few noticed in the general relief. Furthermore, the document promised a free market and private enterprise. One puzzled delegate at the founding conference rose to challenge Walter Ulbricht, asking: 'So right and necessary as this policy programme is, how does it differ from the programme of any other democratic party?' Ulbricht's reply was teasing: 'Comrade, you will soon see the difference, believe me. Just wait for a while.'

The land reform of September 1945 under the motto 'Junker lands into peasants' hands' was laid down by the Soviet military administration (SMAD) under Marshal Georgi Zhukov. This was a radical step in the restructuring of society in the Soviet zone, but accepted by all four parties as fitting punishment for the Junkers who, the received wisdom ran, had been allied with Hitler. The fact that many landowners had been executed or imprisoned for opposing the National Socialists was never mentioned. Only the Christian Democrats ventured that compensation should be paid to those affected, whereupon the Soviet military administration promptly stepped in and removed the party's leader and deputy.

In October the SMAD instigated a major industrial reform, taking over the property of the German Reich, the National Socialists and the Wehrmacht (Hitler's army) to prepare the way for nationalization. The KPD rapidly abandoned its initial pledge that the zone economy would be run on capitalist lines for the foreseeable future and pleaded for the 'sensible steering' of the economy. A referendum on the expropriation of the property of former Nazis and those who had profited from the regime (in effect all major industries) produced a 77.6 per cent vote for the move and just 16 per cent against.

Both the land and industry reforms enjoyed genuine public support and were regarded as fitting revenge on those who had profited from Nazi rule. Ulbricht capitalized on the mood to introduce sweeping nationalization, using barely-disguised sophistry. 'If we were to say we are pursuing nationalization,' he said, 'that would mean that the property of entrepreneurs and shareholders was being expropriated because they were capitalists. But we are not expropriating their property because they are capitalists, but because they were war criminals, Nazis and war profiteers.' The peasants were also gratified to have their erstwhile masters' land carved up between them, little suspecting that it was to be whisked away from them again by the Workers' and Peasants' State a mere five years later.

At this stage, the Communists were careful to have all the fundamental changes voted through by referendum. The votes may well have been rigged, but there was enough enthusiasm for expropriation of land-owners' property for the Soviet administration to achieve a quick and relatively uncontroversial nationalization of key industries in the zone.

The two socialist parties, the social democrat SPD and the communist KPD, had meanwhile established themselves as the most popular parties in the Soviet Zone. Both had histories of resistance to fascism, both presented the hope of a peaceful socialist future for Germany, a welcome message for a people emerging from the actual and moral ruins around them. The rank and file of both were motivated by the desire to create a broad left-wing alliance of forces, hounded by the memory that their refusal to close ranks in the twenties and thirties had left the way to power open to the Nazis.

For the KPD leadership, there was a more pressing problem. By late 1945, the Communist leadership realized that it was on its way to becoming a minority party as the Social Democrats gained confidence and support – particularly across the Western zones. This was brought home to them by similar developments in other former Nazi-occupied countries, particularly the trouncing of the Austrian Communists in the elections of November 1945. Despite their predictions of parity with the Social Democrats, the latter received 76 seats in the new parliament, the Communists a mere four. The leadership realized that its favoured status with the SMAD was no protection against being voted down when it came to an election. They decided to use the power they still had and the backing of Moscow to encourage a merger with the Social Democrats: they would simply absorb the opposition.

In retrospect, it is easy to see why the Communists, inferior in both number and popularity, were so keen on merging with the Social Democrats; it is less clear why the SPD clung to this goal. Gustav Dahrendorf, the respected Social Democrat who was to flee disillusioned to the West when he realised the true terms of the merger, used to tell the following story to convey the emotional power exerted by the idea of a unified left. He was imprisoned with Wilhelm Leuschner for their association with the Stauffenberg plot to assassinate Hitler in 1944. Days before his execution, Leuschner caught sight of his comrade and called to him the single word 'unity' before he was hustled away. Dahrendorf was to say afterwards that he took the task of forging a unified left in Germany as the political bequest of those Social Democrats who had perished in the fight against Hitler.

The attitudes of the Social Democrats between 1945 and 1949 were rooted in the events of 1933. The unity which could have saved Germany from Hitler became the present aim. A merger now was an act of contrition for the failure to stand together previously. The SPD was afflicted by its historical tendency towards drifting in the wind, towards vagueness and inaction, no less true now than then. The Communists could never have been accused of that.

The Utopian goal of a unified left blinded the Berlin SPD to the unsuitability of the Communists as a partner in democratic politics. The period leading to the merger in April 1946 is an unedifying chapter in the party's history. The Communist tail wagged the Social Democratic dog without much difficulty. Ulbricht did not hide his contempt for the SPD, which he still considered as the home of the 'Social Fascists' the communists had blamed for the rise of Hitler in 1933. Erich Gniffke, who shared the SPD leadership with Otto Grotewohl and Max Fechner, described Ulbricht's manner at an early meeting between the two party executives:

He did not look at any of us. His cold glance moved unsteadily from one to the other. When he managed to force a smile, his face was like a mask and his eyes refused to join in. We became increasingly irritated and could not hide our annoyance. In order to end the talks as soon as possible, we finally agreed to his arguments.

'We finally agreed to his arguments' . . . Nowhere perhaps is the weakness of the SPD more apparent than in Gniffke's throwaway line. Despite the distrust and dislike that the Social Democrat leaders – cultivated, tolerant liberals – felt for the pharisaical and dogmatic Ulbricht, they refused to let go of the chimera of an unified party of equals. That the KPD, doused by Stalinism, steered by the Kremlin and run by the tyrant from Saxony, was scarcely a model example of democratic procedures, seemed to escape them. They were to pay dearly for their gullibility in the years to follow.

The main resistance came from Kurt Schumacher and the group of exiles who had spent their exile in London with him. They were now preaching an anti-merger doctrine which drew many eastern Social Democrats away from the pro-unity line but failed to convince the leaders in the Soviet Zone. Soon after the end of the war, the Communists realized that their appeal was waning to the benefit of the SPD in all the occupied zones. They knew too that a gap was opening within the SPD between the party's anti-merger action, led by Schumacher and based in western Germany, and the pro-unity Berlin leadership. The party split along the lines of the respective occupiers in both zones and out of the traditional geographical difference within the SPD. The gentle Rhinelanders had always tended more towards the centre, while the Berliners embraced the more militant traditions of a Marxist-inspired mass movement. Between them opened an unbridgeable divide.

In this most tortuous of courtships it was the communists who had initially played hard to get, with the SPD the keener suitor. Now the roles were reversed. In September 1945 Wilhelm Pieck called for unity of the parties as soon as possible and, in a carefully planned media event to mark his seventieth birthday in January 1946, Otto Grotewohl, the SPD's most prominent pro-unity voice, offered him his hand with the words: 'This handshake not only has meaning for today, but will come to last so long that our hands shall never part.' The subsequent united party was to carry this handshake as its symbol until its collapse in January 1990. During the anti-regime demonstrations of autumn 1989, one of the most popular banners depicted the historical gesture under the cheeky message '*Tschüss*' – 'Bye-bye'.

No referendum on the unification of the parties was permitted in the East. Only in the Western sectors of Berlin was a vote on the proposed merger allowed. Four-fifths of the Social Democrats in the west voted against the proposal and the SPD in the western sectors threw their lot in with Schumacher's version of social democracy, leaving the party in East Berlin to its fate.

In standard East German accounts, the unity of the two left-wing parties is portrayed as an act of sublime free will; in West German memory it ranks as the *Zwangsvereinigung* – the merger by force. The truth lies somewhere between the two. The SPD was the victim of its own Utopian idealism. It wanted unity with a Marxist party which would respect the rules, a party prepared for politics of consensus and compromise. Instead, it got the KPD.

The shotgun wedding took place on 22 April 1946 and the happy couple were renamed the *Sozialistische Einheitspartei Deutschlands* – the SED, Socialist Unity Party of Germany. Its organ, *Neues Deutschland*, was first published a day later and greeted the merger as 'the greatest event for our people since the tragedy of fascism'. Pictures of Marx and Engels appeared on the front page above the pledge 'No one-party system'. The inaugural declarations were inspired by Marx and Engels, who were acceptable figure-heads for the SPD. The party, although firmly reformist since its part in the débâcle of the 'socialist Germany' of 1918, had a traditionally Marxist component which was not disclaimed

18

until the Bad Godesberg conference of 1959, at which official distance was placed between social democracy and socialism.

The more troublesome role-models of Lenin and Stalin were carefully omitted. The only major voice in the party to rumble dissent from the west was that of Kurt Schumacher, who commented that the 'Unity Party' would be 'nothing more nor less than the continuation of the old KPD under another name'. That was precisely what the wilier members of the KPD intended and precisely the way it turned out. Doubtless Grotewohl hoped to triumph over Pieck, whose dithering and signs of senility by this stage, the young Willy Brandt remarked, 'gave the impression of a communist Hindenburg'.

The early promises were to crumble within the next two years. The guarantee of parity within the unified party faded as the gap between the Soviets and the Western Allies widened. By mid-1948 the eastern orientation of the party was unmistakable. Ulbricht, who had quickly departed from promises of inter-party democracy after the merger, introduced the secret 'seven-to-two rule': in all the party's committees, seven communists were to be present for every two Social Democrats. This open discrimination caused many of the more opportunist Social Democrats to knuckle down and become 'new communists'. The more principled fled to the West, further weakening the representation of the Social Democratic tradition within the SED. Erich Gniffke, the deputy leader of the eastern Social Democrats, was one of those who went, leaving behind a bitter letter of recrimination to his party:

Ulbricht has occupied almost all positions in the zone and in Berlin with old and new communists, threaded them through with his chosen cadres and applied to any Social Democrat who did not suit him the curse 'agent'. His political concept has become more and more clear: the destruction of social democracy and its traditionally liberal tendencies, destruction of independent political powers in the other bourgeois parties and the establishment of a dictatorship of the Ulbricht apparatus in the form of 'People's Democracy' in the eastern zone.

He predicted that the course on which the communists had embarked could not end other than in 'separatism and division'.

The pre-war administrative units, the *Länder*, were still in use in the east until the sweeping reforms of the Second Party Conference of 1952 replaced them with districts and localities in order to weaken old geographical bonds and promote centralism. In elections in Brandenburg, Mecklenburg, Thuringia, Saxony and Saxony-Anhalt in October 1946, the SED emerged as the strongest party but failed to achieve a single overall majority. The CDU and LDPD, at this time still genuine political forces in the east, were gaining support fast despite the frequent interventions of the Soviet administration. The restrictions varied according to the region and its local administration, but arrests of candidates, confiscation of materials and disruption of the printing and distribution of leaflets were all common. The message of the elections in Berlin was however unmistakable.

In these, the last to be held across the whole city with both the SED and the western-based SPD standing, the latter gained over 48 per cent of the vote, the SED less than 20. It was a decisive vote against the unified party and a powerful dent to the communists' confidence, especially as the KPD had prided itself on gaining more votes in Berlin than the SPD in the latter years of the Weimar Republic. The next free elections in the east were held in March 1990. Henceforth, the non-competitive principle of the 'unity-list' of approved candidates was to operate. A 'vote' for the candidates was merely an acceptance of the list, without even a mark being made on the voting slip. For the next forty-three years, East Germans reflected the pointlessness of their electoral process by referring to it as merely 'paper folding'.

Documents released from the SED archive during 1991 indicate that, while they encouraged their members to build the 'anti-fascist democratic order', Ulbricht and Pieck may well have been steering towards the division of Germany from the start. Even before the Potsdam Conference, Stalin had called together Ulbricht, Pieck and Anton Ackermann, the Party theorist who had supported a separate German road to socialism without recourse to the Soviet model, to discuss Moscow's policy towards Germany.

Pieck's record of the meeting, kept secret in the archives until the collapse of the East German state, contains the note 'Perspective: there will be two Germanies'. The argument as to whether the founding of the German Democratic Republic was an early Soviet plan or a mere response to the formation of the Federal Republic has raged since 1949. Pieck's note, while it indicates that in the immediate aftermath of the war the Soviet leader was prepared to entertain this solution, by no means resolves the argument. Stalin's tongue was notoriously loose, and he was often no more honest with the German communists than with Churchill or Roosevelt, to whom he pledged not to divide Germany.

The most likely explanation is that the foundation of the socialist German state was the outcome of a long struggle between two separate policies on Germany which had been worked out by the Soviets in 1943 and 1944.

The first concept was aimed at long-term co-operation with the Western Allies in return for a peace treaty, economic assistance for the Soviet Union, generous reparations and a share in the control of the heavy industry of the Ruhr region, the heart of German industry. This presumed a generally co-operative *modus vivendi* with the West.

The second was a safety net against the failure of the first: the securing of Soviet territories in Eastern Europe, including eastern Germany, by absorption into a pro-Soviet bloc, and was predicated on poorer relations with the Western Allies. The change appears to have been less the result of a sudden awakening than of a 'zig-zag course' pursued during 1947 by a Kremlin caught between wishful thinking and panic.

When the Soviet Foreign Minister Molotov attended the Paris Conference in June 1947 with no less than eighty experts in tow, to discuss the Marshall Plan offer (then extended to the Soviet zone as well on condition that a democratic, pluralist system was secured), he conveyed the impression of having no clear brief on which way to vote, and delayed proceedings to wait for a last-minute directive from Moscow rejecting the American suggestion. This move seems to have completed the transition from Plan A to Plan B.

Conflicts between the Soviet Union and the Western Allies had widened rapidly in the first half of 1947. The British and Americans had formed a Bi-zone on 1 January 1947, soon joined by the French; Marshall Aid was announced in that June; and the Cominform – the Moscow-run information bureau succeeding the Comintern – in September. At its inauguration, Andrei Zhdanov, Stalin's ideology chief, announced that the world was split into two opposing and irreconcilable camps, the socialist and the capitalist, confirming Churchill's recognition in his Fulton speech of 1946 of the descent of an Iron Curtain. It is a quirk of German-Russian history that the phrase 'two camps' was initially coined by the fiery nineteenth-century German poet Ferdinand Freiligrath in his call to arms against the bulwark of Russian despotism:

> *Zwei Lager zerklueften heute die Welt*
> *Und ein hueben, ein drueben nur gilt*
> (Two camps today rend the world in two
> And one rules here, while the other reigns there)

Soviet demands for shared control of the Ruhr and 10 billion dollars of reparations, the recognition of the Oder-Neisse line, and a provisional all-German government, including mass organizations as well as political parties, were finally rejected when the four Allied foreign ministers met in London in December 1947. The SED grew rapidly in the wake of the split within the global camp. It began to attract young members motivated by a mixture of self-interest, reawakened idealism and latent anti-Americanism. By now it was clear that the party badge to have if one wished swift preferment in the Zone was the red one with the clasped hands, known disparagingly as the 'bonbon'.

Despite its ropy start in the elections of 1946, the Party boasted 1.8 million members by the following September. How many it really had is open to question – 'we were a bit liberal in our counting,' admitted one statistician from the Party school in Kleinmachnow when I visited him in 1989. 'Some of our "members" had already left the Soviet Zone and joined the CDU in the west!'

After Zhdanov's speech the SED swerved direction to trot after its Soviet masters. The SED of April 1946 had been a reflection in microcosm of the Soviet desire to maintain cordial relations with the Western Allies: the path of 'Finlandization', based on tolerance of western democratic forms, in return for a special regard for Soviet security interests. The SED of early 1949 declared itself a 'Party of a New Type'. In fact, it had developed into a party of an all too familiar type: the cadre-dominated party of Lenin (he was suddenly back on the leadership's lips), identical in structure and general ideology to the Communist Party of the Soviet Union. Following the Soviet model, the Party began to concentrate its organization in the factories rather than the localities, thus strengthening its influence on the economy.

A Soviet-sponsored campaign of intimidation directed at dissident Social Democrats and the Christian Democrat and Liberal parties began with the SMAD using its position as licence-giver for all newspapers in the Zone to censor opposition publications. Ink and paper deliveries were often withheld as well.

Former concentration camps, among them Buchenwald and Sachsenhausen, were used to intern political opponents, including many Social Democrats, in appalling conditions. Only in 1990 was it revealed that some twenty thousand people had died of cold and hunger in the camps after they had been officially liberated by the Soviets in 1945. At Sachsenhausen, outside Berlin, skulls were dug up in the forest outside the camp gates. Older residents revealed that they had witnessed executions in the night in the two years after the war ended.

Investigation of this period was forbidden to historians until the end of Honecker's rule. In June 1991, Chancellor Kohl paid a visit to Buchenwald, the first head of state to commemorate not only the victims of the camps under Nazi rule, but those who perished on the same site under the successor regime. One elderly man watching the events had been imprisoned there as a Social Democrat under both. 'My friends who died here under the Nazis died as part of a carefully executed plan. Those who died under the communists died of neglect. That has always struck me as reflecting both the central similarity and the central difference of the two regimes,' he said.

The SPD's dream of unity with the communists had turned into a nightmare: trapped within the 'Unity party', they were ill-placed to protest at the gradual diminution of their influence. By now, appearance and reality were at odds. Otto Grotewohl and Wilhelm Pieck remained joint party leaders: in reality, however, it was Walter Ulbricht with his Lenin beard and Stalinist views who held power.

The zone was on its way to becoming a republic, with three People's Congresses (at which the oft-cited 'People' were represented by a majority of communist delegates) paving the way to a separate state. In March 1948, the Soviets left the Allied *Kontrollrat* for Germany and a few weeks later walked out of the *Kommandatura*, the four-power administrative body in Berlin. Co-operation with the Western Allies effectively ceased.

The economic climate was disastrous on both sides of the zonal frontier, with the black market dominating trade. As the stream of refugees from east to west increased, productivity in the Soviet Zone slumped. Even with severe rationing (a manual worker was allocated a mere 1,400 calories a day, which amounted to a compulsory slimming diet), the shops frequently ran short of supplies and there was a small fortune to be made by spivs and allotment holders.

The currency reform in the western zones and West Berlin in June 1948 replaced the old Reichsmark with the US-backed Deutschmark. This alleviated the economic misery, but also proved to be a decisive contribution to the final division. Its terms and logistics had been contracted in secret by groups of German economists working under American guard at a military camp and sworn to secrecy. The notes were printed in the USA. The east responded with a monetary reform of its own which, for want of time to prepare, consisted largely of sticking coupons on to the old Reichsmark note. The resulting hybrid soon earned the nickname 'wallpaper notes', a less than auspicious start for the new currency, which rapidly fell behind the western Deutschmark in value.

The move promoted the Soviets to launch the Berlin blockade, in the hope of overwhelming the capitalist island in the middle of what was now clearly a communist sea. They besieged West Berlin by blocking all road and rail traffic, in the expectation that the West would not be prepared to fight for it, and that it could be merged with the Soviet zone. The resistance of the Western Allies and the ensuing eleven-month airlift – of more than 900 flights on some days – served instead to underline the irreconcilability of Soviet and Western plans for Germany and the inevitability of a divided Berlin. The blockade was eventually dropped in May 1949.

It also strengthened support in the West for the Christian Democrat Konrad Adenauer's theory that prosperity and freedom for Germany lay in binding three zones into the Western community, even at the price of losing the fourth to Moscow. His conviction on this point won him a narrow victory in the August 1949 elections over the Social Democrats, who were less keen to tie western Germany exclusively to American security interests and favoured a return to Germany's pre-First World War role between east and west. With the drift towards the foundation of a separate western state no longer ignorable, the east had held single-list elections in May 1949 to approve the constitution of the German Democratic Republic.

These elections provided the first act of the electoral farce which was to run for four decades. On the first count, the communists were horrified to find that even on the restrictive formula of a 'yes' or 'no' vote for their proposals, they had not secured the decisive vote for the founding of the socialist state they had hoped for. The interior ministers of the five *Länder* were promptly issued with orders to recount and to respect the following rules – this example is taken from the *Land* of Brandenburg's archives:

The only 'no' votes are those in which a cross is placed in the circle 'no'. All others are to be counted as valid 'yes' votes. Blank voting papers are to be counted as 'yes' votes. In the case of comments or defaced voting slips, these are to count as 'yes' votes.

Even under these propitious conditions, only 61 per cent of the electorate voted for the proposed constitution (and thus for the founding of a second German state) and 39 per cent against. In East Berlin, despite numerous 'recounts' and a twenty-hour delay in announcing the result, only 51.6 per cent of the voters had approved the unified list. And so began, as the East German playwright Joachim Walthers was to remark some years later, the single most outstanding achievement of the German Democratic Republic: 'The energetic construction of socialism by a people who never expressly wanted it.'

2

The Unimprovables

Above all, I was fascinated by his face. A countenance which aroused familiarity and yet suspicion, an expression which, if one were inclined to think well of the bearer, could be described as purposeful, proud and strong of will, and if one were not, as arrogant and narrow-minded . . . I had encountered men with this expression at every stage of my life. It was the final face of my father.

> Monika Maron, from her novel *Stille Zeile Sechs* (which can be roughly translated as 'Sleepy Hollow, No. 6')

I returned to East Berlin in 1950 and it was wonderful, after everything we communists had been through, to return to a socialist Germany: our dream of the twenties and thirties. I remained a convinced GDR citizen, even after the revelations about Stalin. They were two different things for me, separated in my mind: a mistake that has taken a terrible revenge. Now I see that what we built here had its roots in Stalinism. I thought that I was being honest with myself while I believed and repeated things which I now know weren't true. It is very hard to cope with what has happened . . .

> Ruth Werner, interview with the author, 1991

While the history of the German Democratic Republic is largely that of a passive majority which came to be dominated by a manipulative minority, it is also the history of those members of a German generation who turned to Marx for a solution to their country's *misère* of militarism, war and social discord. It was said of the Socialist Unity Party, when it collapsed in 1989, that four-fifths of its two million-plus members were in the Party out of opportunism or inertia, a fifth really meant it. Many of that small, stubborn segment of believers are old-age pensioners, communists since the twenties. Theirs is a story of courage and cowardice, self-sacrifice and self-deception, wisdom and foolhardiness. It is the story of German communism itself.

The country they created failed to outlast many of its own midwives.

Had the collapse come a decade later, most would have gone to their graves believing in the triumph of their ideology. Now, in the last years of their lives, they have seen the battle between capitalism and socialism on German soil lost, the restoration of a unified Germany on the West's terms: the harshest of punishments for their mistakes and transgressions. While we indulge in a touch of the told-you-sos at the collapse of the Soviet empire, it is sobering to remember those bewildered and broken elderly communists. Known with a mixture of mockery and grudging admiration as *die Unverbesserlichen* (the unimprovables), they can now but reflect that their efforts were largely misguided and ultimately in vain.

At the Clara Zetkin old people's home in the Friedrichshagen suburb of Berlin, where the 'activists of the first hour' spend their old age, a bust of the proletarian woman revolutionary whose name the institution bears stands in the hall alongside a meditative Lenin. On the notice-board there are postcards from old friends in the Soviet Union. 'We are waiting to hear from Erich . . .' reads one, a reference to the deposed leader Eric Honecker who fled there in March 1991 to escape prosecution for ordering the deaths of would-be escapers.

Annette Wilkendorf, who runs the establishment, has the unmistakable mannerisms of a staunch Party member, mannerisms which have not been eradicated by the mere collapse of the Party. Not for her the headlong dash towards consumerism, the blind acceptance of the new order. The day I visited, she had just sent packing members of a west Berlin social services delegation after they looked askance at the socialist memorabilia. 'These are old people who have lived through a century of hardship for their beliefs. These statues are their religion. I would not take that from them. The political present is awful for them: the end of a dream. All they have is the past.'

Known as 'little Wandlitz' – a reference to the compound in which the old political élite lived – because of its comparative luxury, the home was funded by the East German Council of State as a thank-you to the old communists who had made it all possible. Now it has become a refuge for those displaced by the revolution of 1989.

During my visit, the home was preparing for the traditional socialist holiday of May Day, the residents polishing their orders of Marx and Lenin and preparing to give the traditional speeches in support of the proletarian struggle, in grim defiance of the reality outside their door.

On the first floor lives Benny Heumann, a half-Russian architect who as the son of one of the first Bolsheviks spent his childhood in Lenin's company in the Soviet Union and in exile in Switzerland. He declares proudly that he knew the revolutionary leader better than anyone still alive. 'He would have hated what became of his idea,' he says. 'He was a simple and open man, not like the self-deceivers and idiots who ruined this place.' He divides his life into three chapters: the fight against fascism, the hope of building up democratic socialism on German soil and the long decline of that hope, ending in the collapse of the GDR.

The greatest pain of my life has been the daily realization that socialism was slipping away, that my own Party was driving the people back into the arms of capitalism. It is hard to bear this defeat, but we are a generation toughened by our fight against Hitler. We cannot give up the dream even though these days it seems that only the very young and the very old believe in it.

One of the regime's many failures was its refusal to learn from the ancient Greeks, who used the elderly to advise and warn rulers, but left the business of government to the young. The average age in the East German Politburo was sixty-nine, and most of the members with any significant role were in their seventies and eighties. The eldest, the Minister for State Security Erich Mielke, was eighty-three when the government collapsed. With more tenacious determination than even their sibling regimes of the Eastern bloc, the rulers of the GDR clung to power even in their dotage. 'How,' went a popular joke of the eighties, 'will the next party conference begin? With the carrying-in of the Politburo, of course.'

Most of the leading functionaries regarded their power as a right gained in the long years of opposition to fascism. The official description of the country as an 'anti-fascist state' lent weight to their authority: they, after all, had been the original anti-fascists. 'There were two criteria for a place at the top,' the former Berlin Party chief Günter Schabowski was to say after the collapse, 'having been in the Spanish Civil War or in prison under the Nazis. That excluded any of my generation [a mere babe of sixty when the regime collapsed] from a decisive role as far as they were concerned.'

This is the generation of socialists whose development is entwined with the fate of 'the Great Soviet Union', with its myriad triumphs and disasters, its beliefs and mores already set in aspic. They are distinct from the legions of characterless, epigone functionaries who dominated the country from the mid-seventies, having had experience of life outside the rigid confines of their own country, the experience of capitalism, war and exile on which to draw. Their world was governed, not by the self-generating discipline of the Party membership book, but by sheer political passion.

They witnessed the bloody street battles of the twenties, embarked on breathless pilgrimages to Stalin's Soviet Union in the thirties, and fought tirelessly on the open and invisible fronts the war against Hitler. Their reward was the German Democratic Republic, the guarantee of a socialist future. Their curse was that it remained anchored in the past, and that it never emerged from Stalin's shadow. Only with the hindsight bestowed by the state's collapse have they come to realize that the ghost of the *Generalissimo* had hovered over them like a malevolent guardian angel all the time, warding off change, stifling renewal, justifying oppression, rebutting the truth.

Sonya

I didn't know what to call her at first. She was born in 1905 into an intellectual and rather grand Berlin family as Ursula Kuczynski. As the Soviet agent codenamed 'Sonya' she ran rings around British intelligence in the forties. In East Germany she was known as the writer Ruth Werner, although she is married to an Englishman named Beurton. On closer enquiry, it turns out that this is not his real name either, although it is the one he has used for many decades. Seeking clarification, I asked what her husband called her. She considered a moment and pronounced, in an accent in which the Home Counties still competes with a German-Jewish twang, 'He calls me Ducky.'

We decided on Ruth. She is an indefatigable matriarch, ensconced in a small, crumbling house in an East Berlin suburb. On the door hangs a tea-towel bearing the legend 'Workers of the World Unite'; her grandchildren pop in and out on errands, and there is always tea and a home-baked cake on offer. She seems an unlikely candidate for the post of Colonel in the Red Army, a title awarded in recognition of her work for the cause. The Order of the Red Banner, which she received twice, is nowhere to be seen, hidden away in a drawer. 'I'm not a great fan of all these baubles,' she says and only her dark eyes betray a flash of pride in her reward.

She is probably the bravest and most successful female spy in the history of the second oldest profession. For a while she ranked as a strong candidate for the position of Fifth Man, after Chapman Pincher claimed that she had controlled Roger Hollis, the head of MI5 after the war. It has since been confirmed that that particular title belongs to John Cairncross, but Ruth Werner's achievements as a GRU (Soviet Military Intelligence) agent based in Britain during and after the war still inspire speculation among those who cannot work out quite how she got away with it all.

'I am not a spy,' she says, pouring the tea with a steady hand, 'Please don't call me that. I was an intelligence officer in the service of the Red Army. A Soviet military intelligence officer.' She is not the first to insist on the distinction – all the old East German agents I have encountered shared this antipathy to the word spy, preferring the more respectable appellation of *Kundschafter* (emissary). Spying, as far as they are concerned, is something the other side did.

Her name provokes reactions ranging from boundless admiration to shudders. In Soviet espionage circles, she ranked as a heroine – her Moscow handler said that five Sonyas would have brought the war to a close sooner, choosing to ignore that she was spying on an ally, not an enemy. British Intelligence, meanwhile, were apparently so embarrassed at their failure to catch the woman who passed Klaus Fuchs' atomic secrets to Stalin that they let her leave, even after her cover was blown.

Within East Germany her account of her life, *Sonya's Report*, sold half a million copies and inspired a generation bored with the stultifying predictability of their own protected lives under Honecker's 'real existing socialism'. In West Germany, the fact that she had had three children by three different men and prospered in the male world of espionage made her a model for feminists – a role she rebuts.

I was never a great campaigner for women's rights. The simple fact is that I had two great passions – my work for the Soviet Union and children. Between the ages of twenty and forty I was working as an agent. I had to have the children then or not at all. It was not a settled life and it was hard to keep relationships together – hence the three fathers.

In the socially conservative GDR her private life was considered a blot on her career. When she wrote *Sonya's Report* she was asked to blur the fact that her children had different fathers. There was also criticism that she had taken her children with her on dangerous missions abroad. 'I had to point out that if I had stayed in Germany as a Jewish communist, I and my three children would probably have ended up in a concentration camp.'

She enjoyed a successful writing career and at the height of the unrest in autumn 1989, the day after the Wall had been opened by Egon Krenz's rudderless government, made a surprise appearance in front of 150,000 communists gathered at a rally which was to turn into their swan-song. It fell to her, a reedy voice cutting through the parroted slogans of the other, younger speakers, to tell the unpalatable truth: that the party in which German communists had placed their faith had become a stultified, unbending monolith, immune to change or criticism.

'During the last few years I have come so far, that I have told comrades who intended to go into the Party apparatus: don't. You will either end up with an ulcer, break your own neck or you will fall prey to the poison of power,' she told the crowd before urging them to reform the Party. But it was too late. Ruth Werner, like many others of her generation, is having to learn to live in a system she fought against all her life.

Her story begins in 1924 at the age of nineteen when, horrified by the poverty and unemployment she saw around her in Berlin, she joined the KPD. It cost her an agreeable job in a publishing house but, she says, she had read Rosa Luxemburg and Lenin and was 'absolutely convinced, unshakeable'. Even her left-wing father, the eminent academic René Kuczynski, one of the founders of statistical science in Germany and later, during the exile from fascism a lecturer at the London School of Economics, was taken aback at her decision and warned that it would make her life a difficult one.

In 1930, she married a Berlin architect, Rolf Hamburger, who to escape unemployment at home took a job with the British authorities in Shanghai. The couple, fortified only by sausage, bread and tea – they had spent their last money on the tickets – travelled on the trans-Siberian railway. China was in the midst of a civil war between the communists and the nationalists. Jolted by the chaos and poverty she found, she was soon to join the underground communists, although she still moved in bourgeois European circles. 'It was a very dangerous place for communists,' she recalls. 'I knew that my best cover was that of an intellectually inclined, progressive European woman.'

Through the American journalist Agnes Smedley she met Richard Sorge, the most successful Soviet agent in the East, who took a risk on her, banking on the mild left-wing sentiments she had let slip at salon gatherings, to ask her to help the communists. 'He started to talk about communism and I said, "You don't have to tell me all of that, what can I do to help?" He was very relieved.' He gave her the code-name 'Sonya' and trained her in ciphers and explosives.

The Japanese invaded Manchuria in 1931 and reached Shanghai by January the following year. Her work became essential to the communists there, who used her home for clandestine meetings. She hid weapons and explosives in an old wooden chest and learnt more sophisticated aspects of covert work from Sorge. He was to enter the annals of espionage history by successfully predicting the date of Hitler's attack on the Soviet Union in 1941, and was hanged by the Japanese as a spy in 1945.

Ruth was sent to Moscow to be trained in morse transmission, decoding and the making of explosives. She had to leave her baby with her husband's parents so that he wouldn't learn to speak Russian. Moscow sent her back to Manchuria to support the Chinese partisans. 'They used me to buy the explosives because I was such an unlikely suspect. I could pretend I needed the ingredients for the household or the garden, but I would be told to buy massive quantities and I was terrified. They probably thought I was mad about gardening.' In Manchuria, where spies were shot without mercy, she lived in fear of her life. 'I realized then that a basic quality needed in our work was not to have too much imagination, to commit oneself to calculated risk and then just get on with it.'

She was sent by her controllers to Poland to observe German activity there, and then in 1938 to Switzerland as head of an anti-German spy ring. Her first marriage had crumbled when she left China, and by now she had a second child, a daughter, Nina, by a fellow-agent she identifies only as 'Ernst'.

She kept her pregnancy secret from her controllers, fearing that it might end her career, and missed only one transmission because of the birth. The following day, she radioed to Moscow: 'Apologize for failure to transmit. Gave birth to daughter.' In Switzerland she recruited Len Beurton, a British veteran of the Spanish Civil War. Their meeting had been set up by their Moscow handlers on the shores of Lake Geneva. He was to carry *The Times* and a bag of apples, she a string bag of oranges. At her handlers' suggestion, she married him to gain a British passport. Even their wedding day was chosen with an eye to political symbolism: it took place on 23 February 1940, the anniversary of the founding of the Red Army.

More than half a century later, they are still together. 'It was love at first sight,' says Len. 'She was very pretty and had great legs.' He is frail now, hard of hearing and can read only with the aid of a magnifying glass. His thoughts, he says, often turn to England, to his home in Epping Forest. Since he joined Ruth in East Berlin in 1950, he has not been back to Britain. 'It would have been an unnecessary risk,' he says phlegmatically. The East German news agency ADN gave him a job surveying the British press and he worked there for many years in self-imposed isolation, a loner who did not appreciate the collective environment.

He is more withdrawn than his wife on the subject of his past activities as a morse operator in Geneva, less of an ideologue on the whole. He is politely bemused that anyone should be interested in his past. 'It was thrilling to make contact with Moscow, but after that the most tedious job in the world,' he says. In spring 1939, in Munich, he encountered Hitler lunching in a restaurant with Eva Braun and Unity Mitford, and discovered from the manager that this was a weekly affair. 'I proposed to the Party that we should try an assassination attempt in the restaurant, but while they were still thinking about it the war started and Hitler's public lunches stopped. I always regret not having had the chance to kill him. It would have done wonders for the reputation of British communists.'

We talked about literature, his love of American history and the poems of Housman. 'Soon my eyesight will be so bad that I won't be able to read them, so I'm memorizing them all,' he said. He spends his summers listening to cricket on the World Service and consulting his Wisden. From his eyrie in East Berlin he has followed the Cold War as a well-informed spectator. He reminisces about George Blake's escape from prison and is delighted to hear that his helpers Pottle and Randle have been found not guilty. Was there anything I could bring him from England? His eyes lit up. 'You couldn't get hold of a copy of Geoffrey Howe's speech, the one that started Mrs Thatcher's tumble, could you?' After four decades behind the Iron Curtain, he is still tilting energetically at the British establishment, although whether inspired by passion or habit I could not quite tell.

After their marriage, Sonya took a ship to Liverpool and joined her parents, who had been evacuated to Oxford. By 1942 she had moved into a cottage in the grounds of the house owned by the High Court Judge Neville Laski, father of the late writer Marghanita. Ruth strung her aerial for receiving radio messages from Moscow over the washing line.

By now, she was pregnant again. 'That bit was fun. The baby made excellent cover – particularly as the washing line was always full of nappies. No one suspected a housewife and mother – it didn't fit the textbook image of an intelligence officer.' She liked England. The children went to boarding-school and they had a family holiday at Butlin's, after which Nina declared her favourite people to be the distinctly unsocialist heroes of the Queen and Billy Butlin.

'I never had the feeling that what I was doing would harm Britain or the British,' says Ruth. 'We desperately needed the Second Front to open, but Churchill held back. I merely saw it as helping an ally which wasn't doing enough to do more.' Her cheeky definition of high-calibre espionage as unsolicited assistance to a dawdling government is delivered with magnificent, chilly directness. For the first time, I caught a glimpse of Ruth Werner as she must have been: a calculating operator spying not on an enemy, but on an ally. And justifying it with the deeper enmity of ideology.

She says she reckoned on eight to ten years in prison if she were discovered. 'But Britain was civilized in comparison with China, or even Switzerland – they used to deposit spies at the German border, which was equivalent to a death sentence. It was a relief not to have that hanging over me.'

Her close-knit and politically united family provided her with valuable sources of information. It was her father who passed on a conversation with Stafford Cripps when the new Minister for Aircraft Production said, after returning from his post as Ambassador to Moscow in 1942, that aid to the Soviet Union would be wasted because Hitler would go through the country 'like a hot knife through butter'.

Her information was read avidly in the Kremlin, which was hungry for knowledge of political attitudes towards the war among the Western Allies, and she received a rare message of congratulation for this particular snippet. Her brother, the economic historian Jürgen Kuczynski, helped by cultivating John Strachey, the Labour MP who was a Wing Commander in the Air Ministry directorate of bomber operations.

By now she had moved to a cottage called 'The Firs' in the Cotswold village of Great Rollright. Len, caught between orders from his handler in Switzerland and those of his wife, radioed to Moscow: 'Should I, as instructed by Sonya, try to come to England or as Albert (Rado) advises, stay in Switzerland?' The answer was, 'Do as Sonya tells you', and he joined her soon afterwards.

Via Jürgen, a prominent functionary in the exiled German Communist Party in Britain, she was introduced to the German scientist Klaus Fuchs and became his courier, passing the blueprint of the atom bomb he was working on at Harwell to Moscow. 'He was a very sensitive young man: clearly not strong. He was not the spying type, but he truly believed that the world would only be safe if the Soviet Union had the bomb too.'

They decided on the cover of young lovers, and she would cycle through the Oxford countryside to meet him. 'It was also a relief to me to be able to talk to a German communist about politics.' In 1943, Fuchs left 'a big blue book' in a pre-arranged hole in the ground for her. She says she did not know what she was passing on because she had never heard of an atom bomb – 'It was hieroglyphics but I knew that it was something important. When I found out, I thought it was quite right to have passed it on to Moscow.' She conveyed the book to a fellow GRU agent, a Soviet embassy official called 'Sergei', hidden under the child's seat on the back of her bicycle, and within days Stalin had the secrets of the atom bomb.

Why did she spy for Stalin?

'I never did anything for Stalin,' she says stubbornly. 'As far as I was concerned I was working against fascism, for the German people, and for peace.' But of course, she worked for the Soviet Union after the defeat of the Third Reich. 'I could see the Cold War starting,' she says defensively. 'I feared another war and yes, I was on the side of the Soviet Union.' Like hundreds of her anti-fascist colleagues, she carried her zeal into the service of Stalin's tyranny. In the heated, divided days of her youth, she had decided which side she was on in the battle for the world. The commitment grew into sheer stubbornness. Only in 1956, after Khrushchev's secret speech, did she distance herself from the dead dictator.

I had never identified with the personality cult – it went against the grain for me to have to refer to him as 'The Great Stalin' – but the awful thing about that sort of thing is that, when so many people go along with it, you find yourself thinking, 'Perhaps they're right'. When his crimes were revealed, I got the most awful shock. From that day on though, I vowed I would never place all my faith in one person again.

She insists that she had no knowledge of the atrocities before. 'Perhaps some suspicions gathered on the grapevine. But I was only in Moscow for a brief period. If the Party said that only traitors were being killed in the Soviet Union, I was inclined to believe it. The goodness of Stalin was an article of faith: it was not prone to normal scrutiny or doubt.' It is the suspension of disbelief, the stubborn refusal to draw uncomfortable conclusions from ready evidence which is most depressing – and the tendency to explain away complicity to this day. The 'brief period' in which Ruth was in Moscow saw the executions of Bukharin and Yagoda (the former NKVD chief). General Jan Berzin, the director of Red Army Intelligence who promoted her to colonel was also executed.

Sonya's espionage for Moscow was betrayed to the British authorities early in 1947 after the defection from the GRU of Allan Foote, a comrade of Len Beurton's from their Spanish Civil War days and Moscow's initial candidate to marry her. One day that year, two men came to her door in Great Rollright and introduced themselves as being from British Intelligence. They said that they knew of her work in Switzerland and asked for

34

her co-operation. If they had hoped to unnerve her, they failed. She offered them a cup of tea, told them that she was a 'loyal British citizen' and refused to comment on her past.

Remarkably, there was no follow-up to the interview, leaving her to continue her activities undetected. This good fortune led to later theories that she had a protector in MI5, a theme to which she still warms, insisting that she has no longer any reason to hide the name of any British benefactor.

There are only two explanations. Either I was extraordinarily lucky or there was a hand held over me in MI5. We [she and Len] always used to say, 'One can't be so lucky'. We have spent long evenings since trying to work it out. For a time, I thought perhaps it was Philby, but the timing wasn't right. People keep asking me who protected me, particularly from the West. How on earth should I know? Surely you can work out who was doing what in your own service without asking me.

This minor torrent is delivered in a tone of gentle scolding. Ruth Werner treats the world of espionage with a mixture of pride and contempt. Like a strict grandmother, she gives the impression that it was the general sloppiness that annoyed her most about the whole business. In *Sonya's Report* she delivered a brisk verdict of 'Could Do Better' on her several opponents. 'Alongside the thoroughness, I have encountered such incompetence among the security services of the countries in which I worked that I have long since given up trying to puzzle it out.'

Asked whether she had, as some sections of MI5 suspect to this day, penetrated British Intelligence, she snorts. 'I would like nothing better than to say I did, and I have no reason for saying I didn't other than it is the truth. If I had controlled Roger Hollis I would certainly tell you, and would be proud of the fact.' Those who think she was spying on MI5 point to the circumstantial evidence of her base in Oxford – several sections of the service had been evacuated to Blenheim Palace and Bletchley. Ruth Werner says that had she known of MI5's proximity she would have moved. 'I was far too close for comfort: it could have blown my other work. I was simply there because my parents were in Oxford.' This is not entirely convincing, particularly given her father's willingness to help her out with valuable information. But she dismisses as 'trashy' the idea of a family spy-nest.

In 1948, in the wake of Foote's denunciation, the Soviet Union suddenly broke contact, without even a message telling her to move on. 'I was like a fish out of water,' she recalls. 'My whole life had been a rhythm

35

of meetings, messages, drops and above all, this contact with Moscow. Then suddenly, nothing. I was back to being a housewife.' But a housewife in danger. The net was closing in on Klaus Fuchs, she was increasingly exposed and, one senses, aware for the first time that she was a pawn in someone else's game.

She and her husband were probably casualties of a clear-out of foreign-nationality agents whom the Soviet Union considered essential during the war, and in the immediate post-war years, but who were then replaced with fresh soldiers to fight on the new front of the Cold War. Asked if she resented being left in the lurch by Moscow, she denies it hotly but with a rather forced resort to discipline. 'I used to tell myself that the Red Army couldn't take personal notice of all its soldiers.' Len intervenes: 'We fought a war as anti-fascists for the Soviet Union and the Soviet Union won. We walked on clouds afterwards.' But they cannot conceal the strain on their loyalty on this point. She radioed repeatedly to Moscow asking for permission to leave for East Germany and finally received the go-ahead. She left England in some haste, the day Klaus Fuch's trial opened.

Later, when the scientist was released from prison and returned to East Germany, he met Ruth again and told her that his interrogators knew that she was the courier. 'I think that they [British Intelligence] had realized by then that they had made such a God-awful mess of it that they preferred to just let me go,' she says.

She arrived in East Berlin in February 1950, a few months after the foundation of the GDR. It is difficult to imagine how this cosmopolitan free spirit settled down in a small, grey country, governed by the socialist bureaucrats returned from a dogmatic Moscow exile. 'The British had been so healthy, so strong and good-looking by comparison. In my mind it had all been different. One imagined a triumphal return to a socialist Germany and instead there were piles of rubble. It was a shock.'

She took a job in the Information Ministry but was removed in 1952 during the purge of those communists who had spent the years of fascism in the West – particularly those from bourgeois intellectual backgrounds. Having an English husband, although his biography brought him closer to the ideal citizen than ninety-nine per cent of the East German population, did not help. There were no rewards for her years of working for Moscow, no villa or driver, and there was a discretion about her past which bordered on the grudging. The file on her activities was kept closed by the Central Committee, where she had a minder. Even before the building of the Wall she was not permitted to travel to the western part of the city. Only in 1977 was she encouraged to publish her life story, to encourage other young spies.

She has never revised her belief in socialism although, particularly after the advent of President Gorbachev – years in which the hardline GDR was increasingly out of step with the rest of the Eastern bloc – she distanced herself from her old view of the world as a battleground between two hostile ideologies, with spies acting as the soldiers on the unseen front.

We talked at length about betrayal, a word which used to figure prominently in her vocabulary:

For me, people who left us or went over to the other side were *de facto* traitors. I am ashamed now to think that I considered people who were killed or went to prison for treachery as guilty without thinking about their motives. Now I realize that they were sometimes more far-sighted than we were. I still don't like people who sell themselves to the other side or profit from their change of heart, though.

Ruth Werner's life and personality mirror the sum contradictions of her guiding ideology. Throughout our meetings she laid great emphasis on honesty. Too much emphasis? Perhaps, but she is more open about her beliefs and her mistakes than many other East German communists, and she refuses to make use of convenient loopholes.

She was annoyed when I expressed doubt about elements in the account of her life. The cosy atmosphere tightened, she sat back wounded, and suddenly older, in her chair. She has the gentleman spy's schizophrenic belief that one can remain an honest person while pursuing a trade governed by deception. Her mind is sharper, her memory better than most people's half her age, but when pursued on uncomfortable topics she sighs disarmingly and delivers a perfect line of defence – 'Now you are asking an old woman too much.' She attributes the triumph of the callous, bureaucratic element in Leninist socialism to the exaggerated tenet of Party discipline; then points out that discipline was the communist's best weapon in the battle against fascism.

Her eldest son, Michael Hamburger, who spent his babyhood in China, his boyhood and student days in Britain and his adulthood in East Germany, is vice-president of the recently united joint-German Shakespeare society. As one of the first recruits to the opposition New Forum movement, he can claim to have carried on the family tradition as an 'activist of the first hour', albeit campaigning for the end of the system his parents fought to establish. She smiles proudly at the observation and says she admires his courage.

The collapse of communism in the Soviet Union causes her 'the greatest pain' and she admits that she does not feel at home in the new, capitalist Germany. 'My grandson said to me the other day, "Why are you so depressed? You don't think that this capitalism is the answer? In twenty years it will all begin to look different." Well, that's all right for him, but it's a bit long for me to wait.'

I tried to begin a wider discussion on the flaws of state socialism. 'That's far too complicated for me,' she said. 'Go and talk to an intellectual. Talk to Jürgen.'

The Tightrope Walker

The apple blossom outside Professor Jürgen Kuczynski's house was in full bloom and the bell at the side of a sturdy Wilhelminian door still bore the injunction, 'Please ring three times, loudly'. He stood in front of me, at 7.30 in the morning already resplendent in waistcoat, watch and a rather jaunty velvet jacket, unfailingly charming. 'Come in, my child,' he said. Female visitors of whatever vintage are always received with this appellation, males with 'My good man'. All Berlin, all Germany may be in the midst of giddying change but here, as always, nothing has changed.

At eighty-seven he had not altered since our first meeting seven years earlier, his long face dominated by generous bags under the eyes, suggesting a well-read and gentle-mannered bloodhound. Every room in the house is piled with books, ranging from the complete works of innumerable economists to a vast library of thrillers featuring an endless array of Agatha Christies. 'I've read nearly all of them,' he said happily, 'and still I can never work out who the murderer is.' The morning's reading, *Neues Deutschland* and *The Economist*, lay on the desk. He had just dashed off a letter to *The Times Literary Supplement*, correcting a reviewer on the circumstances of Hegel's introduction to French philosophical circles. The mere collapse of his state into the arms of despised Western capitalism has not shaken him out of his routine or unsettled his composure. The very thought . . .

Professor Kuczynski is the embodiment of both a class of thinkers and a social group which enriched Germany before the Nazis and was wiped from the country's intellectual landscape by the Holocaust and by emigration: the grand-bourgeois Jewish intelligentsia. A trip to see JK, as he has styled himself over the years in a whimsical resurrection of the personality cult, has been one of the pleasures of my years in East Germany. His was one of the few doors always open to Western visitors

38

with awkward questions to ply, and his gay disregard for the formalities of registering interviews with the authorities was a rare boon to visiting correspondents. My brown-suited minder from the Foreign Ministry who, rather like my mother when I was a child, always seemed to know what mischief I was going to indulge in before I had even finalized the details of the venture, tried to warn me off with a note: 'Please bear in mind that permission is also necessary to visit Professor Kuczynski, as he sometimes forgets to ask for it himself.'

The question which hangs over Jürgen Kuczynski's life in East Germany, indeed over his whole life as a communist intellectual, is whether he led the authorities by the nose or the other way round. In fact, it is evident that the nose-leading was mutual and mutually beneficial. He has been at once insider and renegade, craved the favour of those whose intellects he despised and then exploited the resulting munificence to challenge them. 'I have as many Party discipline cases against me as I have Party orders honouring me,' he once told me. This parity was, for him, both a condition of his existence within East Germany and a result of it. He is a walking dialectic, infuriating, endearing, wise and foolishly vain: Brecht's *'Mensch in seinem Widerspruch'* – man in all his contradictions, and more contradictory than most. His favourite words are *'Gnade'* and *'Ungnade'* – grace and disgrace – conditions which have governed his life. The bestower of these states was the Party: the *force majeur* behind his existence.

He regarded the position of the intellectual under state socialism in the way Galileo – in Brecht's portrayal at least – saw the position of the scientist under the Church. Both were there on sufferance, both could be scythed down at the whim of the ignorant but powerful. The main thing was to survive, to be able to work, in the name of the Party and for its moral improvement. 'I am fully in agreement with Galileo,' he says. 'Recant when you must but carry on working on the quiet.' The compromises would be justified by the results: that, at least, was the theory.

So he wrote the yearly reports on developments in capitalist economics for Erich Honecker. Having supplied the leadership with comforting theories on the unavoidable crisis of capitalism one week, he would wipe the smile off their faces the following week by accusing them of dangerously exaggerating the stability of their own economic position. His hobby-horse was the absurd media policies of the regime. 'Sugar-bakery' he would call the cosmetically adjusted production figures, the grandiose declarations of the identity of purpose between people and Party which appeared in the newspapers.

His low opinion of the leadership's intelligence was no secret, yet he cultivated Honecker – 'Dear Erich' – so that the cantankerous leader would speed the passage of his articles into publications which would otherwise have shied away from their political tone. 'We had been young communists together,' he explains. 'That meant that when I was in disgrace it was particularly hard going and when I was in favour it was pure sunshine.'

Professor Kuczynski does not so much give interviews as tutorials. Once again I was distracted by the thought of how well he would fit into an Oxbridge Senior Common Room, how reminiscent of the academic milieu of the thirties his study is, down to the detail of a large watch placed conspicuously on the desk, a discreet reminder that his time is a precious commodity.

My tutorial-interviews have always begun early in the morning, by which time he had been up and working for three hours. 'I have forty minutes,' he would say. 'What would you like to know?' I wanted to know whether it was a victory or a defeat, this life of his. I wanted to know if the end still justified the means, even when the end was receding further and further into the distance, leaving the bald compromises, the half-truths, the less than upright means haunting the memory. I wanted to know how a communist intellectual looks back on the century that was supposed to bring a new birth for mankind and ended up with the death of its own ideology.

He was sent to London in 1936 by the Communist Party, with Walter Ulbricht telling them that his unmistakably Jewish looks made him 'a walking danger to all of our blonde comrades'. He had already spent two years at the Brookings Institute in Washington, visited Moscow, been the economics editor of the Party paper *Rote Fahne* (Red Flag) and published thirteen books on economics and economic history. It is a rate of literary production which he has kept up all his life. He has a forty-volume *History of the Working Classes in Germany* to his name and over 3,000 miscellaneous publications. Even now, not a month passes without his name appearing in a handful of left-wing publications on a variety of topics. He has never been shy of repeating himself, elegant variations on an analytical Marxist theme. His prolific output was almost a standing joke in East German intellectual circles, and led to the observation that most academics read a thousand books and then wrote one – Jürgen Kuczynski did it the other way round.

Settled in Belsize Park, he administered the financial affairs of a wealthy friend in return for a share of any profits made on the Stock

Exchange, which he used to help fund the Party in exile. It was not the last time he was to exploit his natural links with the capitalist world to help the communist cause. He worked in the British Library on his history project and became involved in the organization of the exiled German communists in Britain. Together with his wife he set up the Free German Youth and the German Cultural Association in Hampstead. He also made his way into elevated left-wing circles with ease, cultivating Aneurin Bevan, the fellow-traveller novelist Leo H. Myers, and Lillian Bowes-Lyon, the Queen Mother's cousin. He became close friends with Cecil Day Lewis and the inventor Geoffrey Pyke, and began to write economic analyses for *Labour Monthly* under a pseudonym – a penchant for which clearly runs in the family.

Soon after his arrival in Britain he produced one of the odder pieces of communist propaganda, a book entitled *Hitler and the British Empire*, under the name James Turner. Kuczynski, like his fellow-communists in exile, was exercised by the task of awakening British opinion-makers to German fascism, not merely as an unsavoury development abroad, but as a risk to Britain and her interests. He concluded that the way to an Englishman's mind was through his Empire, delivering a fulsome account of the danger the Hun posed to Britain's colonial influence through expansion in shipbuilding, exports, and ambitions in the East and in Africa.

The book makes comical reading, a flawless imitation of upper-class literary mannerisms coupled with an eloquent exegesis on the narrow interests of the British political establishment. The conclusion was the culmination of a precisely executed fugue of patriotic concern:

I am interested solely in Great Britain and the British Empire and it is because of this that I think it very necessary to issue a warning against Germany . . . Caveat Consules! May British statesmen realize the danger and act accordingly! May they take up their rightful position as the foremost guardians of world peace and world prosperity.

The thought of this forgery of literary mores being brewed by an exiled communist German-Jew makes it one of the outstanding pranks played on British sensibilities. Kuczynski still giggles at the mention of this particular *œuvre*, his first victory by deception over the bourgeois establishment, at once his foe and his natural home. It would be churlish to disagree with the self-congratulation he issues in his memoirs, which are written, for some peculiar reason, in the third person: 'There was his capability to circulate easily in all circles and classes and his natural tendency towards secrecy.'

He was a charming and witty young man, never at a loss for influential friends. Interned for three months in a camp at Seaton, near Devon, he was rescued on Roosevelt's intervention, courtesy of the offices of the American ambassador in Berlin who was a friend of both Kuczynski and the President. He dined frequently in Cambridge and made friends with Maynard Keynes and Joan Robinson, although he opposed their economic theories violently. In his memoirs he recalls how Harry Pollitt, the General Secretary of the Communist Party of Great Britain, ordered him to scale down the venom of his attacks on Joan Robinson, who was pregnant and working herself into such a state over the criticisms (published by Kuczynski under yet another pseudonym in *Labour Monthly*) that it was feared she might lose the child. 'I cooled them down for a while and mother and child survived the ordeal,' he recalls.

As Ruth Werner confirms, Jürgen introduced her to Klaus Fuchs and gave her economic analyses which she passed to the Soviet Union, although neither are particularly keen to talk in depth about their cooperation on such projects. The picture both present is one of a casual association. One imagines Jürgen popping round to Sunday lunch in Great Rollright and saying: 'By the way, I've got this atomic scientist you might like to meet.' It is likely that the relationship in England was more formal than that, but when I broached the subject of intelligence work, Professor Kuczynski waved a dismissive hand and murmured, 'There were other people for that.'

We do know, however, that towards the end of the war he was approached by an American intelligence officer looking for German communists to undergo dangerous work inside Germany. Together with Ruth he recruited a number of exiles who were then infiltrated into Germany by the Americans. Any further joint operations are unknown: both brother and sister preserve a perfect consistency in their recollections of this time, though whether this is due to perfect honesty or perfect artifice is an open question.

In October 1944 Kuczynski was given a job in the American Strategic Bombing Survey under Kenneth Galbraith, pinpointing economic targets in Germany. It carried the rank of Lieutenant-Colonel, which amused him greatly. Loyalty to that particular flag, however, was not his strong suit, as he cheerfully admitted to me:

We were on very good terms with the Office of Strategic Services – the forerunner of the CIA. They had superb information about the economic situation of western Germany. I had a couple of friends who had wonderful tricks for getting this information out of Germany and underneath their reports would be written the distribution list, consisting of Churchill and his chief of staff, Roosevelt and his chief of staff. I simply decided to add 'Stalin and his chief of staff' for myself.

He was presumably acting in much the same spirit as his sister when she decided to 'help an ally which wasn't doing enough to do more'. The Allied intelligence services were strangely ungrateful for the Kuczynskis' unsought assistance.

He is unwilling to talk further about intelligence matters – 'that's Ruth's department' – but leaves no doubt that he diverted high-quality information to the Soviets over many years. After he moved back to the family home in West Berlin's Schlachtensee the Americans cut off his telephone, and the Russians responded by cutting the lines of two leading Social Democrats. Walter Ulbricht, for whom intellectuals, artists and writers were baubles with which to deck the bare exterior of the newly-formed state, bade him come over to the east in 1950, luring him with a house big enough for his extensive library and the vague promise of the economics portfolio, which never materialized. He omits to mention that the timing of the move coincided with the arrest of Klaus Fuchs in London.

From 1950–58 he was a delegate to the East German parliament, the Volkskammer, but relations with the stubbornly anti-intellectual Ulbricht cooled and he was ousted in the political purges of the fifties after his support for anti-Ulbricht factions became known. Like his sister Ruth, his privileged Jewish background and his long stint in Western exile made him a target for removal from the spheres of political influence. Never one to hang around in an atmosphere in which he felt threatened, he moved to China for a lengthy research visit until Ulbricht's ire had faded.

Kuczynski, who had established himself in the left-wing intellectual circles around Bertolt Brecht, is scathing about Ulbricht's intellectual capacities. 'He was an absolute petit-bourgeois when it came to art,' he recalls. 'I used to joke with my old friend Brecht that when Wilhelm Pieck quoted Balzac we knew that he learned it from Rosa Luxemburg and Franz Mehring in the Party school in 1912, but when Walter Ulbricht quoted Brecht, as he had a habit of doing, then we just wondered who had taught him the quote that day.'

And yet he liked Ulbricht, which made him something of a one-off, even in communist circles. He has the left-wing intellectual's fatal flaw of admiring the thug, the tactician, the anti-intellectual, while at the same time sensing that these are the very forces intent on liquidating his own contribution to socialism. 'I have no illusions about Walter. I knew that he would walk over my corpse if he felt like it. But I admired his purpose, his ability to manoeuvre.'

But what of Stalin? Kuczynski gave the problems surrounding his legacy a long-overdue airing in his book *Dialogue With My Great-Grandson*, published in 1983. This is an imaginative romp through the problems of the socialist world in the early eighties, using the device of a young man questioning his great-grandfather about his experiences of communism throughout the twentieth century. The sixth dialogue caused a minor stir among the reading public in a country where Stalinism, although officially condemned, had never been subjected to critical scrutiny. What, asked the probing descendant, did Kuczynski now think about his days under Stalin?

The answer is lodged in the folk-memory of East Germans, half of whom recall it as a sign of Kuczynski's honesty, the others as a suspiciously economic attempt at dealing with the dominant factor in the construction and collapse of socialism throughout the Eastern bloc. 'I would say to you first and foremost: I am a child of the Stalin years with its great achievements and negative aspects, in the grip of the eminent figure of Stalin, his policies and his party line . . . In many respects then I resembled a believer rather than a scientist, without even admitting it to myself.'

Kuczynski recalled an encounter in the London of the late thirties with Hermann Dunker, an eminent communist in the Weimar Republic who had been one of the founders of the KPD in 1918 and played a leading role in the ideological battles within the Party during the twenties. Dunker's son, who was in exile in the Soviet Union, had been arrested with Bukharin. Kuczynski's task, as leader of the Party in British exile, was to comfort the old communist and prevent him from 'becoming prone to doubts' after the revelation. 'It took a long time,' Kuczynski admits, 'until I could persuade him that Soviet justice makes no mistakes.' The old man was still crying when he left and said, 'I'm sure you're right. But you must understand how difficult it is for me to believe in the treachery of my son and of my good old friend Bukharin.'

He acknowledges that he was later ashamed of his actions that day, but there is an unintentionally chilling postscript contained in the account. 'We remained on good terms with one another to the end of his life,' he writes, 'and we never again spoke of that hour.'

There are two aspects of Stalinism at work here and Kuczynski still admits to only one of them. The first is the consequences of the purges in the thirties and the false discipline of the other communist parties. But the second and more poisonous legacy is that indicated in the statement that he and Dunker, who later became director of the central trade-union school in East Germany, never discussed the matter again; that the suppression – even of personal pain and injustice – of those days persisted, reinforced by the silence of those who had, in many cases, been close relatives or friends of Stalin's random victims.

His comments on Stalinism are a slight summary of the myriad injustices practised in socialism's name. While he cannot be accused of suppressing them, the dishonesty lies in the superficiality of his treatment. The failure of his generation of intellectuals to deal with Stalinism lies in their habitual *Verharmlosung* – the rendering harmless of a pernicious figure by recourse to relativity, conveniently provided by fascism. No conversation with a communist of his age ends without the reminder that Stalin defeated Hitler, as if this should give the dictator generous remission for every death he imposed on his own people.

'Admiration for Stalin is not Stalinism,' he says. 'Stalinism was a command system of grotesque discipline. It allowed no differences of opinion, no democracy: we all admired Churchill, who had a good deal of these characteristics too.' The game of relativities, once begun, knows no end and the Professor, practised in the convincing defence of the indefensible, plays it with more panache than most.

We have had similar conversations over several years and they never fail to leave a yawning dissatisfaction behind. The admissions of personal guilt run dangerously close to the shallow seam of ritual self-criticism. 'I would admit,' says Kuczynski at the end of all of this, 'that the consequences of the Stalin days remain in many of us to this day, certainly in me, without us being aware of them.' I don't know if it is depressing or consoling that he senses that he has spoken of this without really talking about it; that his discourse on the topic is also a silencing of it; that the manner of the revelation is itself a form of suppression.

Back to the future. Lenin. Ah yes, Lenin was a different matter. Has he told me the story of H. G. Wells and Lenin? Well, yes, several times, but he tells it so well I don't mind hearing it again. Lenin and Wells were taking tea together in Moscow and the author's comfortable glow at the advances of revolutionary Russia had taken a knock after he had talked to some Russian workers. He told the leader that he was concerned at how dissatisfied they were. 'But isn't that wonderful,' said Lenin. 'As long as they are dissatisfied, they are involved.'

The problem in East Germany, he said, was that the people had been dissatisfied but not involved, the overwhelming Party bureaucracy had nipped their creative discontent in the bud, deformed it into straight antipathy. Lenin would not have tolerated that. A future socialism will not tolerate it either. 'In two hundred years, it will all look very different for socialism,' he says blithely. Out of the old *real existierender Sozialismus* – actual existing socialism – has grown an exotic, mutant-creature: a hybrid of past legends hitched to future dreams. The last seventy years are being gradually airbrushed from the ideological record. Socialism is what they had then (1917) and will have again someday. Prognoses as to when vary. Ruth Werner's grandson says twenty years; his great-uncle Jürgen errs on the conservative side at two hundred.

The ultimate failure of communism in the twentieth century is its inability to accommodate reform. All the waiting in the shadows, the precise attention to grace and disgrace, were based on the premise that one could do it better. But the reforms of Mikhail Gorbachev have resulted merely in an acceleration of decline. The intellectuals who so carefully kept their powder dry now find that the final battle is cancelled due to lack of interest. Jürgen Kuczynski's life began under the capitalism of the Kaiser's Reich and will end under the capitalism of the united Federal Republic.

It has been a life of outstanding wealth of experience and insight and yet depressingly typical of a generation of great thinkers under communism. A life spent on the tightrope over an abyss of their own and others' destruction, clutching the unwieldy balancing pole of compromise. His is the psychology of the card-carrying survivor, motivated by the desire to outlive the Stalins, Ulbrichts and Honeckers and finally get down to building Utopia. But the strategy failed. The intellectuals waited so long, devoted such energy to their own survival, that the much-vaunted *gemeinsame Sache* (the common aim) has evaporated around them.

What remains, beyond the fine words and the grubby compromises? Only the faith of the unimprovables, the religion of the atheist. A suspicion Kuczynski betrays in his memoirs when he writes that he could as little imagine leaving the Party as resigning from the human race; or when he says, 'Margerite [his wife] used to say to me years ago, "If you had been born two hundred years earlier, you would have been one of the truest sons of the Catholic Church."'

He has no regrets about his life of strategy. He felt no calling to be a hero: 'It is the task of the reformer to know when a challenge is meaningful and when it is simply a waste of time and energy. Heroism would have been glamorous and cheap but, in the circumstances in which we lived, rarely useful.' The only alternative, he said, would be to have gone to the West.

My patience snapped with this elegant pirouette of a great brain across a mesh of unreason, and I blurted out the tactless question: 'Would it not have been better for you, as an intellectual, to have been able to write the whole truth in the West than the half-truths you wrote here?'

A seraphic smile spread across his face as, struggling to find words simple enough to convey a complex truth to a moron, he resorted to the language of proportions. 'But my child,' he said, 'what a question! I would rather live in a 25 per cent socialist country than a 100 per cent capitalist one any day.'

3
The Fifties

Teething Troubles

Builders, painters, carpenters, sun-browned faces, white linen caps, muscular arms, well-developed necks: we haven't nourished you too badly in this republic of yours, you could see that. Square-built you came thence . . . And as a hand sweeps a touch of dust from a jacket, the Soviet army wiped the city clean. Only those with a reason to fight are prepared to do battle, and you had no reason. Your false friends, the scum from the other side, stole on silver bicycles through the city like swallows before the rain. And were wiped away. But you could go to sleep in your beds by nine that night, like good children. For you and for the peace of the world, the Soviet army and the comrades of the People's Police kept its watch.

Are you not ashamed, as I am?

For you will have to build much and well and behave wisely in the future before this shame of yours will be forgotten.

How Ashamed I Am, KuBa (Kurt Bartel), Secretary of the Writers' Association,
in response to the uprising of 17 June 1953

> After the uprising of 17 June,
> The Secretary of the Writers' Union
> Had leaflets distributed in the Stalinallee
> Stating that the people
> Had forfeited the confidence of the government,
> And could win it back only
> By redoubled efforts. Would it not be easier
> In that case for the government
> To dissolve the people
> And elect another?

> Bertolt Brecht, *The Solution*, August 1953

By the spring of 1953 Lotte Ulbricht was preoccupied with arrangements for her husband's sixtieth birthday at the end of June. What she intended

48

to give him is unrecorded, but she left little doubt about what gifts of gratitude she expected of everyone else. With an eye on the pan-national knees-up which had accompanied Stalin's seventieth birthday in 1949, a committee – the Commission for the Preparation of the Sixtieth Birthday of Comrade Walter Ulbricht – was assembled under her leadership.

But this time the revelling was to have a distinctly feudal character: socialist Utopia was to meet folk-German tradition halfway. There was to be singing and dancing in the market squares of the republic. All church choirs were to hold commemorative performances and a parade before the flag was to take place in schoolyards (the fact that this had once been the form on the Führer's birthday did not deter her). An act of state was to be held in East Berlin. A million copies of a Free German Youth appreciation of the leader were to be printed and an official biography was commissioned from the Minister of Culture, Johannes R. Becher, who combined the useful talents of being extraordinarily literate and extraordinarily sycophantic.

Frau Ulbricht was ecstatic at Becher's eulogy, probably because it read more like a wifely valentine than a political biography: 'All of us who love our homeland and all of us who love peace love you, Walter Ulbricht, the German workers' son.' In fact, not everyone loved Walter: not his own Politburo, which was fast fomenting opposition to his dogmatic leadership and his hostility to intellectuals and non-communists, and certainly not the population, alienated by his authoritarian style and economic mismanagement.

Not even the most elaborate stage-management could suppress the spontaneous shows of dislike for the leader. In 1950, a Dresden football crowd in his native Saxony had pelted guest of honour Ulbricht with tomatoes at the final league match of the first season. Dresden-Friedrichstadt, a privately-run club and Horch-Zwickau, a workers' co-operative, had been level on points before the match. Assisted by some creative refereeing, Zwickau won 5–1. The entire Dresden team voted with its feet and transferred *en masse* to the west.

Ulbricht's grip on the political apparatus was so strong, however, that no one dreamed of telling Lotte to down-play the personality cult. Not, that is, until her plans received a disturbing interruption. On 5 March, Josef Stalin died in Moscow and was succeeded by the collective leadership of Georgi Malenkov, Laurentij Beria and Nikita Khrushchev. The dictator's death was the last birthday present Ulbricht needed, particularly when his successors lost no time in introducing some mild reforms aimed at softening the East-West conflict on which the East German regime thrived.

At the beginning of June, the newly-appointed High Commissioner of the Soviet Union in Germany, Vladimir Semyonov, called the leading lights of the SED to a meeting. He recommended that Ulbricht should spend his sixtieth birthday as Lenin had passed his fiftieth. Sensing a rare opportunity to put the comradely boot in, the ideology chief Fred Oelssner, one of the growing guard of Ulbricht critics in the Politburo, politely enquired how the great revolutionary had marked the day. 'Comrade Lenin,' said Semyonov evenly, 'invited a few friends round for the evening.' The encounter left Lotte Ulbricht and the birthday-present commission with the awkward task of turning a national celebration into a non-event. It was a cleverly executed public humiliation, intended to reveal to the world Moscow's displeasure with Ulbricht. It made him look foolish – something that he, like many insecure politicians, could not stand – and it was read by his critics within the apparatus as an encouragement to challenge him.

His own policies and arrogance had brought him to the edge of the abyss. In autumn 1952, at the second Party Conference, he had set the course of the state full tilt for socialism with the declaration, 'The democratic development as well as the consciousness of the working class and the majority of our working people are now so advanced that the construction of socialism in the GDR has become the basic task.' The congress buried the 'anti-fascist democratic order' which had been promised in the late forties.

A clamp-down began on small businesses and private tradesmen, with draconian tax increases and the withdrawal of ration cards from those in the private sector: a crash course in constructing a command economy. The Congress also declared that the power of the state was behind the rapid construction of socialism under the dictatorship of the proletariat, a phrase which had until then been studiously avoided. Concerned at the economic decline caused by a steady stream of migrants to the west, Ulbricht imposed a 10 per cent increase in production norms, which in real terms meant a salary decrease for many manual workers. The measures were to be implemented 'with the support of the state organs of control', a transparent euphemism for the police and state security.

The retrenchment caused a leap in the number of refugees from socialism. From December 1952 to March 1953 the number of emigrants rose from 22,000 in the previous three months to more than 58,000 – the highest figure in any quarter until the mass exodus of 1989. It was no longer possible to ignore the transformation of the second German state into a Soviet satellite of the strictest variety: but now a different wind was blowing from Moscow.

Although scarcely known for his liberalism, Beria was anxious to instigate a quick departure from Stalin's economically ruinous ways, and make a fresh attempt to secure German unification on terms strategically favourable to the Soviet Union. He had indicated to Rudolf Herrnstadt, editor of the Party paper *Neues Deutschland*, and to the Chief of State Security Wilhelm Zaisser, that the Kremlin was prepared to back them against Ulbricht, whose stubbornness and lack of charisma were regarded as liabilities.

Herrnstadt and Zaisser favoured a thorough reform of the Party – although how far this would have got in the light of subsequent developments in Moscow is dubious – and the removal of Ulbricht and his youth leader Erich Honecker, by now already established as the crown prince. They wanted a greater degree of economic freedom within a socialist structure, and a popularization of the Party outside the ranks of Ulbricht's heroic proletariat. 'The Party must become a party of the people,' their platform announced. 'It must respect the legitimate interests of all classes and groups in order to secure the support not only of the working class but of all classes and social levels.'

The ensuing power battle in East Berlin was a microcosm of that which preceded it in Moscow, Ulbricht banking on the conservative Soviet Foreign Minister Molotov and the deputy Prime Minister Kaganovich, while his opponents crossed their fingers for Beria, Malenkov and Khrushchev. The reformers appeared to be in the ascendant. Their secret platform was betrayed to Ulbricht on 16 June and a Politburo sitting called to discuss the challenge. But while the wrangling leaders confronted each other behind closed doors, an unexpected and previously dormant force was about to upset the calculations on both sides: the East German people.

On 16 and 17 June, workers in East Berlin and the country's industrial centres took to the streets. These protests rapidly evolved into an uprising which brought the country to the brink of collapse, less than four years after its foundation. Discontent had been growing since the second Party Congress in spring 1953, and the post-Stalin Kremlin, concerned for the stability of Ulbricht's GDR, took matters into its own hands by ordering that the 'hard course' be softened. Ulbricht, whose obsessive attachment to the former Soviet leader left him ill-prepared to take orders from others, refused, considering the reform – any reform in fact – a betrayal of Stalin's infallibility.

Instead he ordered 'heightened watchfulness' and the 'unsparing exposure of agents, good-for-nothings and blatherers' and used these extraordinary decrees to instigate the removal of Party members – such as Ruth Werner – from significant positions. The Kremlin, worried by the haemorrhage of East Germans to the West, responded at the beginning of June with a secret memorandum instructing Ulbricht to change course. On 9 June, after he had failed to comply, High Commissioner Semyonov ordered the East Berlin government to recant the hardline reforms of the past nine months and cancelled Ulbricht's birthday party. 'If you're not careful,' he told the still hesitant Politburo, 'you won't have a state left at all after the next fourteen days.'

It was the first time that the regime had been prevailed upon to eat its words, albeit in a recipe cooked up in Moscow. The declaration of a 'new course' appeared in *Neues Deutschland* on 11 June but without any editorial comment:

The leadership admits that a number of mistakes have been made in the past by the SED and the government of the German Democratic Republic. One consequence of this was that many people have left our republic ... For this reason, the Politburo believes it necessary that in the days to come, measures be carried out relating to the correction of plans for heavy industry and that the living standards of workers, farmers and the intelligentsia should be improved.

And so it went on, in the strangled tone of the unwilling penitent. The decree ended with a restatement of the East German leadership's will to work towards the unity of the two German states: a plant by the new troika in Moscow to revive Stalin's failed strategy of unification. The only failure it did not mention was the one which was to drive the first flock of workers on to the streets a few days later: the draconian rise in production norms which hit hardest the numerous manual workers employed in rebuilding the country, often resulting in a sizeable loss of wages.

On 16 June the building workers employed in the construction of the grandiose Stalin Allee – 'the first socialist street in Berlin' – downed tools. The symbolism was engaging but slightly at odds with reality, as the workers were not initially concerned with Stalin or his legacy, as Frank Meyer, a builder from one of the first sites to strike and now employed renovating the Allee, told me. 'We didn't want to start a revolution. We were just mad as hell,' he said in the Pünktchen, a pub just off the street which still carries the name of Karl Marx but is probably heading for yet another rechristening soon.

The government had already repealed most of its crazier suggestions and softened the old course but not a word was said about the raised norms. They were set so high that we would have all lost our extra premiums for the week's work – either that or work overtime every day. It was a financial grievance to begin with.

The arrogation of the role of sole major employer by the state meant that any industrial dispute automatically turned into an ideological confrontation.

That wasn't what we intended. I can't even say that at that point we had anything against the system as such, although Ulbricht was never popular with the workers. We were just sick of being the human toys of his grand designs. But at the back of our minds there was a bitterness about the way this Party, which was supposed to represent us, the workers, was treating us – the same way as the old capitalists before the war, with random demands and no arguments accepted. Once we started to talk about that, people just became more and more heated.

In the middle on the early shift on 16 June, at nine in the morning, eighty workers set off down the Stalin Allee with a single banner reading 'We demand the revision of norms'. By the time they reached the Strausberger Platz, Meyer recalls, they had been joined by hundreds of their colleagues and the original call was soon complemented by the more adventurous cry 'Away with the goatee-beard' (Ulbricht) and 'We want to be free people'.

This is probably the point at which the home-made protest ended and the uprising began. By the time the procession reached its goal, the House of Ministries, it had been joined by both East and West Berliners. The exact point at which the West became involved is controversial. Karl Eduard von Schnitzler, the chief commentator of East German television who was sent out to talk to the mutinous builders that morning, swears that they had already been infiltrated by 'people I had never seen before in snowy-white overalls who didn't know how to handle a spade'. But it is a long time since anyone believed Herr von Schnitzler.

All other indications are that the west was completely unprepared for the uprising and that only when the march began did West Berliners – many of whom had crossed the zonal border from the east to escape Ulbricht and his policies – join in. When the first reports of trouble ran on RIAS, the radio station of the American sector, the major news agencies even refused to use it because they suspected that the strike was a ploy by the East Berlin government to boost its democratic credentials in the wake of the mild reforms. Despite calls by the demonstrators for Ulbricht and his Prime Minister Otto Grotewohl to appear, there was no movement from behind the heavy lace curtains of the Central Committee building. Having come face to face with its citizens for the first time, the Politburo decided that it did not much like the look of them and locked itself in.

Instead, the leadership communicated with its masses in the only way it knew: by publishing a statement. This repealed the raising of industrial norms. It is enlightening to compare the language of this second back-down with the Soviet-inspired declaration of a few days earlier. The statement of 16 June was characterized by a lamb-like meekness which was not otherwise a salient feature of Ulbricht's rule:

The Politburo considers the raising of labour norms in the state-owned factories by 10 per cent via administrative means to be completely erroneous. The raising of norms cannot be forced through by purely administrative methods but solely on the grounds of conviction and voluntary action ... The Party is departing from a course it recognizes as false and commencing on a new and corrected one.

But the statement came too late to calm the masses gathered on the streets of East Berlin and by now in Leipzig, Magdeburg and Dresden too. Instead it acted as a catalyst to strike action in the smaller industrial centres. According to East German figures there were strikes in 27 towns and cities: the east counted 300,000 participants, the west 372,000. By the morning of 17 June the strikes had spread across the republic. Towards midday, Ulbricht was smuggled out of the Central Committee building in a Soviet tank and taken to Kienbaum, a small village outside Berlin close to the Soviet military airport and thus a guaranteed route out should the protestors gain the upper hand.

By now the demonstrations had taken on the significance the regime feared most. The *Deutschlandlied*, the West German national anthem, could be heard on the streets, the red flag had been torn down from the top of the Brandenburg Gate and the anti-norm slogans had given way to cries of 'Unity'. Undirected violence spread throughout the republic. No leaders emerged from the ranks of the workers to steer the proceedings. Alfred Kantorowicz, the diarist, who travelled from Leipzig by train that day, remarked on his arrival that the journey had been 'a trip through enemy territory'. Like many intellectuals, he was shocked to discover how thin the layer of public tolerance for the communist leadership was, and how readily the venting of small grievances unleashed a violent reaction against the regime.

Analysing the event afterwards, the SED resorted to its familiar trick of blurring the distinction between anti-communism and fascism by suggesting that the instigators were aiming for the restoration of the Third Reich. While this is plainly absurd, it would also be misleading to ignore the brutality of some of the demonstrators. Several jails were stormed and war criminals – whether for political ends or not remains unclear – were among the prisoners set free. In Leipzig communist functionaries were attacked, and one died when he was thrown from his window.

Nor was the uprising a homogeneous affair. Many in the crowd outside the SED's headquarters in East Berlin were reform communists who held aloft portraits of the old KPD leader, Ernst Thälmann, murdered by the Nazis in 1944, as a way of declaring their opposition to the bureaucratic Ulbricht while stressing their adherence to the communist cause. In the provincial cities, however, the mood was deeply anti-communist.

At midday a state of emergency was declared and the Soviet occupation powers took control by special decree. The number of known deaths, twenty-one, was doubtless supplemented by many victims of instant retribution, whether practised by the mob or the security forces. Then came the tanks, supported by teams from the People's Police (then still known, as the People's Police in Barracks), followed by obedient silence.

By the evening, the uprising had been quashed and Ulbricht returned to Berlin. Arnulf Baring, a West Berlin historian with no sympathy for the communist cause, whose 1957 study of the 17 June uprising remains the most thorough, points out that the Soviets acted 'carefully and with restraint'. The tank commanders were ordered to show their strength but avoid casualties wherever possible. The uprising died a natural death towards the evening. The presence of the tanks was deterrent enough against further action:

Let us make no mistakes. The uprising was not put down by the Soviet tanks. The revolutionary wave had been broken before the Russians marched in. Their intervention was not a turning-point but a closing-point. The strike and demonstration movement had exhausted itself during the course of the day.

Nevertheless, the incident was the Soviet Union's first military intervention to counter undesirable domestic developments in an Eastern European state, and it had been smooth and successful. A government working party which is currently researching the true extent of executions in the east, with access to Stasi files, has revealed that the figures of deaths during and after the uprising were much higher than even the west had believed, and probably stands between 100 and 200. A still unspecified number of executions followed in the next few years, disguised by the authorities as natural deaths in prison.

The Party was well aware of the responsibility it carried for the events of 17 June. Prime Minister Otto Grotewohl acknowledged the Party's responsibility soon afterwards when he observed: 'If the mass of workers fail understand the Party, then it is the Party's fault, not the workers.' But the view was quickly silenced at the helm as a bitter power struggle took place in the Politburo between Ulbricht and his challengers Herrnstadt and Zaisser. Initial signals from the Kremlin, that it intended to drop the leader in favour of the reformers, gave way to support for the existing leadership.

The backing Herrnstadt and Zaisser had gained from Beria proved to be their political death sentence. On 9 July, Beria's arrest was announced in Moscow and he was denounced as an 'enemy of the Party and the state'. Ulbricht and his backers were saved, Herrnstadt and Zaisser stripped of their offices and Party membership. In his memoirs Herrnstadt was to state that his intention and Beria's had been internal liberalization in both the Soviet Union and the satellites, coupled with concessions towards the Western powers aimed at breaking through the ice of the Cold War. Ulbricht indulged in the required self-criticism to satisfy his Moscow masters and then proceeded to use the atmosphere of recrimination and distrust for which he bore responsibility to purge the Politburo of those he suspected of harbouring unhealthy hopes of restoring German unity.

Anton Ackermann, the proponent of a separate German path to socialism uncoupled from Soviet structures, was ousted, together with the East Berlin Party chief Hans Jendretsky. The tragedy of 17 June is that it saved Ulbricht's neck at a time when the constellation of forces around him brought him to the brink of destruction. In the wake of the event, the Kremlin considered stability in East Germany to have a priority over reform, and the obstinate leader profited from this judgement.

Although he was forced to accept the 'New Course' prescribed for the Kremlin, Ulbricht received a favourable deal after the near-disaster his intransigence had unleashed. Anxious to avoid further disturbances with economic roots, the Kremlin dropped its crippling reparations demand of 2.5 billion dollars, handed back to the GDR 33 factories it had bagged as the Soviet share of companies 1945–49, and placed a ceiling on the amount East Berlin was to pay Moscow for the privilege of having Soviet troops stationed on its soil – a protection racket which persisted in the

Eastern bloc until the very end of the Soviet domination and which continues to this day in a politer form. Until the final withdrawal of the 380,000 Soviet troops from eastern Germany in 1994, Bonn will finance their upkeep and the building of homes for them back in the former Soviet Union.

In practice, there were few reforms of note other than the wider acceptance of 'bourgeois culture' – the state film company DEFA was finally allowed to make a love story which did not begin with the scenario which its frustrated directors used to describe as 'man meets tractor' – and the placing of greater emphasis on raising living standards. Far from being the Day of Unity that the west had hoped, 17 June effectively buried the chance of unification. This probably explains why, despite being the first popular uprising against the Soviet-installed regimes of Eastern Europe, the date has failed to capture the international imagination.

The inability of historians to pinpoint the prime movers – if indeed there were any – behind the events gave rise to opposing and equally unconvincing theories. East Berlin believed that it was essentially masterminded by American and West German secret service agents, attempting to capitalize on the dissatisfaction of the workers in order to bring about the collapse of the GDR and achieve German unity under a reactionary flag. This version of events was however scorned even by communists such as the dissident scientist Robert Havemann, whose sober balance, drawn in 1970, probably comes closest to the truth:

Nowhere in the world does anything happen on the political stage without the secret services of East and West having their fingers in it somewhere. In the Berlin of 1953 they were certainly not far away. But it is naïve to believe that these fingers can move world history. The eruption of the June uprising was a surprise for everyone.

Bonn meanwhile preferred the more gratifying explanation that East Germany in the fifties was a tinderbox of unification hopes waiting for a match, and that the raising of the norms produced a spontaneous uprising throughout the country, culminating in a cry for German unity.

Each side proceeded to write the history of the day as it suited their needs and on its anniversary every year the East celebrated the defeat of a counter-revolution inspired by old Nazis and imperialist reactionaries, while Bonn dubbed it the Day of German Unity. This was something of a cheat, given that the overwhelming tone of the protests was against the SED and its hari-kiri economic policies, with cries for unification an afterthought.

The historian Fritz Stern caused one of the Federal Republic's perennial rows over the interpretation of Germany's recent past when in 1987 he followed the tradition of public figures using sensitive anniversaries to say what most people feel privately during the rest of the year. In his speech to the Bundestag on the anniversary of the uprising, he rejected the conventional pieties by interpreting the event as a call for liberty rather than unity: 'One of the great moments in which men stand up against force and inhumanity ... it was not an uprising for reunification.'

The main boulevard in West Berlin still bears 17 June as its name but few Germans, east or west, could put their hands on their hearts and say that the date bears any great significance for them. Since unification on 3 October 1990, that date has supplanted it as the German national holiday. As a caesura it lacked the passion of the Hungarians' revolt against the Sovietization of their land in 1956, or the stark symbolism of Prague in 1968. The events of 17 June confirmed the adage that Germans and revolutions do not mix well, and its muddled history, overlaid by the propaganda requirements of both German governments, ensured that it never caught on as a symbol.

Not, that is, until the anniversary in 1990 when the first democratically elected Volkskammer and the West German Bundestag held a joint sitting to mark the day. Several East German MPs were so overcome by the re-emergence of the date as a national holiday that year that they proposed that its role as the Day of Unity should be taken literally, and that the autumn date for the unification of the two Germanies should be brought forward in favour of an instant accession of the GDR to the Federal Republic. The vote was narrowly defeated, to the great relief of most East Germans, who preferred a little more time to gird their loins for the event. Jens Reich of the opposition New Forum group commented that he had nothing against being unified, but he would prefer it not to take place 'by caesarean and under an anaesthetic'. The cloakroom lady in the Volkskammer told me the next day that she had had 'quite a turn' when she realized that she had 'nearly woken up as a *Wessi*'.

The lost battle had two clear victors: Walter Ulbricht, who strengthened his otherwise shaky position with his Soviet backers, and Konrad Adenauer, the West German chancellor, who turned it to rhetorical advantage in defence of his refusal to do business with the regime. But the greater strategic advantage was the East's. The West had shown that, despite its verbal commitment to roll-back policy, it was not prepared to risk intervention in the Soviet sphere of influence (a useful precedent for Ulbricht when it came to building the Wall); and by its intervention the Soviet Union had made it clear that it considered the GDR as a satellite, to be defended with military means if necessary. The major victim was the possibility of democratic reform in East Germany.

As the fifties continued, Ulbricht's paranoia intensified. Inspired by the show-trials of alleged Zionist sympathizers in Prague in 1952, and confident that the policy would not provoke undue domestic opposition, Ulbricht exploited anti-semitism to have several opponents sentenced as 'agents of world Judaism'. The courts were used ruthlessly to quell dissent, making even the mildest criticism a criminal offence, as demonstrated by the case of Herbert Gaedecke. This case was cited by Ulbricht's biographer Carola Stern, who had herself witnessed the development as a young teacher. In an off-the-cuff remark Gaedecke, a lecturer at a technical college in Dessau, told a class of insatiably curious students: 'I'm not omniscient. Not like Walter Ulbricht.' He was sentenced to six months' imprisonment for slandering the state. 'The accused delivered his comment in such a manner that it could in no way be understood to refer to the evident knowledge of Comrade Walter Ulbricht,' said the judge, clearly fearing that he could be the defendent in another case of state slander if his ruling were to be interpreted as a denial of Comrade Ulbricht's omniscience.

While Stalin's death and the subsequent revelations of his atrocities caused shock waves in communist movements across the world, and prompted many of his supporters in East Germany to review their slavish adoration, Ulbricht carried on as if nothing had happened. One of his few recorded comments on the revelations was that Stalin could now no longer count as a classic exponent of Marxist theory. But he deftly stifled a thorough discussion of the personality cult by proclaiming that those who aimed at pushing the matter into the foreground were influenced by counter-revolutionary forces and ordered the nation to concentrate on its future economic welfare rather than past problems. The Politburo passed a resolution to 'investigate to what extent there might be elements of a leadership cult in the GDR', then carried on as before.

It would not have needed to look far. Hand in hand with Ulbricht's growing conviction of his own infallibility went his obsession with styling himself the moral father of the nation. This was to take on a warped theological overtone when, in 1958, he swerved wildly from his previously materialist conviction by proclaiming the Ten Commandments of Socialist Morality.

They began: 'Thou shalt engage thy efforts without fail for the international solidarity of the working class and all working people as well as for the invincible bond of all socialist countries,' and enjoined the populace: 'Thou shalt protect all socialist property and aim to enlarge it,' and culminated in: 'Thou shalt educate thy children in the spirit of peace and socialism to adults firm of character and physically steeled.'

Ulbricht's reign was essentially Victorian, and despite his fanatical attachment to Lenin and to his beloved 'scientific-technological revolution', many of his utterances reflected the concerns of *fin de siècle* capitalism. Of the ten refashioned commandments, his favourite remained: 'Thou shalt live in cleanliness and decency and show regard for thy family.' East Germans remain perversely proud of this enterprise as one of the rare occasions where their leadership outstripped the lunatic Romanian dictator Nicolae Ceaucescu in the megalomania stakes. Ceaucescu saw himself as the successor to the Dacian dynasty; Ulbricht would stop at nothing less than being the universal lawgiver.

Kindergarten teachers were instructed to familiarize children with Ulbricht's portrait, and the 'recognition that he is a good man'. In their yearly report of 1963, the Association of Small Allotment Holders and Animal Breeders issued the following fervent pledge: 'We in the Association spend our free time raising the productivity . . . of our output of fruit and vegetables, eggs, meat, honey, milk, wool and hides for our common good and the honour of Walter Ulbricht.' Or, as Orwell had put it in *Animal Farm* a few years earlier, 'You would often hear one hen remark to another, "Under the guidance of our Leader, Comrade Napoleon, I have laid five eggs in six days".'

While paying lip-service to Moscow's liberalization, Ulbricht tightened the security services at home, instituting the *Kampfgruppen* – standby groups of workers trained to combat internal dissent and whose cheerful ditty ran, '*Arbeiterbataillonen treffen und schlagen zu*' ('Battalions of workers gather and put the boot in').

When Ulbricht heard of unrest in the Leuna chemicals plant in 1956, he dispatched Erich Mielke, then state secretary in the State Security Ministry (and later the feared head of the service) to find the inevitable 'agents' responsible. Several arrests later, the work-force went back to their machines. A further challenge by his deputy Karl Schirdewan in 1958 also failed and Schirdewan was put out to grass at the state archive in Potsdam. By now Moscow had changed tack on the German question, preferring to stick with the territorial gain represented by the existence of the GDR rather than risk *détente* with the Western powers. Little as Khrushchev liked Ulbricht, he decided that his uncanny ability to survive crises was a suitable symbol of the impregnability of the East German state. By the end of the fifties, Ulbricht seemed invincible.

His widow and mentor Lotte is still alive in east Berlin at the age of ninety. She lives in Pankow's Mayakovsky Ring, an apple-blossomed suburb inhabited by Ulbricht and his Politburo before the nervousness occasioned by 17 June and the Hungarian uprising prompted them to move *en masse* to the remote Wandlitz in 1958. After the fall of the regime in 1990, the Mayakovsky Ring was used to house the ousted leaders, among them Erich Honecker's brief successor Egon Krenz. On their first encounter, Frau Ulbricht told her new neighbour that he ought to be ashamed of himself for allowing the collapse of the GDR. It would never have happened under Walter, she said. Why hadn't Krenz sent in tanks to crush the counter-revolution?

She ventured out on the day of the first free general elections in March 1990 to cast her vote in the tiny polling station once reserved for the political élite. Without a word to the gathered journalists or officials, she walked to the ballot box shaking her head and, like 12 million other East Germans, submitted her multiple-choice voting slip for the first time since Hitler suspended the free vote in 1933. In the neighbourhood, she is regarded as a kind old lady who frequently entertains the children of the locality in her kitchen. She is less fond of adults, and declines to discuss Walter even with old friends from the communist movement. When I tried to visit her, she would not let me past the garden gate.

Difficulties with the Truth

As the state prosecutor's speech by now no longer held any surprises for me, I stopped paying attention to it and looked at the audience in court. Anna Seghers looked mortified and stared ahead or looked at the ground. She listened to the defamation of her friend Lukács and myself – her comrade from Mexican exile – without a word. The same went for Helene Weigel. Johannes R. Becher was informed daily of the progress of my trial but there was no word from him. Nothing. Not a single word from any of them. Do you understand? As for my workers in the publishing house, I do not blame them. They had no means of defending themselves. But I won't have that said of the writers. They had all lifted their voices against the brutality of the Nazi regime. So why did they fear to speak out when another justice, our own justice, was abused?

Walter Janka, conversation with the author, April 1991

Walter Janka, former head of the East German prestige publishers Aufbau, is a talkative man, the result of thirty years of silence. As the most prominent victim of Ulbricht's persecution of those intellectuals unwilling to place their brains solely in the service of his grand designs, his name and his story were kept alive on the grapevine of East Germany's cultural circles. And yet he was unknown to the mass of the population.

When in 1989 he finally told his experiences in public it came as a shock to the national consciousness. 'How could we not know?' was the response to the publication of his memoirs. He was sentenced to quiescence by the Party to which he had pledged his life as a young man, rendered an unperson by the communists he believed were his comrades, sentenced to prison and oblivion by the complicity of some of the most respected names in German literature. And yet he too kept to the rules which made his persecution possible, confounding his supporters by accepting a belated honour from the very Party which had condemned him.

His is a story which reflects better than any other the darkest period in the country's history: the fifties, and the shadow of ignorance and fear they cast over later years. If there was a 'fifties sound' behind the Iron Curtain it was that of crashing silence.

Janka lives in Kleinmachnow, a rural village-cum-suburb on the edge of East Berlin which used to be jammed up against the Wall. On the day of my visit, tractors and steamrollers, restoring the road across the former death strip to the well-heeled neighbouring district of southern Zehlendorf, drowned out the bird-song with the sound of mechanized reunification. The proximity to the border and the presence of the Party school there made Kleinmachnow a functionaries' suburb. Only the most reliable were rewarded with homes there and the village consists of low bungalows with generous gardens, middle-class idylls for the champions of the proletariat.

As a young communist, Janka was imprisoned by the Nazis. As an older communist he was back behind bars under their successors whose ideology he still calls his own. His is a face one sees less and less frequently these days, the unmistakeable features of a proletarian intellectual. His eyes betray the weariness of his seventy-two years and myriad disappointments, but after every description of recognized injustice he sets his chin obstinately to declare his allegience to the state which hounded him. His frame is frail but his mouth is pursed in constant readiness to attack, rebut, correct, and above all to explain.

He came from a communist Berlin family and his brother Albert, at twenty-six the youngest communist representative in the Reichstag, was savagely beaten to death by the Nazis. Walter, sent to a concentration camp, was later released and fled via Czechoslovakia to the Spanish Civil War, where as a battalion commander he fought at the front throughout the major battles and was badly wounded. Together with other Spanish Civil War veterans and writers, such as Anna Seghers, Ludwig Renn and Paul Merker (the earliest victim of Ulbricht's purges), he chose Mexico for his exile and founded there the communist paper *El Libro Libre*.

When he returned to East Germany in 1950 it was with a sense of deep relief:

For the first time in my life I was in a country whose basic ideology reflected my conviction that one must remove the social roots which had allowed fascism to flourish. I had realized by then that we communists had made a mistake by rejecting a partnership against Hitler with the Social Democrats, even to the extent of calling them Social Fascists: a terrible thing to say and also untrue. But it annoys me when people say that we were responsible for Hitler's accession to power. It was German capitalism which heaved him there, hoping to find a way out of the world economic crisis. What they got instead was the most terrifying chaos imaginable. It seemed to me that one needed a completely new social order to eradicate the risk of anything like that happening again, and as an alternative to capitalism all that was on offer was the socialism of Karl Marx.

Besides the ideological conviction, Janka – in common with other returning communists – was ready for respite from persecution and harried exile. Bertolt Brecht was to acknowledge the weaknesses and compromises of his peers in his poem 'To those Born Later', which anticipated the discredit of the later years, asking future generations to 'think of us with forbearance'. They [the early communists] had spent their lives 'changing countries more often than [they] changed their shoes'.

Examining the complicity of Germany's communist intellectuals in the erection of the regime which followed, one is confronted time and again with the all-too-human factor of sheer exhaustion and relief. While this can never excuse their moral inertia, it should at least help us understand its roots. 'I was overcome with a sense of peaceful victory,' says Janka of his return. 'I felt that my brother's murder had been avenged at last.'

The initial euphoria did not last long. Janka soon realized that the German communist movement was divided between those thinkers who had spent their exile in the West and those returned from the Soviet Union.

For Johannes Becher and Walter Ulbricht, the aim was quite clearly that of a socialist republic on the Soviet model. Anything else, like the so-called 'anti-fascist democratic period' of 1945–48, was a mere tactic for them. But for me, returning from Mexico, the ideal was something different, an alternative to capitalism, constructed on a partnership of social democracy and socialism, a democratic system with checks and balances but without the dominance of capital. The same vision persists on the left today, although hopefully they will have learned from our mistakes.

He soon established himself at the apex of cultural life in the newly-formed country and was appointed editor-in-chief of the Aufbau publishing house, entrusted with the publication of Thomas Mann and Bertolt Brecht, both of them also friends.

At first I thought I was in heaven, given such wonderful authors to deal with. Then the problems started. We were refused permission to print Brecht because he was too pacifist. We were refused permission to print Hemingway because he was anti-communist. Bloch (the Marxist philosopher) was out as being 'Un-Marxist', which came as a bit of a surprise to him as well. Hanns Eisler was denounced as a *Kosmopolit*, Picasso as a formalist . . . I was beginning to wonder who would be left on our lists at all apart from the hammer-and-tongs-socialists.

The cultural policies of the early fifties were dominated by unseemly scuffles over how to define socialist art. Formalism, indeed almost any experiment with form, was condemned as bourgeois decadence to which the curse of *Kosmopolit* (cosmopolitan) – imported from the Soviet cultural purges – was added if the writer had lived abroad in the West for long enough to suggest that he might have shed the provincialism considered essential to ideological reliability. The twelve-tone scale as employed by Eisler (a former pupil of Schönberg and thus suspect to begin with) in his score for Brecht's opera *The Trial of Lucullus* was treated as the musical expression of imperialist war-mongering. Jazz, abstract art and 'Western unculture' were banned, together with the further abominations of ringed socks, crêpe-soled shoes, blue jeans, and chewing gum.

In 1950 the Party confidently declared that an adequate reception of Bach was 'only now possible, after the defeat of German fascism by the armies of the Soviet Union'; and the Central Committee marked the 125th anniversary of Beethoven's death by combining clammy adoration with an attack on Adenauer's government:

The American cultural barbarians and their lackeys desecrate the memory of Beethoven by misusing Bonn, the town of his birth, for the most pernicious national degradation . . . In Bonn, Beethoven's sublime demand for peace and friendship among the peoples is trampled underfoot.

The events of 1953 shook the intelligentsia's faith in Ulbricht, although Wilhelm Pieck, in his go-between role as the thinking man's

Stalinist, smoothed the ruffles of dissent by persuading the philistine Party leader to allow some relaxation in the draconian guidelines of Zhdanov's potty socialist realism. But the cultural reforms which accompanied the economic 'New Course' were skin-deep, grudging concessions coupled with ritualistic self-criticism as mocked by Brecht in his poem 'Unidentifiable Errors of the Arts Commission':

> Invited to a session at the Academy of Arts
> The highest officials of the Arts Commission
> Paid their tribute to the noble custom of
> Accusing oneself of certain errors, and
> Muttered that they too accused themselves
> Of certain errors. Asked
> What errors however, they found it wholly impossible to recall
> Any specific errors. Everything that
> The Academy held against them had been
> precisely no error, for the Arts Commission
> Had suppressed only worthless stuff, indeed had not
> Suppressed it exactly, had just not pushed it.
> Despite the most earnest ruminations
> They could recall no specific errors. Nonetheless,
> They were most insistent that they had
> Committed errors – as is the custom.

The same autumn, Brecht wrote an article for *Neues Deutschland* stating that most artists and writers in the country felt alienated from the government's cultural policies. The newly courageous cultural association openly demanded freedoms of expression and scientific theory (even these were strictly controlled by the Party, which for reasons too Byzantine to contemplate, considered quantum theory 'un-Marxist'). The Arts Commission was replaced by a Ministry of Culture, headed by Johannes Becher – a development initially welcomed by the intelligentsia as a normalization of relations between themselves and the state.

Emboldened by these mild reforms, the Aufbau publishing house was to grow into a centre of critical discourse. By 1956, however, Becher had become a paper tiger, unwilling to challenge Ulbricht on fundamental issues of cultural freedom and, most important, unable to bring himself to depart from his compulsive hero-worship of Stalin. On the occasion of the Soviet dictator's death he wrote the following paean of thanksgiving for his life:

> Germany, remember your best friend.
> Oh, be thanked Stalin. No one was ever
> So deeply entwined with you.
> East and west are united in him.
> He crosses the seas, and the mountains
> Are no barrier to him.
> No enemy can resist him . . .

Even Brecht, despite having written his fair share of Stalin eulogies, disliked his rival's German-Soviet pathos intensely and had provided an apt critical response to this sort of mush several years earlier in his notes. 'At least,' he lamented, quoting an over-excited Becher, 'the Pied Piper knew how to whistle . . .'

The distance between intelligentsia and government could no longer be hidden even by Wilhelm Pieck's occasional ministrations. Khrushchev's secret speech had caused the murmur of dissent, in Aufbau as elsewhere, to swell to a volume which could no longer be ignored. Walter Janka encouraged his staff to hold open debates about the development in cultural policies and invited his friend Becher to attend, 'with the intention of showing him how bad the atmosphere really was among the intelligentsia'.

In October that same year came the Hungarian uprising. Janka received a call from Anna Seghers, a friend from Mexico who had established herself on her return to the east as the first lady of German letters. Seghers was worried about the fate of the critic Georg Lukács, who was also one of Janka's authors. With the eastern media reporting counter-revolution provoked by the treachery of the Petofi Club intellectuals, and the western stations reporting the lynchings of communist functionaries and the burning of Party buildings, it was little wonder that she feared for Lukács, who as both a communist and a pro-reform intellectual was guaranteed to be unpopular with whichever side gained the upper hand.

Her solution was a rescue bid, as ill-conceived as it was ludicrous, demonstrating just how out of their depth the socialist intellectuals were in the brutal power play of the fifties. Dan Dare in the guise of an East German publisher was to rescue the maiden in distress – here a rebarbative Hungarian critic – from the peril of political conflagration. Stranger still, she had already secured Becher's agreement for the operation, although whether the culture minister was intent on an elaborate set-up from the start is unclear. In any case, there was little

Janka could do save agree to the mantle of heroism which was being thrust upon him, and arrange to be taken to West Berlin next day by Becher's nameless driver who was to secure passports and money for the journey. 'I felt like the unwilling protagonist in a seedy crime story,' he recalls, with the first hint of a smile.

He says he was saved from the adventure by a last-minute intervention from Ulbricht. An hour before he was due to depart, Becher called off the mission, saying that the leader feared it would be seen as an insult to 'our Soviet friends'. Janka heaved a sigh of relief and returned to his Aufbau desk. Lukács was duly imprisoned and later released after international protest.

Nine months later Janka was arrested for activities hostile to the socialist state, amongst them the accusation that he had conspired to bring Georg Lukács – 'the intellectual father of the counter-revolution in Hungary' – to East Berlin as 'the spiritual chieftain of counter-revolution in the GDR'. As the move was primarily intended to deter other intellectuals, it was carried out on the unmistakable model of a show-trial. In court were a clutch of prominent intellectuals: Brecht's widow Helene Weigel, the writers Willi Bredel and Bodo Uhse, the chief commentator of the East German media Karl Eduard von Schnitzler – and the inspirer of his Hungarian journey, Anna Seghers.

His request to call Johannes Becher and Anna Seghers as witnesses in his defence was turned down. 'The state prosecutor said that I was attempting to provoke a state crisis by calling the minister of culture as a witness against the public prosecutor, and to undermine Seghers' reputation as the bearer of the Stalin Prize for Literature by dragging her through the mire.'

We were drinking tea as he talked and, at this point, Janka's hand began to shake so violently that he could not replace his cup in the saucer. It is not the infliction of a show-trial by his own Party which pains him over thirty years later, nor even the five years in prison; it is the silence of his friends and comrades which echoes back at him, down the years.

That Janka's case was intended to stifle debate among the country's intellectuals is clear. It will be some time before the Party's archives, only now being opened to historians, will reveal whether the ill-fated Hungary mission was simply seized on by the hardliners around Ulbricht to add to the list of spurious charges they had dreamt up against Janka, or whether Becher as Culture Minister had set up the episode as an *agent provocateur* from the start, with or without the knowledge of Anna Seghers. It scarcely matters. What makes the case of Walter Janka the most shameful chapter in the history of East Germany's intellectuals is their failure to speak out for him.

Janka is too disciplined a communist to expect that all his comrades would cry 'foul' at his arrest. He told me that he had later reasoned with himself that Becher had considered it 'more beneficial' to the country's authors to stay in office than to forfeit it. And Helene Weigel doubtless wanted to keep hold of the Berliner Ensemble, the theatre company she had founded with Brecht in 1949. But Anna Seghers, holder of the Stalin Prize, and the most renowned woman writer in Germany?

In the case of the others, I can understand that they thought heroism would be pointless. They would simply have been arrested as co-conspirators, which would have been neither pleasant for them nor useful to me. But Anna . . . she could have changed things by doing very little. If she had simply got up and left the court, it would have been a signal. But she stayed.

When he was released from prison in 1961, the literary community welcomed him back, but studiously avoided asking anything about his time behind bars. 'It was as if I had disappeared for five years to a health farm,' he says. The writer Stephan Hermlin came round for dinner, ate Frau Janka's fillet steak with gusto while enumerating the idiocies of Ulbricht's policies, then a week later wrote a lengthy article in *Neues Deutschland* pledging his support for the government. Helene Weigel offered him a job at the Berliner Ensemble for the wage of a manual worker, and Willi Bredel surreptitiously gave him money to tide him over unemployment. Seghers recommended a course at the Party school. Not one of them asked whether he was guilty. Refused a post at Aufbau, he was eventually allowed to take up a job writing screenplays at the film company DEFA – on condition that he kept quiet about the past.

He now ranks as one of East Germany's rediscovered heroes: but does he deserve it? Listening to Walter Janka's life story, I was reminded of the remark of a friend about German communists of that generation. He maintained that their outstanding common quality was a capacity for suffering, last seen in the early Christian martyrs. More than that even, they display a masochistic urge to impose suffering on themselves in the name of a higher good which is barely discernible through the lies, corruption and defeats of a lifetime – other people's, and their own.

He is a victim who showed considerable courage in withstanding persecution twice in his life. Yet he is also a prime example of the kind of intellectual whose unshakable faith in the regime which maltreated him made its continuation possible. Asked why he took up his membership of the Communist Party again in 1972, he says that it was not he who belonged outside the Party, but his persecutors. However, it was his persecutors and their successors who directed the farce of Party 'democracy' right until the end. It was from their hands that, in spring 1989, he accepted the Fatherland Order of Merit in Gold: the staggering regime sought to avoid present confrontation by priding itself on the symbolic righting of wrongs which lay far enough in the past not to be damaging. He was not rehabilitated until a year later, after the fall of the regime.

Although begged by contemporaries to publish his story and reveal the full cruelty of the Ulbricht regime, he refused until 1989. 'Such a book would never have been published here. To have it published in the West would have been taken as a vote of no confidence in the GDR. I never wanted to be a dissident,' he explains.

So the concentration camp survivor, Spanish Civil War veteran, show-trial victim and graduate of Bautzen jail chose by silence to defend the system which had falsely imprisoned him and countless others. Is it too harsh to demand to know how socialism was to be reformed when those whose personal fates could have given the impulse for change refused to speak out for fear of toppling a system they knew, by their own experience, to be mercilessly unjust?

We are left with bravery flawed by pointlessness. The West German literary critic Fritz J. Raddatz wrestled with this conundrum recently when he reviewed Janka's memoirs and recalled the devastating but irrefutable comment of a young poet who said of Janka, 'In the end, he arrested himself.' Raddatz said that he could not withhold criticism of the man, while at the same time feeling that it would be unworthy to write a polemic against him. He chose the elegant way out by concluding that Walter Janka's story was 'a case for the philosophers'.

The case is not simply one for them, but one for all who aspire to a society based on ideals, of whatever colour. Walter Janka holds firmly to a creed he has seen discredited, to an 'idea' or 'ideal' whose definition now eludes him. Like many German socialists inspired by Hegel, he uses these words interchangeably.

His fate revealed the humiliations, the deceptions, the contradictions of the ideology as practised. The comrades who ranked in the history books as heroes turned out to be cowards when heroism would have signalled the negation of their belief, the admission that the enemies of progress and humanity could wear the jackboots of the Volksarmee just as well as those of the Wehrmacht.

Our conversation was becoming unnervingly reminiscent of the salon games of definition played in Prussia in the nineteenth century. What was the 'it' of socialism, to which he still aspires, once stripped of all of the qualities evident in its previous manifestation? 'An alternative to capitalism', as prescribed by Eastern Europe's reform socialist parties, is cheating because it is too easy, and because it does not tell us whether the medicine will be more harmful than the illness it intends to cure – a risk the populations of the Soviet Union and of Eastern Europe will be in no hurry to take again.

Does the flaw lie, not with Stalin, always handy as the great deformer, but with Lenin, who clothed Marx's philosophy with the garments of power politics, or (heresy of heresies) with the originator himself? Or was the deformation due to the cultural and historical environment of the century in which his idea was summoned to life? Ernst Bloch pointed towards an uncomfortable answer when he asked whether Stalinism had deformed socialism to the point of unrecognizability, or made it truly recognizable by revealing its negative potential.

But just as true beliefs can produce evil actions, false ones can have noble results. Janka and his peers were among the bravest opponents of fascism in the days when most of Europe slept. The same purposeful conviction made them unwavering dupes of wishful thinking when their time to rule arrived. They thought they were the bearers of a scientific ideology but were, all along, devotees of a mythology. The irresistible dialectic has revealed itself as no more or less binding than the good old-fashioned leap of faith.

Johannes Becher died a broken man, his reputation as a poet subsumed by his notoriety as apostrophizer of Stalin and silent witness of injustice. Only in his verse did the truth sometimes penetrate the haze of complicity. His later works are laden with the admission that the system he had helped to implement was doomed to failure, that it was unworthy of the name it bore. In his poem 'The Tower of Babel' he recognized, in the debasement of language by the state, the seeds of communism's destruction. The word, he said, was being emptied of meaning to echo senselessly back at the speaker. The tower, like its biblical predecessor, would collapse into dust.

4
Erich Honecker:
the Banality of Dictatorship

An *Apparatchik* Ascends

He had the main characteristic I would consider essential for success as a young functionary: absolutely average intelligence. In a communist party on the Stalinist model, you have to have a good memory and an ability to absorb reams of resolutions and turn them into directives, so you need a certain basic intelligence. You can't be plain dumb, as was required under the Nazis, because the ideology is much more complicated. But you can't be too intelligent, because people of above-average intellect have a tendency to challenge the arcana, to spot its flaws, which makes them disobedient. When the system is in a crisis, then the bright people come to the fore: Kadar in Hungary, Dubček in Czechoslovakia, Gorbachev in the Soviet Union. But during normal times it is the average who rule: the Ulbrichts and Honeckers. The system demands them.

Wolfgang Leonhard, former comrade of Erich Honecker,
conversation with the author, 1991

It is a neat arch of historical dramaturgy that the German Democratic Republic effectively began and ended with the secret take-off of a Soviet plane. The instructions of fate seem to have read 'Moscow-Berlin-Moscow'. The first journey, on 30 April 1945, brought the core members of the Ulbricht Group from Moscow to Berlin to re-establish the Communist Party in Germany after Hitler's defeat and to lay the ground for socialism in the east. The second took off under cover of night from a Soviet airfield near Berlin on 13 March 1991. Its cargo was Erich Honecker, the country's erstwhile leader, who preferred to flee into the arms of Mother Russia rather than face the charges of manslaughter and corruption that the authorities of the unified Germany had prepared against him. A few months later, he was fighting to escape extradition as the Soviet Union itself disintegrated around him.

Honecker's fate provided a timely reminder that throughout its entire history, and even after its demise, East Germany never escaped Moscow's political embrace. The federal government accepted Moscow's explanation that it had a duty to stand by its dethroned ally in time of need; that Erich Honecker, post-GDR, was the Kremlin's business rather than Bonn's. Indeed, Chancellor Kohl was probably relieved to be rid of him. A trial of the former leader for crimes – principally the deaths of those shot trying to cross to the west – which had been known about when Honecker was received with state honours in Bonn in 1986, would provide more embarrassment than satisfaction. While the Soviets under Gorbachev had been relieved at the fall of Honecker, who, like Ceaucescu in Romania and Husak in Czecho-slovakia, was an inconvenient vestige of pre-perestroika days, they clearly felt that it would be uncomradely to abandon him to his fate after his country first turned against him and then dissolved itself.

After he had been released, on health grounds, from prison in East Berlin (an imprisonment resulting from initial charges brought in January 1990) he found asylum with a compassionate minister in the religious enclave of Lobetal (literally 'the valley of praise') near the capital. The Protestant community had been set up to give shelter to those rendered homeless in Berlin by the city's sudden sprawl in the early years of the century, and the numbers of outcasts it dealt with spiralled during the economic depression of the twenties and thirties.

Under the communists, the community was allowed to continue as a refuge for the mentally and physically handicapped. Its symbol was the figure of Christ, arms outstretched above the motto 'Come unto me all ye who are weary and I will give you rest'. Even Honecker's most bitter foes would have to admit that, by March 1990, the haggard and demoralized former General Secretary was a fitting candidate for that particular offer of Christian kindness.

'We are here to help the people who cannot otherwise cope in our society,' the minister, Uwe Holmer, told me when I visited him that spring to enquire about his guest. Yes, he said, he did put the one-time leader and his wife, the former Education Minister Margot Honecker, in this category. Honecker did not appear, but we could hear his footsteps in the room above.

The minister was a straightforward, rather dour man, intent on giving the Honeckers 'a decent old age' despite the fact that his own children, as practising Christians, had not been allowed to go to university. He cited the commandment 'Love thy neighbour', and the Gospels' call to forgive one's enemy, with a quiet self-evidence that was strangely unnerving

72

amidst the wild abuse which was showering down on the former leader. The solution, however, soon proved to be impractical. The peaceful community was overrun with the newcomers' old citizens, intent on pilgrimages of revenge. Pastor Holmer received death threats, and his beneficence was viewed askance even in Church circles, where it was thought that the Communist Party should bear the responsibility for Honecker's future well-being.

Soon the Honeckers were on the move again, to a secluded house provided by the government. The delivery van carrying them and their few belongings did not even make it to the door of their new home. The residents of the village made clear their objections to the newcomer by chasing after the van bearing their former leader, throwing tomatoes, jeering and banging pan lids together in a chilling re-enactment of feudal custom: driving away the outcast by a show of noisy mass contempt.

Like a modern King Lear, Honecker found his kingdom dismembered, his influence forgotten and his presence undesired wherever he turned. After his eighteen-year rule of increasing tyranny, there was cause enough in nature for these hard hearts. None the less, the gaunt figures of Honecker (who had undergone two cancer operations in just over a year) and his grim, staunch wife were beginning to inspire an uncomfortable mixture of sympathy and guilt. So it was with relief that the interim government accepted Moscow's offer of a place for the couple in the Soviet military hospital at Beelitz, deep in the woods south of Berlin. If anywhere could be considered a safe haven in the GDR, it was the Soviet camps. Tiny impregnable Soviet republics in the midst of Germany, they were secured by high perimeter fences and permanently guarded. Honecker, the man who had effected the imprisonment of his own people behind concrete and barbed wire, was happy with his voluntary incarceration. He could be glimpsed through the trees, chatting to his guards and taking a daily walk with Margot and a minder in tow, through the woods.

The sight of him enjoying a peaceful, if isolated, rural life was too much for the families and friends of some of the 200 East Germans shot trying to escape. The federal authorities had opened investigations into the killings and began the search for concrete evidence that Honecker had ordered them. They eventually unearthed the minutes of a meeting of the National Defence Council, chaired by the leader in May 1974. These recorded the directive that 'ruthless use of firearms' was permitted to counter illegal attempts to cross the border, and that 'Comrades

73

who make successful use of their weapons should be rewarded'. It was not, strictly speaking, a shoot-to-kill order, but it sanctioned shooting without specifying that the killing of the escapers was to be avoided. It would provide an adequate basis for a manslaughter charge which, even if it were dismissed by the court, would grant the outraged populace the sight of their warder in the dock. Most newspapers were candid about the fact that this constituted a response to the people's anger rather than a *prima facie* case.

In farcical conditions, the Berlin police attempted to serve an arrest warrant in December 1990, only to be refused entry to the Beelitz camp by the Soviet guards on the grounds that they needed an order from their commandant to allow this. (As Germany had regained its full sovereignty on unification two months earlier, this was not the case – the police were fully entitled to walk in if they wished. Their political masters held them back.) The commandant was, mysteriously, nowhere to be found until the next day, by which time the Russians announced that their charge was too weak to be removed from the camp and that a nervous and physical collapse had confined him to a hospital bed. On 14 March 1991, a brief statement was issued from the Soviet representation in Berlin – the former grandiose embassy to East Germany – to the effect that Erich Honecker had been removed to Moscow for urgent medical treatment.

It was a transparent excuse for Moscow to snatch its old ally away from the threat of being brought to trial. The very absurdity of the reason given indicated that not even the Kremlin expected it to be taken seriously. What treatment could be at once so urgent as to require Honecker's removal without consultation and so rare as only to be found in the Soviet Union rather than the richly equipped hospitals of the united Germany? This was the logical extension of the diplomatic colds which had been a feature of East-West relations for years: now a serious, sudden and ill-defined diplomatic illness was upon us.

Honecker's lawyers had not been warned of the move, and arrived for their weekly consultation with their client to find him gone. 'We were totally dumbstruck,' said one. Bonn sources hastened to insist that the Soviets had only informed them of what happened a day after the impromptu removal. This had to be corrected when German journalists recalled that in the parliamentary debate the previous day, the Chancellor had absentmindedly referred to the then leader of the opposition, Hans-Jochen Vogel, as 'Herr Honecker'. Herr Vogel's middle-of-the-road Social Democrat credentials were so impeccable that not even the most virulent conservative could harbour suspicions that he was a bedfellow of

Erich Honecker. The Chancellor finally owned up: he had heard of the former leader's flight just before entering the Bundestag chamber and had the matter on his mind, hence the slip. There had been no time, he said, to prevent the escape.

This has now become the official version. It is, however, unlikely that President Gorbachev would have risked a major disruption in the newly cosy German-Soviet relations by approving the snatch without prior consultation. It directly contravened the treaty on the withdrawal of Soviet troops from Germany, which states that the Soviets would 'honour the sovereignty of the Federal Republic of Germany and of German law and renounce any intervention in German internal affairs'. It is much more likely that the removal was an informal agreement, made between the two countries the previous week as the final German concession for Moscow's ratification of the two-plus-four agreement on unification.

Bonn expressed its displeasure but failed to sound very convinced. Foreign minister Hans-Dietrich Genscher even went so far as to assume a hurt scowl and demand that Honecker be sent back to face trial, safe in the knowledge (it was before the Moscow coup) that the united Germany and the former East German leader were not likely to see one another again.

But as the Soviet Union collapsed around him and his protector Mikhail Gorbachev ceded influence to Boris Yeltsin in late 1991, Honecker's safe haven became increasingly vulnerable. The Russian leader made clear that, unlike Gorbachev, he felt no loyalty to Honecker and would offer him no protection in the republic after the Soviet presidency had been dissolved. Neither were there any offers of asylum forthcoming from the other republics. In December, the Honeckers approached Clodomiro Almeyda, the Chilean ambassador in Moscow, an old friend of the couple from the days of the Allende government, and asked for help. Almeyda offered them a room in his residence and thus *de facto* protection against extradition. The man who had driven thousands of his own desperate citizens to seek refuge in the embassies of East Berlin, Prague and Budapest in 1989 was now undergoing the same indignity. An offer of hospitality from the North Korean government was turned down: Honecker, while still defending the benefits of communism, was in no hurry to experience the variety practised by the deranged dictator Kim Il Sung. In February 1992, he was allowed to leave the embassy for medical treatment. Despite the protestations of their government, most Germans assumed that he was unlikely to return home.

In the chronicles of East German history, Honecker's life had been

75

carefully stylized as a heroic saga of 'Rags to General Secretaryship'. The story of the convinced young communist, imprisoned by the Nazis only to continue the underground struggle in Brandenburg jail and escape over the roofs of Berlin in the final stage of the war, had acquired the status of socialist legend in kindergartens and schools.

His position in the communist party went unchallenged, even when it was clear to all who worked with him that he was no longer master of his work. Doubts were swiftly extinguished by referring to the virtues of his youth. Honecker's ten years in prison in Brandenburg were interpreted as giving him *carte blanche* to govern as long as he saw fit. Egon Krenz, his brief successor, told me that even when he had finally decided to go ahead with a long-overdue challenge for Honecker's job, 'I felt as if I were about to play Brutus. The older comrades had presented their power as a natural right after what they had suffered under fascism. That was deeply instilled in our political culture. It meant that we, the younger ones, did not have the right to challenge them.'

East Germany's treatment of age as a virtue recalled its Prussian, authoritarian roots. A common image of the leader was as father figure to the nation or '*Volkspapi*' (People's Daddy), as the more daring detractors used to mock. The incumbents were judged not on their (often fading) abilities, but on their longevity. 'Isn't he wonderful?' I heard one delegate to the Party Congress of 1986 remark. 'All of seventy-four and he can still make a one-and-a-half hour speech.'

The Federal Republic also forsook strict judgement for kid-gloved discretion during his years in power. The press and the Bonn establishment treated him with surprising leniency for a man who, charged under Ulbricht with security matters, had been the architect of the Berlin Wall and the proponent of *Abgrenzung* – physical and cultural demarcation of the two states. The negative iconography of Honecker as a monstrous criminal and hypocrite largely emerged after his fall. Naturally, much of the kind treatment he received in Bonn was due to *Ostpolitik* and its goal of keeping the channels between the two Germanies open, but the residue of respect for those who had fought fascism often obscured the less pleasant aspects of his regime.

Born in 1912 into a family of six, Honecker grew up in the impoverished Saarland on the border with France. His father, a miner and communist trade unionist, was frequently unemployed. At the age of ten he enrolled in the Young Spartacists and was rapidly promoted to the position of drummer in the street band of the Red Fighters' Front. It was his first experience of leadership, which he looked back on proudly in

1990, telling a visitor, 'The drummer is the most important man in the whole orchestra. I wasn't so interested in the music, I wanted to have a position in the Red Fighters' Front on our marches. Even today I could still play you the accompaniment to "Sportsmen, Join the Battle".'

Somewhere between 1926 and 1928 he joined the Youth Section of the Communist Party. It is difficult to date his entry exactly because he had a tendency to alter the dates in his curriculum vitae in order to exaggerate his early devotion. He insisted that he had been the political leader of the Young Communists in Wiebelskirchen 1926–28 when in fact he had spent most of these years hundreds of miles away in Pomerania, working as a farm hand. Even disregarding his exaggerations, however, he appears to have been a convinced and active young communist, who enjoyed a reputation as a good speaker, and who used to address rallies in the village argot of the Saarland.

Spotted as a prospective talent by the regional Agitprop functionary, he was dispatched to the Party school in Moscow in 1930 to brush up his scanty knowledge of Marx, Lenin and – times being as they were – Stalin. 'We hardly recognized him when he came back,' says Artur Mannbar, a childhood friend and later comrade of Honecker. 'He obviously thought that it was more impressive to speak in High German, and strained himself to speak without his native dialect. Unfortunately, he couldn't quite manage it, and bits of Saar-German kept breaking through his posh bits. It sounded as though he was being strangled. We kept interrupting him, shouting, "For heaven's sake Erich, you don't have to put that on for us." He looked a bit cross, but at least he began to talk properly again.'

At eighty, Mannbar is an exact contemporary of Honecker, and bewildered by the collapse of a system to which he pledged himself as heartily as did the erstwhile leader. Until his retirement he had been editor-in-chief of the state East German ADN news agency and accompanied Honecker on his trips abroad to report on the speeches in which the leader often seemed to have the same old trouble, swinging between stilted High German and his native Saarland accent. Even at the height of his strength, he often had trouble pronouncing borrowed foreign words, and he always travelled with a coterie of advisers whose main task was to give discreet tips on required behaviour and on pronunciation.

In the days of East Germany's existence, Mannbar was the traditional first port of call for keen Free German Youth chroniclers in search of sanitized accounts of the General Secretary as a young man. He still

77

scurries off to produce, with a mixture of pride and embarrassment, several tomes of excruciating hero worship to which he contributed. 'I used to say that Erich had never lost his roots. Now I see that he lost them a very long time ago,' he says, and his face fills with sorrow, the anguish of a child who discovers the weaknesses of his hero.

In common with other East Germans he had been reading the newly-published files that Erich Mielke, the Minister for State Security, had kept on his boss. Their content disclosed several significant departures from the official account of Honecker's life.

In 1935, the files reveal, Honecker received orders from the Young Communists' headquarters, an organization by now illegal in Germany and based in Prague, to move to Berlin and assist Bruno Baum, the head of the Young Communists there. A courier named Sarah Fodorova met him with funds and documents. On the way back from the meeting, by now with the briefcase in tow, he noticed that he was being followed, panicked and ran from the taxi, leaving the incriminating papers behind. He was arrested next day in his apartment by the Gestapo.

Later, Honecker was to describe his week on remand as 'days of fortitude', in which he had not flinched from his ideals. In fact the Gestapo were less interested in the conversion of a minor youth functionary than in details of the communists' illegal operations in Berlin. Under interrogation, he revealed the identity of Bruno Baum and the nature of his own task in Berlin. The Gestapo had more difficulty with Sarah Fodorova, also arrested but who, ignorant of Honecker's confession, kept to the rules of covert activity and refused to dispense information, even after 'difficult negotiations' – the Nazi interrogators' standard shorthand for maltreatment.

Honecker had good reason to fillet the episode from his later recollections. This had been his first major conspiratorial task and he had made a thorough mess of it. His behaviour stood in stark and unfavourable comparison with that of the steadfast Fodorova and of the Young Communist leader Bruno Baum. Baum was arrested and sentenced to thirteen years in jail, the harshest sentence available, on the grounds that he had consistently refused to betray information about his comrades and their work. His name was not mentioned in East German histories of the Resistance. Fodorova was released but soon rearrested. She never returned to Prague and there is no record of her fate in the Gestapo files.

In June 1937 Honecker joined the existing communist contingent in Brandenburg prison, after having been sentenced to ten years in jail. There was already a thriving illegal network among the prisoners, led by

Eduard Wald, who later recalled in his memoirs that Honecker 'was colourless, shy and not particularly comradely. He checked the work of others (in the prison workshop) with unpleasant accuracy and liked to play the role of the boss's right-hand man.'

At the beginning of 1945, with a German defeat in sight and Berlin badly bombed, the Nazis delegated 'reliable' prisoners with the relevant skills to undertake repair work. Honecker and a fellow inmate were given the task of mending roofs in the city. They were accommodated in the women's prison. Here he befriended a young warder named Lotte Grund who was later to become his first and, until 1991, undisclosed wife. She was not a communist and had little interest in politics, coming from a family of Jehovah's Witnesses. Honecker doubtless felt that the combination would fail to impress the KPD leadership after 1945. On his application for Party membership he placed a line after the question 'Are you married?' Further embarrassment was provided by the fact that she became mentally ill. She died in 1946 and her existence was never mentioned thereafter. Artur Mannbar held the panegyric. 'Erich wanted a small service. The matter was never mentioned after that,' he recalled.

During his stint at the women's prison he seized the chance to escape, although the underground communist organization in Brandenburg forbade individual flight because it endangered the lives of those left behind. He was sheltered by Lotte Grund's mother in her back room but, when half of the tenement was brought down in a bombing raid, he feared capture and returned voluntarily to the prison. After the liberation of the jail, at the end of April, he headed back to Berlin to seek out the Ulbricht Group, newly arrived from Moscow and scouring the city for young resistance people with whom to set up a new administration.

When the wrathful Brandenburg communists arrived, however, he was hauled in front of a Party disciplinary committee to explain why he had risked their lives by fleeing. Not for the last time, he was extraordinarily lucky. No executions had resulted from his flight because the rigour of the Nazi political commandants responsible for the jails had faded as the end of the war drew near; and the communists, in the chaos of May 1945, had more on their minds than the energetic pursuit of retrospective disciplinary procedures.

His official biography was riddled with so many little lies that he was often forced to compound them with bigger ones, to keep the whole structure from toppling. His reticence over his first marriage made him unwilling to put a date on his second, to a Social Democratic functionary, Edith Baumann. Even after his fall, he stuck to the legend he had created, telling an East German interviewer in 1990, 'I married Edith in around 1948 – so far as I can remember.' Günter Schabowski confirms that the marriage to Edith Baumann was 'a Party affair' directed by the leadership, which often suggested suitable partners to its functionaries.

Nor did he seem to remember when he divorced her. At any rate, he soon exchanged her for the more promising Margot Feist, a communist who had the twin advantages over poor Edith of being both attractive and ambitious. The falling-off in relations with his second wife and his affair with Margot seem to have taken place in uncanny harmony with the move of the Socialist Unity Party away from its Social Democratic component and towards undiluted Marxist-Leninism: the much-vaunted unity of theory and practice, perhaps.

In the early months after the end of the war, lightning careers were made by young functionaries in the Soviet zone and Honecker was one of the first to profit. By June 1945 he was already youth secretary of the Communist Party of Germany (KPD) with his own office in the Einbeckerstrasse 41, where the Party chief Ulbricht was ensconced.

Ulbricht admired the functionary's ability to inspire young people with rhetoric which sounded less formal than that of the veterans of the pre-war KPD (such as himself and Wilhelm Pieck) without ever departing from their Stalinist message. The Free German Youth of the late forties and fifties was not quite the dour organization of devoted activists later presented in its official histories. It was, as one former activist coyly described to me, 'the forerunner of the permissive society'. Its school in the countryside outside Berlin soon gained the undignified local title of the 'Red Brothel'.

By all accounts, Honecker enjoyed the privileges on offer within the FDJ's ranks. 'Like a lot of communists who had spent the war in prison or in exile, the new freedom rather went to his head,' said Schabowski. 'He had quite a taste for blonde girls in blue uniforms.' It was a taste which lasted. Every year at the FDJ's Whitsun festival, the organization had to come up with a slender, blonde comrade to present him with the inevitable flowers. 'It would have been unthinkable to send him a dark, plain one,' said an acquaintance who had served in the organization's Central Council. 'We knew what he liked.'

Under Ulbricht he advanced quickly. His closeness to the leader shielded him from challenges except when his mentor came under fire. By 1953 it was clear that Honecker was Ulbricht's favourite, as Elli Schmidt, the sole woman in the Politburo, commented acidly during one of the rare attacks on the leader which followed the 17 June uprising.

'Only those who are well-behaved and parrot what you say have any freedom: like Honecker, for instance, that good child.'

By 1956 he was honoured with a seat on the 'Commission for the Repression of Counter-Revolutionary Activities', aimed at rooting out anti-Stalinists in the Party. Karl Schirdewan who was, as he puts it, 'catapulted out of the Politburo' when as Ulbricht's deputy he challenged him for power in 1958, recalls that the young Honecker was the driving force behind his dismissal. 'He was young enough for one to assume that he might side against the old guard, so he often got wind of anti-Ulbricht challenges before the rest. He would play along for a while and then, when things became critical, leap back into the Ulbricht camp.'

As a reward for his loyalty during the nearly successful Schirdewan challenge, he was declared a full member of the Politburo in 1958 and a year later, Secretary of the Central Committee's Security Commission. It was in this capacity that he was to co-rdinate the building of the Berlin Wall two years later.

His role as Wall-builder also strengthened Honecker's position in the Politburo, particularly as the half-senile, fully megalomaniac Ulbricht was becoming increasingly intolerable to his comrades in both East Berlin and Moscow. In 1963, Ulbricht declared the New Economic System, intended to make East Germany the model economy in the Eastern bloc – an arrogation of the leading role which annoyed the Kremlin. Overnight, he changed from an uncritical admirer of the heavy-industry-based economy of the Soviet Union to a technocrat blinded by the possibilities of robotronics. Investment was switched from industry to ambitious computer developments and the goal was to be 'world standard', a euphemism for achieving western standards with eastern methods. That this was a sheer impossibility was clear to all except Ulbricht. The change was carried out at the price of cutting back the badly-needed housing programme and curtailing production of consumer goods. East Germany began to borrow heavily from the Soviet Union and the West.

How concerned Brezhnev was at these developments was not revealed until 1990, when a secret transcript of a conversation of the Soviet leader with Erich Honecker in July 1970 was released from the Party archives. It ends the long speculation amongst Western observers as to the tone and manner in which the Kremlin dealt with East Berlin, and put paid to the myth that East Germany had ever been treated as anything other than a dependent satellite, to be scolded and corrected at will. Brezhnev remarked:

You can believe me, Erich, the situation which has developed in your country disturbs me deeply. Things have reached the stage where they are no longer simply your own affair. The GDR is for us a socialist brother-country, an important outpost. It is the result of the Second World War, our conquest, won with the blood of the Soviet people . . . We must and will react . . . I tell you quite honestly, we will not permit him to go his own way . . . After all, we have troops on your soil, Erich. I say to you frankly, never forget that.

The conversation gave Honecker the authority to proceed against Ulbricht, and he soon gathered supporters in the Politburo. In January 1971, on Honecker's prompting, the challengers wrote to Brezhnev requesting permission to unseat Ulbricht, who was by now seventy-eight and in the grip of what the plotters politely described as 'a human and biological problem'. They had been particularly perturbed when, after a controversial Party conference, the leader had refused to change his economic course, stating that he was 'without equal' and that he enjoyed 'unparalleled insight into developments in the GDR'. In April Brezhnev replied, approving his removal, and at a Central Committee meeting in May Walter Ulbricht was ousted from the leadership which he had effectively assumed in 1949.

Eastern Europe's communists loved titles but were quick to empty them of meaning when it suited them. Ulbricht was given the retirement present of Chairman of the Socialist Unity Party, and kept his post as head of state and his seat in the Politburo without keeping an iota of power in the state. His main function until his death in 1973 was presenting medals to those agitators, sportsmen and functionaries for whom Honecker did not have time. After his death there was a lengthy disagreement about what to do with his remains. After a delay lasting a month and a half they were interred in the Friedrichsfelde cemetery for socialist heroes, albeit in a modest grave.

Honecker's accession to power was greeted with relief by the popula-tion, particularly by the intellectuals who had suffered under Ulbricht's maniacal attachment to the sterile Soviet theories of 'positive represent-ation' in art and literature. His successor began with concessions to the masses and the intelligentsia alike. Watching western television was no longer treated as a criminal activity, and soon millions of aerials were adjusted in a westerly direction. The wearing of jeans and long hair was also declared acceptable, with the new leader sensibly observing that what was important was not what went on on top of the population's heads, but inside them. This was a new and welcome tone. At the Eighth

Party Congress in June 1971, the old vocabulary of obedience and discipline was replaced by the buzz-words of variety, imagination, experimentation and tolerance. It was as if the cultural thaw which had followed Stalin's death in 1956 had belatedly arrived in East Germany.

As the seventies progressed, however, relations between the intelligentsia and Honecker worsened, particularly after the Biermann affair (the decline is described more fully in Chapter Seven). Outside the chattering classes, Honecker's policies in the early years were not unpopular, which is the best that can be said for a dictatorship in which the dictator governs by bureaucratic means rather than on the strength of his personality. He introduced a consumer-orientated economy: a pale shadow of the West's superabundance but a large improvement on his predecessor's ascetic policies. The shop windows, particularly in the cities, were filled with goods. Highly priced and of uncertain quality, they often owed their appeal more to appearance than reality, but by comparison with the rest of eastern Europe East Germany became a consumerist cornucopia. Poles and Czechs began to embark on shopping trips across the border to stock up on the goods they could not get at home.

The television menu was broadened to include such delicacies as *Petites Folies* – French soft-porn films on a Saturday night. In the cinema, an idiosyncratic selection of films was imported from West Germany and the USA. Woody Allen was a firm favourite of the People's Own Film Import Company, presumably on the reckoning that a society with as many neurotics as Allen's America must be seriously flawed and ripe for revolution. There were bread and circuses in abundance.

All of this was made possible by the great leap forward of his time in office: the diplomatic recognition by the Federal Republic of the German Democratic Republic.

Changes

German observers are fond of referring to 'favourable constellations' in politics, as though these were written in the stars for the mere mortals of government to observe and act upon. In the case of *détente* between the two German states, however, the fates did indeed play a decisive role. With the Christian Democrats appearing jaded and old-fashioned, and ripples of the 1968 unrest pervading mainstream politics, the Social Democrats, in coalition with the liberal Free Democrats, came to power in West Germany in October 1969 with the energetic Willy Brandt at the helm.

Konrad Adenauer's Christian Democrats had steadfastly refused to recognize the East German state and practised the so-called Hallstein doctrine, which denied the recognition by the Federal Republic of any state which recognized the German Democratic Republic (with the exception of the Soviet Union). But Brandt, who had been the ruling mayor of West Berlin during the building of the Wall, had a different outlook on the division of Germany. While reiterating the view that the German people were one, he admitted the existence of two states. 'They are not foreign countries to each other: their relations with each other can only be of a special nature.' He undertook to end the physical separation of German families by promoting relaxation of the draconian ban on travel to the east.

In March 1970 Brandt travelled to Erfurt to meet the East German Prime Minister Willi Stoph, the first encounter of the two German heads of government. Not even the careful formations of plain-clothes Stasi men in the crowd could suppress the townspeople's spontaneous welcome for the most significant Western visitor in the country's history. It fell to Brandt, waving from his hotel balcony, to try to calm the cheering masses for fear of offending his hosts.

The beginnings of this *rapprochement* fell foul of Moscow. In his conversation with Erich Honecker on 28 July 1970 Brezhnev was clearly annoyed at the East Berlin Politburo's receptiveness to Brandt's overtures. 'There is the socialist GDR and the imperialist Federal Republic. What is the problem? ... There must be no process of *rapprochement* between the GDR and FRG ... let us be honest. Nothing good came of Erfurt and Kassel (the return visit by Stoph to the West the following May). Brandt's aims are not ours.'

By August, however, Brezhnev had signed a renunciation of force treaty with Brandt and was less hostile to the idea of *détente* between East and West Germany. After his ascent to power Honecker, fired by the desire of a new leader to set his mark on foreign policy, began to consider a route to recognition which would not weaken the second German state's precarious identity.

Throughout the Ulbricht years, East Germany had maintained that there was a single German nation, divided into two states, which one day would be united in socialism. Both the 1949 constitution and its 1968 redraft committed the East German state to the re-establishment of German unity. Walter Ulbricht was apt to intone that unification was 'an unavoidable historical imperative' and hopefully christened as many of the country's institutions as possible 'National' and 'German', believing that they would, in time, become the institutions of a unified Germany.

But with the Brandt initiative (two states: one nation), *Ostpolitik* caught hold of imaginations east and west. The Party abruptly changed its line. The official description, 'socialist state of German nationality' was replaced by 'socialist national German state'. As fast as West Germany moved towards the acceptance of the two-in-one theory of state and nation, East Germany moved the other way, emphasizing its national sovereignty. Honecker declared that the national question had been 'finally solved ... according to its class content'. He declared the old German nation to be defunct and produced the new theory that there were now two separate German nations developing: the 'bourgeois nation' of the west and the 'socialist nation' of the east.

The intention was to counter the Federal Republic's advances by stressing the Democratic Republic's separateness, making clear to the population that there would be no movement towards unity. At the same time it tacitly admitted that the original intention of the founders of the state – to create a unified, communist Germany – was no longer realistic.

The reassessment also had an essential practical application. Having established its new status, the GDR declared itself ready to begin talks on a basic relations treaty with the Federal Republic. What Honecker took to calling the *Grosswetterklima* – the broader meteorological climate – was favourable, especially after the Four-Power Berlin agreement of September 1971, in which Moscow and the Western Allies pledged themselves not to use force to solve their differences over Berlin's status, and West Berliners were granted the right to visit the east of the city. The basic treaty, which was signed in December 1972, promised, a shade optimistically, that the two states would hold 'normal, good-neighbourly relations' with each other and concluded that both Germanies respected the other's authority within its own borders 'in both internal and foreign affairs'.

The unloved country had finally found acceptance. Bonn acknowledged the second German state's independent existence and opened the door for diplomatic recognition by other countries. Honecker was touchingly proud of his country's acceptance into the international diplomatic community and insisted that each new establishment of links be prominently recorded in *Neues Deutschland*. His four great ambitions were to make state visits to Bonn, London and Washington and to give a speech to the United Nations. Only the first was ever fulfilled.

The signing of the treaty also recognized East Germany's borders, and *de facto* the loss of a quarter of the territory of the 1937 frontiers, although the Oder-Neisse line was formally recognized as Germany's border with Poland only in the wake of unification in November 1990. While Willy Brandt successfully presented his *Ostpolitik* as an attempt to promote gradual change in the east by opening it up to western influence (a policy which bore the tag *'Wandel durch Annäherung'* – 'change through convergence') the sacrifice of Germany's claim to its eastern territories was greeted with less satisfaction, particularly among the older generation and among the Christian Democratic opposition. To this day, the conservative newspapers *Frankfurter Allgemeine Zeitung* and *Die Welt* refer to eastern Germany as *Mitteldeutschland* on the grounds that what was historically called *Ostdeutschland* – Upper and Lower Silesia and Pomerania – is now in Poland.

In his memoirs Brandt recalled that as late as 1988, in the run-up to his meeting with President Gorbachev, he was still receiving acid enquiries from the public as to whether he intended 'to sell off any more of Germany'. He also admitted to a residual unhappiness about the loss of historical territories, but justified his decision: 'We cannot give away what is no longer ours to give. We no longer have at our disposal what history has already disposed of.'

While the treaty opened new channels of communication and co-operation between the two Germanies, it could not resolve the basic difference of interpretation of the national question, and the Federal Republic never renounced its claim that there was a single German nation. While East Germany treated the Federal Republic as a foreign power and placed inter-German affairs in the charge of the foreign ministry, which also appointed diplomats to Bonn, West Germany ran its relations with the east from the ministry of intra-German affairs and the staff of its representation in East Berlin were delegated from the Chancellor's office.

The departure of Willy Brandt from office in 1974 was occasioned, ironically for the architect of improved intra-German relations, by the discovery of the East German spy Günter Guillaume in his office. It ended the period of initiatives. His successor, Helmut Schmidt, continued to pursue cordial relations with East Berlin but without embarking on any significant advances in the relationship.

The Free Democrats switched sides to support the Christian Democrats in 1982, bringing Chancellor Helmut Kohl to power through that anomaly of proportional representation, a change of government without an election. The new generation of Christian Democrats, who had been children when Germany was divided, did not share their predecessors' hankering for unification, and the new government made no fundamental changes to the Social Democrats' policies towards the east. Relations between Bonn and East Berlin remained prone to sudden spurts of warmth and *froideur*, but these reflected broader superpower issues, such as the decision by Helmut Schmidt in 1982 to approve the stationing of NATO medium-range missiles in the Federal Republic.

Ostpolitik had fallen into a fitful slumber as tensions between Moscow and Washington heightened over the nuclear arms race in Europe. Honecker's first visit to the Federal Republic, intended by the Christian Democrats to set their mark on relations with the east, was mooted in 1984 and scheduled to be held in the bland, ahistorical spa town of Bad Kreuznach to avoid giving the leader full protocol status. Moscow vetoed the idea, and several other attempts to arrange a meeting, seeking a time when the visit would carry significance for the superpower relationship. Autumn 1987, on the eve of the treaty scrapping medium-range weapons in Europe, was finally deemed propitious.

The event, as a senior diplomat in West Germany's East Berlin representation told me later, was 'a protocol nightmare: the slightest mistake on either side could have upset relations for years'. No wonder then that the mood was strained.

Bonn's red carpet was unrolled outside the Chancellery and a guard of honour provided, albeit smaller and less impressive than usual, and led not by the commander but by his deputy. The guest was to be made welcome, while at the same time reminded that he was being served with only the second-best tea-set. Both leaders stood to attention, the bulky westerner Kohl towering over his slight eastern counterpart. It is a snapshot which lingers in the memory as a true reflection of the difference in stature and confidence, not so much between the two men, but between their respective systems.

The band played both national anthems, and the two delegations sat down for mundane talks about trade, transit and that disregarder of even the most fortified of borders, pollution. But both sides knew that it was the style rather than the substance of the visit that mattered. Kohl and Honecker exchanged ritual salvoes of rhetoric, the former stressing the 'suffering of separation' division had brought, the latter intoning that capitalism and communism were 'like fire and water: they cannot mix'. In private, they indulged in harmless chit-chat about their neighbouring home regions, Honecker's Saarland and Kohl's Rhineland Palatinate.

The formality faded when the East German leader visited his home town of Wiebelskirchen, a depressed coal and steel area. For the first time, the West saw Honecker at ease, nostalgia eclipsing his usual tense guardedness. He laid a wreath on his parets' grave overlooking the now defunct colliery where his father had worked, and clinked glasses with the town's pipe band in whose forerunner he had marched as drummer. The visit, he told his old friend Artur Mannbar when he returned to East Berlin, had brought him 'my happiest days for years'. Yes, his old comrade agreed, it had been the proud confirmation of East Germany's acceptance by Bonn. 'That too,' Honecker said. 'Actually I was thinking about Wiebelskirchen, about home.'

Honecker's characteristic wariness and pervasive distrust of the Federal Republic's politicians meant that he was unable to prise open the channels of communication by means of unofficial contacts. Yet the closest political acquaintance Honecker developed in the west was also the least likely. The bruising, arch-conservative Bavarian premier Franz Josef Strauss, demonized by the West German left because of his blood-thirsty rhetoric and illiberal tendencies, developed into the East German communist's closest foreign confidant and a practical ally. Having once denounced Strauss as 'a militarist who would not stop at marching through the Brandenburg Gate' to recapture Berlin, Honecker later insisted that he had 'never viewed Strauss as an enemy of the GDR . . . He was a pragmatist, a very dynamic man.'

In 1983, Strauss negotiated a one-billion Deutschmark loan with Honecker's financial fixer, Alexander Schalck-Golodkowski, to stabilize the East German economy. The precise nature of the pact between Bavaria and East Berlin remains unclear. Strauss claimed that he agreed to help the East economically in order to ease the harassment on the frontier of Bavarian visitors to Thuringia, but a billion did seem to be a high price to pay for a little more courtesy from the border guards. Strauss's critics in the government accused him of wanting to embarrass Kohl by embarking on his own foreign policy offensive. The left scented major financial corruption. Strauss visited Honecker in his hunting lodge on the Werbellinsee in 1987 and recalled with characteristic lack of restraint in his memoirs how he had whisked away the East German leader for a spin in his Mercedes 380 SE: 'a very fast car'. Honecker must have found it an exhilarating change from the stolid government Volvos, known by East Germans as 'chariots of state' or 'big-wigs' scooters' because the sight of them among the Trabants, Wartburgs and Ladas guaranteed the proximity of a clutch of functionaries.

'We don't know the half of what goes on between Bavaria and East

Berlin,' became a head-shaking refrain of tantalized German journalists (on both sides) throughout the eighties. Since the collapse of the East, they have all realized that this was a generous understatement. Schalck-Golodkowski, a Stasi colonel responsible for acquiring hard currency to keep the East German economy afloat and its political élite in the style they desired but could not finance with Ostmarks, absconded to the West in the midst of the peaceful revolution, poured out his heart to the West German secret service, and was rewarded by being released to live in the idyllic village of Rottach-Egern in Bavaria. There he is treated, so the local landlord told me straight-faced, 'like one of us'.

An investigation into his financial affairs and his role as East–West go-between has begun but, with 2,000 files to be examined (and probably that number again missing), it is likely to take some time. In the mean-time, several million Deutschmarks are still mysteriously unaccounted for. What has emerged of the business between Schalck and Strauss is deeply unflattering to the memory of the Bavarian leader and reads like a communist caricature of the devious evils of capitalism, except that one of the protagonists was a representative of the Workers' and Peasants' State itself.

The two would meet in the luxury Bavarian guest house of the März brothers, millionaire butchers from Rosenheim. In return, the März's got mass deliveries of cheap, high-quality meat from the East, untaxed business which was recorded neither in the Federal nor the Democratic Republic's trade records. Payment would be arranged in hard currency which Schalck would take back (he was ferried in a Bavarian state car to the border, and from there home in one of those unmarked East German official Volvos). Schalck would then pass scraps of information from his conversations with Strauss about politics and security issues to the Stasi: according to one file released, the Bavarian leader described the Chancellor as 'a petty bourgeois and a coward', an opinion which is not surprising in itself, but a bizarre thing to confide to your sworn enemy.

Schalck now claims that he is a mere scapegoat for the broader guilt of others who remain hidden. In a tearful interview with the *Frankfurter Allgemeine Zeitung* he sobbed, 'It was only my job. I had to get Honecker his tailored suits, Günter Mittag (the elderly and infirm Party economics chief) his prosthesis, and whenever Mengistu needed bread and weapons for Ethiopia it was my telephone that would ring.'

It would be unwise for any journalist to claim to have worked out the full implications of the secret deals for both East and West Germany, but the tale did at least go a long way towards solving a conundrum prompted by years of eating in East German restaurants: why did the chickens seem to have an inordinate number of legs but no breasts? How could the entire bovine population of the GDR have such a predominance of shins and shoulders, when rarely a rump reached the diner's plate? I have never had any complaints about the quality of the beef in Bavaria.

If you had asked an East German what he or she thought of Honecker, before his fall, the chances were they would have looked at you blankly and murmured something about 'one of the old school . . . better than Ulbricht . . . some achievements in his time . . . a modest man'. If you ask the same question now, the liturgy is likely to differ: 'That coward . . . a criminal . . . ordered deaths on the border . . . robbed us of the best years of our lives.' The discrepancy is not due solely to the revelations of the last couple of years. There is little known about Honecker now that was not known then, bar the falsifications in his biography.

The difference is that, in the aftermath of the country's existence, its injustices are tethered to his person, rather than being treated as a vague if regrettable fact of life. Those who were not members of the Party would often vent their spleen at it but rarely, as far as I remember, at Honecker personally. If there was criticism, it tended to come from intellectuals, who recognized his limitations as a retarding influence on their society.

The fact of the border shootings was known by all East Germans, but only recently has it become common to judge them a reason to despise their leader. In the top-down system known as 'democratic centralism' – but extremely short on the former – no one would have imagined other than that the command came from Honecker. Public ire was more frequently directed at his wife and Education Minister Margot, known as the 'Lilac Dragon' because of her impeccable blue rinses and her ideological ferocity. The hatred of her husband is largely retrospective, if latent all along.

In December 1989 thousands of outraged East Berliners trudged through the snow of the Wandlitz compound, 'the bosses' colony' stranded gloomily in the middle of the fir trees in the woods north of Berlin. It exuded the modest, small-minded prosperity one would have expected from looking at the leaders who had recently vacated the premises, but in the envious eyes of the visitors it was vile extravagance. One woman lashed a kick at Honecker's oak front door, her face beetroot with fury. 'They preached water in public and drank wine on the sly,' she shouted, and everyone nodded vigorous approval. By all accounts, he had kept a cellar more renowned for quantity than quality. The ex-leader of the Italian communist party, Enrico Berlinguer, used to snipe that he hated visits because 'you didn't even get a decent glass of wine at the Honeckers'.

Of course, the fact that the Politburo isolated itself from the people was an affront, but the fact that they lived in Wandlitz in conditions considerably superior to those of the average high-rise tenement was an arrangement few would have previously challenged. If the visitors had been honest with themselves, they would have admitted that they were not in the least surprised. But they felt that the revolution owed them a dose of righteous anger and they were there to have it.

One man who has watched Honecker's prime and descent closely is Clemil de Wroblewsky, a clown and satirist by profession, who used to perform for the Politburo and was stripped of his East German citizenship when his act was no longer found a laughing matter by the authorities. Since 1986 he has run the Café Jenseits (Café Beyond) in West Berlin's Kreuzberg, which used to be the first stopping-off point for artists ejected from the East in search of some familiar company and perhaps a job behind the bar to tide them over. He also compiled the definitive encyclopaedia of East German jokes which, as elsewhere in eastern Europe, served as a rapid bush telegraph to convey information that the official media withheld. One such joke reflects the tendency of East Germans, in the last years of disillusionment and indifference to politics, to carefully cultivated duplicity:

Honecker is lying on the beach of his private island on the Baltic coast. 'Good morning, dear President of the State Council,' says the sun. 'I wish you an agreeable and relaxing day and will shine as well as I can for you.'

'Why, that's kind of you,' says Honecker, and settles down happily.

In the evening, the sun begins to sink and Honecker says, 'Thank you, dear sun, for shining with such conscientious enthusiasm all day for me.'

'Lick my arse you old fool,' replies the sun. 'I'm in the west now.'

Wroblewsky points out that Honecker's enthusiasm for improving living standards was a policy which undermined East Germany's economic well-being by switching funds from investment to the production and import of consumer goods. It resulted in not only the population orienting itself increasingly towards the West, but the regime too.

Ulbricht wanted a self-sufficient GDR, as unlike the Federal Republic as possible. Under Honecker, there was an active convergence towards the west. He tried to buy our goodwill by allowing Intershops (hard currency stores) and buying in West German shoes and small luxuries. Of course, it was fatal. Once the demands were awoken, people became dissatisfied that they couldn't have more and ended up just as dissatisfied as before. He sowed the seeds of his own destruction.

My own indelible memories of Honecker's character are his steadfast belief in the rightness of his project, and his puritanism. He was not one of nature's revolutionaries and often sounded ill at ease declaiming the grander tenets of theory and struggle. But he devoted endless attention to the tiniest details and could recite by heart and with inordinate pride the yearly increase in the number of indoor lavatories in every region. Monika Maron, a writer whose step-father Karl Maron was one of the country's founding communists, distilled the essence of Honecker and his peers in the novel *Stille Zeile Sechs* which settles her generation's account with that of their fathers. In it she wrote of 'the intoxication which power induced in these children of the proletariat, their fear of everything they could not understand and therefore forbade'.

The withdrawal of power has accelerated his ageing, and since his flight to Moscow his health has declined further. In the first TV interview after his escape he was often inarticulate and was constantly prompted, corrected and censored by Margot. Asked if he would act differently given his time in power again, he smiled. 'Everything we did was for the good of the people,' he said. 'There will be another attempt some day. I have no doubt that socialism will triumph. It is the only possible way forwards for the human race.'

5

The Stasi: Sword and Shield

Look, Listen and Grab

The worst thing about our tyrants
Was not their red-dipped tyranny
The worst thing about them was us,
Our crawling cowardice.
We were the evil unto ourselves
Yet that is our chance and our good fortune.
You see! It can be done. And we will recover
The old, the eternal human right for ourselves.

We breathe out again. We sob and laugh
The indolent sadness right out of our breast.
Man, we are stronger than the rats and the dragons
And had forgotten it. But knew it, all along.

Wolf Biermann

Comrade Minister Mielke: And how are things in the factories? What is the mood like there?

Comrade Major General Hähnel: That is a very complicated question at the present moment, Comrade Minister.

Comrade Minister Mielke: No. That is a very easy question. It is a question of power, nothing else.

From the minutes of a meeting between Erich Mielke, Minister of State Security, and Major General Hähnel, Chief of Security, East Berlin area, 31.8.89

On 13 November 1989 Minister of State Security Erich Mielke, unsteady on his feet at eighty-two and with the stubborn glint of senility in his eye, tottered to the podium of the People's Chamber to deliver a barely comprehensible farewell speech before his enforced resignation. 'We are the sons and daughters of the working classes,' he said of his legions of informants, controllers and bullies. 'We have, dear comrades, extremely intensive contact with all working people.' This most cautious of descriptions of the comprehensive net of fear, suspicion and distrust which Mielke's Stasi cast over the whole of East German society unleashed a hail of giggles from the assembly.

The minutes of the parliamentary session record merely 'mirth' at this point. In fact it was the loudest, longest laugh ever heard in the staid chamber, and it provoked Minister Mielke into a peroration of brotherly affection. 'But I love everyone!' he cried. The mirth had by now grown into a chorus of undisguised mockery.

It was an exit more befitting a gone-to-seed nightclub singer than a feared minister of state security. As he fought to be heard above the noise, one almost expected him to launch into 'I did it my way'. His garbled statement was the swan-song of a man who for thirty-two years had run a paranoid security service whose abuse of human rights remains a legacy that post-unity east Germany is incapable of coming to terms with. Its restless ghost still stalks a society in thrall to old repression.

The Stasi, which defined itself as 'the sword and shield of the Party', kept files on 5.5 million East Germans and 500,000 westerners. Details of the habits, views, weaknesses and movements of one in every three citizens resided in their headquarters throughout the country. Four miles of files were held at the East Berlin Stasi headquarters alone. The walls had to be reinforced to stop the weight of the documents pulling them down. Known affectionately to its 600,000 employees as 'the firm' or 'the family', and to the public fearful of its long arm as 'Look, Listen and Grab', the *Staatsicherheit* (literally, state security) held the country in a grip at once subtle and strong.

At the top of the organization sat Erich Mielke. Born in 1907 and the oldest member of the Politburo, his fondness for white uniforms and gold braid lent his otherwise squat appearance a hint of the panache of an ageing Caudillo. He had joined the Communist Party in 1925 and graduated to its paramilitary wing which, in the name of defending itself from the National Socialists, also engaged in violent vendettas. From this time he had a chequered history which East German historians were discouraged from researching. In 1931, at the height of the battles which took place around the Karl Liebknecht House (the KPD's headquarters), he and a colleague allegedly answered a call by the Party's self-defence wing to perform a symbolic assassination of policemen deemed particularly hostile to the communists, and shot dead two local constables in cold blood.

Both the assailants fled abroad, leaving the rest of the Party defence committee to be hauled before the courts and answer for the assassination. Three functionaries were sentenced to death, several others to long spells in prison. The murders turned out to have been a harmful miscalculation. The result of the provocation was a clampdown by the authorities – Karl Liebknecht House and its inhabitants were constantly under siege by a police force taking its revenge. The official annals of East Germany's Communist Party latterly condemned the campaign of 'individual terror' indulged in by the Party's paramilitary wing, but drew a discreet veil over Mielke's role in it.

In Moscow exile, Mielke survived the purges of German communists by aligning himself firmly on the side of Stalin's secret police, the NKVD, and went to the Spanish Civil War as a battalion commander in the International Brigades and later the head of an officers' school. After Franco's victory he fled to France, where he was briefly interned, and then back to the Soviet Union. What he did there 1940–45 is not clear, but from the range of high Soviet military honours that he bore from those days it can safely be concluded that he worked in military or internal Soviet intelligence.

He returned to East Berlin in 1945 entrusted with security tasks, and became head of the rapidly expanding Stasi empire in 1957. There had been disasters with Wilhelm Zaisser (1950–53) and Ernst Wollweber (1953–57) as security ministers in the republic's early years. Both were removed after supporting anti-Ulbricht coalitions. To avoid such embarrassment occurring again, Ulbricht decided to choose a politically naïve but operationally excellent minister. Nevertheless, he was not allowed into the Politburo until 1976: perhaps they feared his thuggishness would bring down the tone of the gathering.

Bone-headed and immature, Mielke had a child-like devotion to his Politburo peers. Extraordinary footage has come to light of him receiving the title 'Hero of the German Democratic Republic' from Erich Honecker, weighed down with ribbons and medals and stuffed into a uniform he had long outgrown. Grinning and grunting with pleasure, he looks like a teddy bear in military fancy dress. In his excitement he can hardly respond, and stammers: 'It has been such a pleasure, always a pleasure, delightful to live here in the GDR.' But he was also thorough and wary, with a limitless suspicion for the antics of 'the enemy' which kept his workers in a state of perpetual nervous anticipation. He made no secret of the fact that he was having even the homes of his Politburo colleagues bugged, and leering, would accost the wives of Wandlitz to repeat details of conversations and rows he had garnered.

The service included a vast espionage service called the *Aufklärung* (Enlightenment), run with great success since 1953 by Markus 'Mischa' Wolf, who doubled as deputy minister for state security. Wolf, who was younger, brighter and more inventive than Mielke, had gradually established total control over external espionage and barely hid the fact that he considered his boss an outdated oaf. He was prone to sneer at his superior's indiscriminate snooping: 'Mielke's idea of absolute state security is that he has to know absolutely everything.'

East Germany also had extensive military intelligence, although this was considered too complicated to be left to Mielke to supervise and was dealt with by Wolf's team in close co-operation with the Soviet GRU. He does, however, seem to have played a leading if not decisive role in the decision to grant asylum and operational aid to Western terrorists such as the legendary Venezuelan 'Carlos' – a frequent guest of the East German state which allowed him to fly in and out of Schönefeld airport on a fake passport with his luggage unchecked – and several Red Army Faction members wanted in West Germany for murders, kidnappings and bombings.

The Stasi ranked as a 'state within the state', with weapons, educational institutions, hospitals, holiday camps, prisons, prostitute rings and even troops of its own – the élite Feliks Dzierzynski regiment which guarded Stasi and government buildings. Under the elegant pseudonym 'College for Juridical Affairs' it ran its own training college in Potsdam. Its students dominated the criminology and forensic science departments of Humboldt University; and on every foreign language course in any university you could be sure that there was at least one student delegated to improve their communication skills for future use abroad.

In the seminar group to which I was assigned at East Berlin's Humboldt University, there was such a young man. He stood out only because of his fierce intensity and enthusiasm for any task he was given, and later his excessive panic about the course of events in the East. At most we suspected him to be a lowly informer. It came as a shock when, after the regime's collapse, and terrified that the 'enemy' would now exact a dreadful revenge, he broke down and confessed that he had been sent to the university as a trainee from the Stasi to create a 'cover' for future infiltration into the West.

It was intended that, armed with his German and English degree, he would 'defect', claiming dissatisfaction with career prospects there, and work his way into a position of influence in West Germany – the tried and tested method of 'settling' young agents and banking on them to rise through the ranks in the West while still controlling them from East Berlin.

My student colleague had been well prepared by his masters. He had been sent to West Berlin on courier jobs to test whether he would take the opportunity to abscond. After his reliability had been established he would be given tasks to familiarize himself with capitalist life. The *Aufklärung* knew that many of the mistakes which had led to the discovery of its agents had been the result of foolish slips rather than major miscalculations. They had learned the lesson the hard way with Günter Guillaume, the spy in Chancellor Willy Brandt's office, to whom they had sent a congratulatory telegram on the birth of his son reading, 'G. Congratulations on the second man.' This had been decoded by the West Germans, and narrowed the hunt for a leak to a man in a position of responsibility in the Bonn hierarchy with a new baby in the family.

In the eighties they jettisoned many of the methods which went back to the days of the Spanish Civil War and the Third Reich, including the sentimental habit of broadcasting coded birthday messages. The next generation of spies was to be flawless. My classmate was drilled in the tiniest subtleties of life in the West. He would be sent to eat in West Berlin to familiarize himself with exotic menus and learn to order wines unheard-of in the East. He would even go to the Stock Exchange and study the workings of capitalism.

From their seats in the centre of the monstrous Normannenstrasse complex in East Berlin, protected from prying eyes by a reinforced outer wall and cast-iron metal gates, the Stasi's top men devised ways to infiltrate the West and keep its own population's dissatisfaction at bay. Mielke ran a weird, amoral kingdom, where the worst in human nature was elevated into the desirable, the essential condition of successful operations.

He had picked up from Romania's Securitate the tip of stealing the work clothes or underwear of troublesome suspects, to be filed in carefully catalogued jars. When the next opportunity arose, they could thus be hunted down with sniffer dogs. The body odours of thousands of 'internal enemies' lined the walls of a 'smell laboratory'. In 1983, when the first signs of economic decline and a sharp rise in the numbers of East Germans trying to leave had been recorded, he planned internment camps for dissidents, should it come to a conflict between the state and 'religious forces and Social Democrats'. Opponents were to be held in trains shunted into the sidings of remote railway stations, and in holiday camps and hotels turned into detention centres. The models were to be the post-war Soviet internment camps for politically suspect Germans, often established in the very Nazi concentration camps they had just liberated. It was an appalling echo of persecution. No other single revelation of the Stasi's intentions caused more revulsion and horror in both parts of Germany.

The Stasi treated operations of vast and dreadful significance with the same unbending seriousness as utter trivia. It ran prisons where the interrogations were conducted as psychological warfare, and delivered opposition or criminal elements it could remove from society without arousing the attention of neighbours and family to a primitive psychiatric unit called Waldheim. It ran special teams who patrolled cities by night on the trail of the unseen hands who were daubing anti-government graffiti on walls, first measuring the letters and analysing the brush strokes for the records before painting over the messages of discontent. A file from the Leipzig headquarters records the fruits of one agent's work in the men's lavatories at the main station, where he found 'degradation of the state on the inner side of the door of the second cubicle from left'.

The observation files it kept on its citizens indicated everything from character weaknesses and blackmail potential to favourite pubs and the time they went to bed and got up, and cross-referenced the subject extensively with his or her contacts. The only weakness of Erich Mielke's operation was that it was too exhaustive; the state's collecting mania had long got out of hand.

To satisfy their bosses' desire for omniscience the agents often felt compelled to provide sheaves of totally useless information. Ten volumes were kept on the writer Erich Loest. Round-the-clock supervision was set up outside the homes of peace protestors in East Berlin. The Stasi had long taken the threat of disruption in the country far more seriously than even the dissidents themselves.

The internal service was Mielke's pride and joy, aimed at combating dissent and stifling potential opposition. In a dictatorship, the security service has two diverse functions: first, to intimidate the population by its universal presence, and second, to pass accurate information back to the centre about the mood in the population. The second function has a certain perverse honesty in that the leaders accept that the views they officially elicit from the public are not their real feelings, and that the channels of communication between the rulers and the ruled are blocked, so that genuine information from the bottom up has to be passed via internal spies.

The balance between these roles is of the utmost importance. If the intimidatory part gets out of hand, as happened in Romania, not even the state security can elicit the real views of the citizens, because everyone learns to keep their mouths shut or parrots expected statements of approbation of the system – what the Stasi called the 'feedback effect'. The agents also begin to fear that they will become the targets of the leaders' wrath if they report too much that is negative, so they begin to adjust their reports cosmetically and their information becomes virtually useless.

If the analytical side becomes overdeveloped the service tends to overestimate its own importance and think that it, rather than the government, should be running the country. The tendency to dominate the government it nominally serves has been seen over the last decade in the Soviet Union, where the KGB took to giving the Party orders, rather than vice versa.

East Germany's Stasi on the whole avoided these two traps, by keeping its repressive side under wraps and information flowing upwards until the very end. When the Stasi's secret 'State of the Nation' reports were released at the end of 1989, it was astonishing how accurate their descriptions were of a society which had lost the political will to live. Nowhere was the mood in the country as accurately characterised as in the report which reached Mielke on 9 September. On being allowed access to the Stasi's political analysis files after the revolution, I was astonished at their bluntness and how similar their conclusions were to the judgements on the demise of the regime by the opposition and pro-reform voices in the Party, the high number of informants within the opposition notwithstanding.

One report read:

While the advantages of socialism, such as social security and its protective nature, are acknowledged, these are no longer seen as the decisive factor when compared with the problems which arise and with the deficiencies. In part the advantages are seen as self-evident and no longer even enter into the citizens' final judgement as a factor. Quite often, they play no part at all. There are doubts and disbelief about the realizability of the goals of our Party and government and their correctness, particularly as far as internal political developments are concerned, about the attainment of corresponding quality of life and the satisfaction of personal needs. It all adds up to the opinion that the developments are not bringing any tangible improvements for the citizens of the GDR. These views are also now current among such groups of persons as were previously socially active but, for the reasons just mentioned, have become tired, resigned and are now giving up the struggle.

Mielke seems to have registered the seriousness of the situation in mid-1989 and this is probably the reason why, against all expectations, he supported the dismissal of Erich Honecker. Time after time he is quoted in the minutes as shouting at his underlings, 'What can we do? What is there left for us to do?' He was horrified when many of the factory henchmen, the volunteer *Kampfgruppen* units, refused to go on duty in the streets in October and bemoaned the fact that they had not been sufficiently prepared for armed conflict with their own people.

When one hapless regional security chief ventures that the exodus of thousands of young people is the main element in weakening the people's resolve, Mielke says, 'Can't we get the Free German Youth to talk to them?', as if a mild knuckle-rapping was all that was needed to change their minds. As the reports continue he is seen to be stranded in the position of a man who knows all the problems besieging the system but realizes that it has neither the will nor the resources to combat them. He begins to seek refuge in barely coherent reminiscences of the Party's glory days in the twenties and thirties, interrupting one lieutenant-general's catalogue of disasters with an outburst:

In our day, in the avant-garde of the KPD, we worked day and night, Saturday, Sunday. That's what's needed today. Now people have cars, go their own way. They can't be bothered with us, they tell us they just want their peace and quiet. But the enemy is always active.

Mielke was arrested on corruption charges and kept under house arrest for several weeks after the collapse of the regime – illegally, as it turned out, for in East German law there was no provision for such detention. It was none the less a fitting lesson for a man who had never shown much attachment to the state of law. After unification he was rearrested by the West German authorities and kept on remand in Berlin's Moabit jail.

Rumours of his senility spread. It was reported that he spent his days bellowing orders at the warders and that they had brought him a toy telephone so that he could dial imaginary inferiors and shout at them instead. Gradually, however, it dawned that these stories were suspiciously colourful, and that Mielke's doctor son Frank seemed unusually happy to help the press with amusing accounts of his father's gaga antics. Senile or not, Mielke remembered the old ruse of playing the fool so convincingly that people began to be more fascinated by his clowning than by his culpability.

In February 1992, his case finally came to court, but as tragedy clad in farce. Lacking sufficient evidence to prosecute him for the atrocities of his security services, the justice authorities charged him instead with the murder of two policemen in one of the street battles of Berlin in 1931. The former minister indulged in a panoply of tactics to convince the judge that he was unfit for trial, moaning softly to himself behind the glass of his bullet-proof dock, 'Shame and treachery', 'I'm ill', and, after he was ordered to remove his pork-pie hat, 'Where is my hat? They have stolen my property.'

The contradictory evidence of two psychologists was produced. One recorded that Mielke tried to hide under the bed whenever he had approached to interview him and could therefore be safely considered mentally confused. The other countered that there was no record of Mielke hiding under the bed when his lawyer or family visited but only at the entrance of his doctor or psychologist. Far from being senile, he argued, Mielke's behaviour betrayed an extremely accurate grasp of his position. The judge accepted that while the defendant was clearly unwilling to be tried, he was not unfit for trial. Mielke promptly recovered his sensibilities, began giving interviews blaming Honecker for the outrages of the GDR and explained his own revival thus: 'I thought I was going mad. But I am not completely mad yet.' He claimed that the Stasi had provided 'peace and order' in East Germany. The only sign of confusion was his declaration. 'I am prepared to die for my Party,' which he followed up with the qualifier, 'Well, there was a Party in those days'.

We know what it was like to be a subject of the Stasi's attentions from writers such as Erich Loest, the minutiae of whose multi-tome file defies belief. His apartment was observed and bugged twenty-four hours a day. There was no need for him to keep a diary: the Stasi did it for him, devoting to him a degree of care and attention which is horrifying and absurd in equal measure. Their findings include such valuable information on the 'negative-hostile subject' as: 'L. kissed his wife. L. then proceeded into the kitchen and made a cup of tea. L. returned to his study with cup of tea and sat at typewriter for two hours.'

We know less about the people who did the domestic spying, whose own lives were dominated by their work for the secret regime without the glamour or mitigation of working abroad in a hostile system. Like all successful dictatorships, East Germany had long mastered the art of entwining vast numbers of its citizens in its dirty work.

Over 100,000 people acted as official informers, and far more gave occasional snippets to the ministry. Most of them have remained undiscovered, their double life unknown to families and friends. Only a handful have publicly admitted their role and then usually under the threat of that nasty German habit of denunciation, as rife in the aftermath of communism as in the years after the collapse of fascism.

Monika Haeger is a rare exception, a former *Spitzel* (informer) who, no longer able to live with 'the feeling of revolting myself', confessed to her role as a full-time, paid informer in the Stasi's service. One of its most valuable internal agents, she infiltrated the East Berlin opposition in the early eighties and spied on the dissidents who had emerged from the peace movement. One, Katja Havemann, widow of Robert, wrote of her, 'People like Monika were used by the Stasi to gain secret access to our souls and minds, to poison our lives.'

Now barely a day passes when the former agent is not spat on, verbally attacked or threatened, both by those with a grudge against the Stasi and those who worked for it and who consider her confession a fresh treachery. The day we met she had been in her local supermarket, where she found herself surrounded by a group of women shouting 'Stasi-pig'. One fellow-shopper, overcome by the desire for revenge but lacking the tools for the job, tried to attack her with a frozen chicken.

It is hard for a society to forgive internal traitors like Monika Haeger, not least because the society is still ashamed of its own treachery. In the Stasi, they see their own opportunism, their own willingness to live with dictatorship, enlarged and named. Meeting with a former Stasi agent is never a comfortable affair, even for an outsider. The desire to know what made them do it is balanced by a fear of coming to accept the unacceptable, of mitigating a terrible phenomenon, of the tempting, flabby humanism of *tout comprendre, c'est tout pardonner.*

When I first met her, in a quiet café, I was surprised by the extent of my own paranoia. Was there a message of disgust in the way the waiter slammed down our coffee? Were the two girls at the next table glancing at us because they knew her from her television appearances? Did people think that I was an old accomplice? It felt like connivance. Perhaps it was just the apprehension that comes of sitting in a public place with someone prone to incur such wrath that people attack her with the contents of the deep-freeze.

She is a nervous woman in her forties with the chain-smoking intensity of the psychotherapist's outpatient – which she is. Since her confession she has suffered a breakdown and spends her days in a west Berlin therapy unit. 'I refused to go into a clinic in the east. Too many of the doctors worked for us [the Stasi]. I can't let those people near me again.'

The organization used a familiar and effective three-level method to deal with the opposition. The first was the age-old tactic of open surveillance, in which agents would follow their charges and sit outside their houses. This was carried out in such a way that the subjects knew that they were being watched, and limited their actions accordingly. The watchers even wore the official uniform – leather jackets – and their vehicles were always dark Ladas rather than the standard Trabants and Wartburgs. Katja Havemann explains, 'I knew my observer very well by sight. He was part of my life, almost as normal as friends and neighbours: always there.'

The second was the sort of covert surveillance which Monika Haeger conducted, and the third was 'disruptive action' aimed at sowing distrust among the members of the opposition groups and thus impeding their co-operation with each other by discrediting their members. Ironically, one of its favoured tactics was to drop hints that other innocent people in the group worked for the Stasi.

People like Monika gave their officers the information needed to get the balance right, to help them decide whom merely to watch, and whom to target with what sort of disruptive action, and when. As a member of the group she was entrusted with confidences about future projects and also the state of morale within it. After leaving their homes she would meet with her officer at varying secret addresses throughout the city and tell him what had been discussed that night.

She was, she says, 'tailor-made for the Stasi', at once unconditionally committed to the communist state and psychologically vulnerable. Abandoned by her mother as a child, she had been brought up in a children's home, a popular recruiting ground for the ministry. 'We were exactly what they needed. More ideologically pliable than other people because we were spoon-fed on socialist thought undiluted by family life. And we were deprived of attention, like all children who grow up in institutions. The Stasi was like a parent to me. The officer who ran me as an agent was always there. He was interested in my views. I was praised and rewarded. It was lovely.'

There are many reasons why people informed for the Stasi. Conviction, material gain, blackmail (active or passive), the desire to snoop or bully, the power which knowledge brings, or simply the pricking satisfaction of standing outside normal society, are usually factors in varying proportions. Some gained from the Stasi the security and care that they otherwise lacked. Not for nothing was it called 'the family'. The service was anxious to bind its agents with the suggestion that they belonged to an exclusive, noble social group. There was even a special recording by the Stasi choir honouring the work of the agents:

Your service is enlightenment
Names remain secret
Your achievements are inconspicuous
But always in the eye of the enemy
Stay watchful always! Never rest
Protect the peace of the world
You soldiers of the invisible front

Many both at home and abroad developed split personalities, identifying both with the regime and its opponents. In a conversation with Günter Guillaume, the spy who was infiltrated into Willy Brandt's office and whose discovery brought down the father of *Ostpolitik*, it occurred to me that he used the phrase 'my party' to refer to both the communists in East Berlin and the Social Democrats in Bonn. 'They were both my parties,' he countered. 'Like all good spies, I was at home in both environments.' The big fish like Guillaume still inspire admiration and envy. I doubt whether anyone ever spits at him. It is the minnows who are caught in the net of revenge.

Monika Haeger was also a good spy, albeit in the less glamorous environment of secret cabals around kitchen tables rather than ministerial meetings in the offices of Bonn. She was twice decorated in secret ceremonies for her performance. 'We weren't allowed to keep the medals in case anyone found them. Now when I think of those awards I am filled with self-loathing and ashamed at how proud I was of them. I was rewarded for my treachery and deceit. I find that most difficult to bear.'

The opposition in East Berlin was a small club, a cosy network of friends bound together by their frustration with the moribund system around them. The pictures which Monika took, ostensibly as an enthusiastic amateur photographer but in truth for the Stasi files, show smiling groups of people at parties in tenement courtyards, playing piggyback races, or huddled around kitchen tables planning their future tactics. For this reason Monika's duplicity cut to the core of the dissident movement in East Berlin. Her old friends have protested against the hounding of former Stasi agents but cannot bring themselves to allow her into their circle again.

Devoid of old friends, despised by her former colleagues and distrusted by new acquaintances, she is paying the price for her past actions. But her fate should also act as a case study for the well-meaning priests and liberal writers who encourage a full airing of the Stasi cupboard. The idea, current in Germany since the end of the war, that one can programme a society to run through *Vergangenheitsbewältigung* (coming to terms with the past), by making people confront their personal responsibility for it, is still dominant. It sounds noble in theory, but unfortunately most East Germans' idea of coming to terms with the past is to suppress it, or simply to channel their aggression towards any scapegoats who come their way.

The files are now opened to those who want to know whether they were observed, and by whom. It will take years before the process is completed and we do not yet know what the full cost to the new German society will be in terms of shock, revenge and misery balanced against the satisfaction of knowing the truth. Joachim Gauck, a former church minister who administers the aftermath of the Stasi on behalf of the German government, says that the step is necessary for 'spiritual hygiene' and that people cannot live comfortably in the future without knowing what was said about them in the past. The first stage of the process is complete, the sealed cupboards have been opened to daylight. Whether the new Germany is strong and wise enough to deal sensibly with the contents is another question. Early indications suggest a tendency to gawp and blame rather than consider and forgive.

Erich Loest has said that the collapse of the Stasi has unleashed 'a human tragedy of no small dimensions'. It has left in its wake damaged people, while the officers who exploited their underlings' conviction and weakness remain unpunished. Those who look in the files find the names of the people who sat in the cars outside their flats, who eavesdropped on their conversations, who passed on unguarded comments in the workplace or pub. They do not find the names and addresses of the men with military rank who controlled the game. And if they did, their old fear of authority would triumph. Few would dare to confront them.

Most east Germans feel that the files should be used in rehabilitation cases, and to check the background of candidates holding or seeking public office. This laborious process is under way at institutions such as Humboldt University, although assessing those who worked within the old system throws up an endless series of 'grey cases' where people tacitly operated alongside the Stasi without committing themselves as informants, often on the calculation that this was the most effective method of dealing with the ubiquitous service or in the mistaken belief that the more the Stasi knew of the extent of dissatisfaction the sooner things would begin to change.

The Stasi is a bacillus which continues to poison the body politic, even in the new Germany. Witness the case of Lothar de Maizière, East Germany's first and last democratically elected prime minister, rewarded after unity with the post of deputy leader of the all-German Christian

Democrats and the presidency of the party in the eastern region of Brandenburg. He quit politics in September 1991 after it was claimed that he had, as a human rights lawyer and church activist, passed on information to the ministry of state security.

It appears that de Maizière did have contacts with people he knew were agents of the service. He remains adamant that he was not an informer himself. Quite possibly, like many other East Germans, he reached the conclusion that the most effective way to continue his work on behalf of his clients was to palm off low-quality information on known agents. This way he could get the Stasi off his back by satisfying its lust for knowledge and be free to carry out his work without harassment. To western ears, such compromises sound grubby. But they were often a condition of life in the east for anyone involved in wringing justice out of an unjust system.

In Bonn they are shedding few tears over his departure, but the timing of the episode (the first allegations emerged when the December 1990 elections were safely over) and the revelation that the incriminating documents were fed to *Der Spiegel* magazine by prominent CDU politicians close to Chancellor Kohl, has given this affair the nasty whiff of a smear campaign. In a country where the hushing-up of scandals is the rule rather than the exception, the government was strangely quick to trumpet this one. It is hard to resist the conclusion that the main purpose of the exercise was that of removing a cuckoo from the political nest, of eradicating an awkward reminder of East German identity from Bonn's cosy milieu.

Even more difficult was the case of Manfred Stolpe, the popular Social Democrat president of Brandenburg and the 'Mr Clean' of east German politics. As the lay head of the Protestant Church in the East, he had performed a complicated role as go-between for the Church and the State, representing the interests of dissidents and conscientious objectors. That this job entailed a certain amount of Stasi contact and double-talk is clear to all. It was nevertheless a shock to discover from the opened files how far Stolpe had gone in flattering the Party that its aims and those of the Church could be accommodated together. His defenders appeal to the tactical necessity of softening up the regime to win concessions. Few doubt Stolpe's own integrity of purpose. His case is a sobering reminder that the Stasi's files were compiled by a dictatorship for the purposes of that dictatorship. It demands an almighty effort of understanding and insight if these same files are to be used to help establish and strengthen a new democracy.

Unlike de Maizière, Stolpe has said that he intends to fight the accusations and remain in office. Whether he is successful or not, it is already clear that the united Germany's political culture can only be declared in good health when those from the east can argue against the Stasi's interpretation of their past and have their defence accepted in Bonn. Otherwise, simply the raising of a suspicion, backed up with a few carefully selected excerpts from a Stasi document, will end career after career – often unfairly.

The Stasi has been unanimously declared the scapegoat for the evils of the East German system, and there are many who hide behind its reputation to lessen their own responsibility for what has happened. There are as many victims of the country's bureaucracy as there are of the Stasi's whims. The case of children removed by the state from parents who tried to flee the country was one of the most shocking abuses of human rights to emerge from East Germany after the fall of the regime. Yet the people who signed the orders were lower-caste bureaucrats working in the innocuous-sounding 'office for family and youth affairs' in local authorities, not sinister secret service agents.

The officials who ordered the expulsion of innocent villagers from sensitive border communities were indifferent mandarins in provincial town halls. No expression of regret is demanded from them. Although the information on which such judgements were made came from the Stasi, the political will behind them emanated from the Communist Party and their implementation was made possible by lack of resistance at every level. Repression was as often effected by resignation and indifference as by force and fear.

It is too often forgotten that the Stasi was, as it declared itself, the Party's 'Sword and Shield'. To dissect the workings of the state security system, name the informers and look in horror at its methods and aims will not alone help Germany come to terms with this chapter of its past. There is a serious risk that overexposure and overpromotion of the topic in the media and in politics will result in people drowning in a sea of ghastly detail rather than gaining any useful perspective on the Stasi and its legacy.

The Nuremberg principle – under which the top Nazis were pursued and the rest effectively left to go free – has effectively been turned on its head in east Germany. The battle over blame is being scrapped out on the lowest level, while the silver-haired generals and majors are honoured with swivel chairs from which to explain away their past for a fee on TV talk shows.

Markus Wolf – The Spy's Spy

He was the very clever, quiet type: I would call them the back-room functionaries who always stand in the background, who see everything, that other comrades take completely seriously and enthusiastically, as a huge game of chess. They never allow themselves to lose their calm, they control the proceedings as if through a pane of glass. They are excited by nothing and nothing ever disturbs their countenance.

Wolfgang Leonhard recalls the young Markus Wolf

It is no easy business meeting Markus Wolf. First, you wheedle your way into his attractive, canalside apartment block in East Berlin and ring the bell. His (third) wife, a pleasant, homely woman, says she's terribly sorry but Mischa doesn't have anything to say at the moment – things being what they are with the West Germans. You know. Perhaps if you got in touch with E. . . . .

E., a fair-skinned, rather foxy-looking former agent, controls access to Markus Wolf and insists on lengthy, anonymous meetings to establish what the man he invariably calls 'the boss' is to be asked – and what's in it for 'the boss' anyway. We wanted to film him for a television documentary, which clearly flattered his vanity. Shortly before unification, Wolf agreed to be interviewed. Which was just as well, because by the day U-Day dawned he had fled to the Soviet Union to avoid arrest by the West German authorities for espionage.

The PR lady in east Berlin's ghastly Grand Hotel was appalled by our thoughtlessness in simply rolling up with the former head of East German intelligence. 'Why didn't you say?' she scolded. 'We would have given you a better room and some flowers. He is a very special guest.' For over twenty years at the top of the service, he ranked as the 'Man without a Face', managing to elude the long lenses of the Western services. By 1990, however, his aquiline features, an interesting muddle of faintly sinister half-tone spectacles, puckish mouth and the ruddy complexion of the *bon viveur*, had celebrity status around the smarter haunts of east Berlin – the result of a well-timed and stylishly-executed swivel in the direction of *perestroika* in the pursuit of whose import into East Germany he left office after thirty-four years in 1987.

He is tall, charming and unfailingly *soigné*, the apotheosis of the German-Jewish *Schöngeist*, a lover of music, chess and literature. He likes to read le Carré: 'He seems to know an awful lot about me.' As usual, E. is in wary attendance. His presence seems justified only to smooth out any minor difficulties which may arise for 'the boss'. One does: Wolf, resplendent in a fine woollen suit which is definitely not a product of the People's

Own Menswear Factory, realizes that he is tieless and insists on having one before he faces the camera. 'British spies are always well dressed. I don't want to look like a country cousin.' E. produces one. Wolf waits while he ties it for him.

Wolf is one of those rare, favoured children of life who earn the respect and envy of friend and foe alike. There were many in the hierarchy of both East and West Germany who disliked him, but no one I ever met was indifferent to him. He enjoyed near-mythical status as the perfect spy chief, masterminded the spy-swap of the U2 pilot Gary Powers for the Soviet agent Colonel Rudolf Abel on the legendary Glienecke Bridge at Potsdam, and later the freedom of Anatoly Sharansky in a multi-sided exchange. He also reduced the rival West German service to the level of what one intelligence man described to me as 'two large Swiss cheeses'. He became a part of spy fiction in his own professional lifetime: the model for John le Carré's icy Karla.

One commentator concluded that he was 'highly gifted, extremely cultured, with good manners, fascinating in conversation, quick-witted, in possession of extraordinary leadership qualities'. It reads like the propaganda of his own side: in fact it was the conclusion of a special report on him commissioned by the West German security services. The writer decided that Wolf's main weakness was 'a lack of feeling and emotional potential'.

As if to confuse the enemy one last time, Wolf promptly produced a well-written and sensitive appraisal of Moscow exile and its effects on the lives of the émigrés thereafter. The Troika traced his brother Koni's friendship with two young German exiles and their later fate on opposing sides in the Cold War. It also condemned the false dawn of Stalinism and dropped elegant hints about the necessity for reform. The Wolf-watchers shook their heads in perplexity.

He was born in 1923, the son of the Jewish communist dramatist Friedrich Wolf. The family emigrated to the Soviet Union, where the young Wolf grew up attending the Karl Liebknecht school and later the Comintern school. He was a child of Stalin's Russia and a product of those years, as he later admitted: 'Stalin was my everything, a part of my whole existence. It would be impossible for me to imagine my time in the Soviet Union without Stalin.'

He arrived back in Berlin in 1945 shortly after the Ulbricht Group, and was delegated by the Party to a reporting job at the Berliner Rundfunk, the radio of the Soviet sector, where he worked alongside the old propaganda chief Karl Eduard von Schnitzler. Sent to the Nuremberg trials and reporting under his pseudonym Michael Storm, he made a name for himself. After East Germany's foundation in 1949 Wolf was briefly sent as adviser to the new republic's mission in Moscow, but the Russians soon decided that they had more ambitious plans for him and returned him to East Berlin to build up an offensive counter-espionage service. It is enlightening that Wolf's very first steps on the espionage ladder were taken not at the bidding of East Berlin, but of Moscow.

Despite his unrivalled success he was never close to the hearts of the East German leadership, and was not rewarded with the place he sought in the Central Committee, to which far less inspiring figures ascended with ease. He was always rather too obviously Moscow's man, in thrall to the dream of the Soviet Union as the model for mankind. Half-Jewish, he kept the channels of private communication open with Israel even while the state was unrecognized by the Soviet bloc, and is said to have been trusted with the sensitive (and still not officially admitted) bridging role between Moscow and Jerusalem.

Wolf's triumphs captured the imagination of the Western media. Spies are only as good as the people who run them, and Wolf was never happier or more motivated than with the discreet reins of power in his hands. He was personally responsible for running Günter Guillaume in Willy Brandt's office and used him to elicit valuable details of how the West Germans would conduct their *Ostpolitik* negotiations on co-operation with East Berlin. 'I would go as far as to say that the *détente* between East and West Germany was only possible because of the role of the security services,' he says. 'Without us to confirm the genuineness of the other side's intentions, the negotiations would never have got off the ground.'

Until 1978 there was not a single picture of him, beyond those taken as a teenager, in the hands of the Western services. He was finally 'identified' on a trip to meet an agent in Sweden in the early seventies. 'Actually, it didn't matter in the least that no one knew what I looked like,' he told me cheerfully. 'It just became one of those ridiculous games one played with the West Germans. After they finally got me, I was quite relieved.'

He is still coy about the reasons for leaving office in 1987. 'I had wanted to go much earlier, on my sixtieth birthday in 1983, but even I was under the discipline of the Party, and the leadership said the time was not right for a change. I felt the need, which I had not had before, to write books, to think critically about my own life and about our history and its causes. That was the reason I wanted to go.' His actions after retirement, however, indicate that he had other things on his mind besides bookish contemplation.

Having realized that Honecker was not going to accept Mikhail Gorbachev's *perestroika* and that the political structures of East Germany were locked, he set about preparing the ground for change. Predicting a leadership crisis in the next few years, he prepared his old friend and fellow Russophile, the popular Dresden party chief Hans Modrow, to take over, backed by a group of reform communist economists and social scientists at Humboldt University. The idea received the approval of the then KGB chief Vladimir Kruchkov, who later revealed his true political nature by supporting the coup against Mikhail Gorbachev in August 1991. What the Russians coyly describe as 'unofficial channels' of communication were opened, through which Wolf and Modrow communicated with the Kremlin without the knowledge of the East German government.

Modrow recalls the preparations for his ascent to power thus: 'There were times when I would be picked up in an unmarked Lada somewhere in town and driven into the Soviet Embassy, so that it would not become clear to the leadership here that I was their guest.' Wolf confirms the story:

Hans Modrow and I had similar views and frequent conversations about the necessity for change. We both feared that the government was steering towards a confrontation with the people which, like 17 June 1953, would be violent, and which it could not win. Modrow was a great hope for me. As for the others who stood in line for power, I didn't expect much from them. Egon Krenz did not have the strength of personality one needed to enthuse the people for *perestroika*.

Wolf realized, however, that it was impossible to heave Modrow to a position of power from outside the Politburo. He intended Krenz as a Chernenko figure, who would begin changes and bring Modrow and other reformers into the government, while banking on the fact that he would fail to find acclaim with the public, so clearing the way for Modrow and his pro-Gorbachev team to take power.

With the intention of destabilizing Krenz's shaky control and re-establishing himself in the role of political savant, Wolf made his appearances at the opposition demonstration of 4 November. To his disappointment, he was greeted with a chorus of boos and whistles. The Stasi mantle was proving difficult to shake off. That Gorbachev knew of and supported Wolf's plan is indicated by the fact that Wolf's communications with the Kremlin continued at a high level during Krenz's early days in power. According to the record of the new leader's first conversation with the Soviet president, one of the first questions he asked was, 'Where is Hans Modrow?' When Krenz and Modrow visited Moscow together, Gorbachev was seen talking animatedly to Modrow – by then prime minister – while Krenz, still leader, hung around uncomfortably on the outside.

The opening of the Wall was a catastrophe for Wolf and his plans, and one for which he still blames Krenz's mismanagement:

It was a shocking development for anyone who wanted to change the GDR from within, for reform communists and the opposition alike. The way in which the border was opened, in panic and without any concern for its effects on internal development, made it immediately clear to me that the consequence would not be unity by steps but merely the melting away of the GDR into the West German system. I regret with all my heart that we were not allowed a chance at true reform.

Markus Wolf is no shrinking violet and there is much in his nature which speaks against the standard analysis of him as a chess-player on the board of international affairs. The image is accurate in so far as it describes his mental processes, but it neglects another equally powerful side of his nature and operations: sex. Markus Wolf clearly likes women. So much so that Erich Mielke believed his womanizing to be a security risk, and had his own chief of espionage bugged. He would not, of course, be the first spy chief with a weakness for women, but he had the most dangerous fascination of all – a desire for ordinary women. For the man who ran a business based on sophisticated manipulation of human weakness, his own was very straightforward.

He disliked the vacuum-packed safety of the high-ranking Stasi's social world. After his first marriage to Elli Schmidt (a fellow-graduate of the Comintern school and a Politburo member under Ulbricht) ended, he began to frequent a corner pub in a suburb of Berlin where he would chat up the barmaids. In a society where the entire Politburo, the majority of whom knew far less about anything of consequence than Wolf, lived incarcerated behind the guarded walls of Wandlitz, the idea of the head of espionage consorting with the locals made Mielke apoplectic with rage and fear. A marriage with another agent was practically arranged for him. Not that this discouraged him. He began an affair with his wife's best friend, a plump beautician, and divorced the distraught second wife to marry the third, insisting, to the Party's dismay, on a lavish and public ceremony. Andrea Wolf is, to the amusement of her husband's former colleagues, entirely uninterested in espionage and political gossip and enjoys clucking about his wellbeing almost as much as he enjoys being looked after.

Wolf's own enthusiasm for romantic adventure gave him the cynically brilliant idea which opened up new channels in the espionage game: 'Casanova agents' who would pose as enthusiastic suitors to woo the government secretaries of Bonn into passionate affairs and morning-after co-operation. He boasted of fifty-three major successes by this method, many of which have only just come to light since the breakdown of confidentiality among agents after unity. Some of the women involved became so entangled in East Berlin's web, and so fearful of discovery in the West, that they followed their Casanovas back to the East. It was far from being a harmless scrape. Many were exploited over many years by Wolf's agents and then deserted. Others were blackmailed into co-operation beyond their own free will. 'Oh really,' says Wolf, 'don't be so censorious. A lot of happy marriages arose from that little escapade, even if our methods were not always those of the drawing-room.'

Wolf and his fellow-spies are campaigning for an amnesty to free them from prosecution for their former activities now that West German law is applicable in the east as well. 'We did no more and no less than any other service in the world,' he said, leaning back in a large leather chair bestowed on us by the Grand Hotel as a fitting throne for the guest. In its attempt to upgrade us, the management had planted us in the lugubrious isolation of the 'hunting suite', decked with stags' heads and antlers. This had the effect, from where I was sitting, of making it look as if Wolf had horns growing out of his head: an image which may well have also appeared to his pursuers in West German intelligence over the years.

'Sometimes we did it with rather more success, but it was a short-lived victory, circumscribed by the failings of our political system.' Nevertheless he is proud of his penetration of the West German government. 'My chaps were everywhere,' he says cheerfully. Sometimes, he admits, it got a little out of hand. While his major coup, settling Guillaume into the Chancellor's office as Brandt's right-hand man, shook Bonn to the core and added to the legend that there was nothing and no one safe from Wolf's agents, the spy's discovery and removal did more harm than good to the East, deepening distrust between the two states and preventing East Berlin building on the triumph of its recognition by Bonn which Brandt had championed.

I asked him whether he enjoyed his reputation of having run one of the most effective espionage services in the world. There was a hint of a wince in the practised, witty reply. 'Our country has collapsed without trace,' he said. 'It couldn't have been that much of a success.'

Since unification, Germany has been faced with the thorny problem of what to do with East German spies. The Basic Law of West Germany was initially intended to apply to all Germans, giving Bonn a legal if not practical right to apply its law to the East. Bonn had long stopped expecting the entire hierarchy of the *Aufklärung* to fall into its hands overnight, but the regular uncovering of new espionage nests has provided a legal headache. East Germany built up an extremely large network of spies and of people running them, and the public prosecutor Alexander von Stahl has said that he reckons with 'at least 4,000 court cases'.

The matter is complicated by the avowal of the Basic Law that all Germans are equal under it. This means that it is difficult to try eastern spies for carrying out the same activity as those working for the west. The Justice Minister Klaus Kinkel, who as a former head of the West's security service, the *Bundesnachrichtendienst* (BND), has a particular animus against Wolf and his spies, has tried to construct a case on the lines that West Germany's spies were defensive (i.e. sought to protect the Federal Republic), while East Germany's were offensive (i.e. sought to undermine it). It is hard to deny Wolf the hearty laugh in which he indulges when this is put to him. 'It comes down to the justice minister saying our spies were good guys and yours were bad guys,' he says. 'Do you really think people swallow that? Do they believe it themselves? This is just the victor's revenge on the vanquished, nothing more.' There is also the thorny matter of whether West German law can be applied retrospectively to East Germany, when the spies can legitimately claim that they worked in the service of a state which was recognized by West Germany. While the conviction of border guards for deaths on the border has provided a precedent for trials of east Germans under the western legal system, the judge's ruling was based on recourse to a higher moral law which would not stand scrutiny in an espionage case.

The constitutional court in Karlsruhe, the ultimate arbiter on the question of what the country's other courts may and may not try, will have to decide whether the trials can proceed. One cannot avoid the impression that much of the discussion has been conducted to satisfy the grievances of the home security service. The politicians of Bonn have also suffered so long from the fear of infiltration (what might loosely be called the 'Secretaries' Syndrome') that they cannot bear the thought of East Germany's intelligence getting off scot-free.

The spectacle of lengthy trials against former eastern agents will become increasingly absurd as the memory of East Germany fades. The spy for a defeated power is a sorry figure, even when he cuts the dash of Markus Wolf. In the handful of symbolic trials, a grudging amnesty is the most likely outcome.

On the morning of Unification Day, 3 October 1990, it was the turn of the Berlin criminal police to wheedle their way into Wolf's apartment block; but he had gone, offered sanctuary by his colleague and old friend, the KGB chief Kruchkov. He used his exile to write a second book recalling his progress and admitting to his political errors – a clever piece of pre-emptive sympathy-gathering. He frequented the writers' colony of

Peredelkino and was seen strolling around Moscow, temptingly beyond the grasp of the German authorities.

His past caught up with him in the form of the Moscow coup, after which Kruchkov was arrested. The new masters made it clear that they would no longer extend protective hospitality to him. He decided to try the rather different political climes of Austria and arrived with a request for political asylum. Vienna had already tweaked Bonn by allowing Wolf to holiday in Austria (he had long been *persona non grata* in the Federal Republic) but it did not want to be stuck with him for good and refused his request. The Austrian authorities nevertheless seemed sorry to see him go and offered him a long weekend in a guesthouse in the Burgen-land mountains to prepare for his departure. 'He told us that he didn't know when he would smell fresh air again, so we invited him to stay for a few days and gather his strength,' said an unembarrassed spokesman for the Vienna foreign ministry.

The holiday ended on 24 September 1991. Wolf was arrested on charges of treason at the tiny border crossing of Gmain between Austria and Germany, on his way to give himself up to the authorities in Karlsruhe. He was given bail, but the public prosecutor's office there insisted that no special deal had been done and that justice would now run its course. Wolf has repeatedly insisted that he will not swap information about the activities of his agents for a more lenient sentence. The thought of the elegant master spy slopping out a prison cell defeats even the liveliest imagination. Perhaps he will take E. with him to do it for him.

While the laborious inquiries into the scope and success of his service continue, he is forbidden to leave Berlin. 'I have no great desire for more adventure anyway,' he said, adding that he prefers a quiet life divided between his apartment and a cottage on the outskirts. 'I need time to come to peace with myself and the new Germany and carry on writing.' There was just a hint of a pause for effect. 'Perhaps a book for children would be nice,' he said.

6

Concrete Horizons

The Cruellest Cut

I understand your question to mean that there are people in West Germany who wish us to mobilize the construction workers in the capital of the GDR to erect a wall. I am not aware that any such intention exists. The construction workers of our capital are mainly occupied in building housing and that demands all of their energies. No one has the intention of building a wall.

Walter Ulbricht at a press conference on plans to solve the Berlin problem,
15 June 1961

Silver-fish in the intersection
Of the window: Pan American DC10
You swim across the roof
Without me. Come along! Blinking lights
Under the carriage,
Come along! But I remain. I do not
Open up the newspaper
Coughing in the Paris dawn
In some fashionable bistro
On the Boulevard Saint Michel
I look to the heavens
Dark as a yet-unborn mouth
O heavens, I say, I do not
Fall to my knees
In a strawberry-filled supermarket
Nor in the Prado
The British Museum, nor the Louvre.
I am not invited to breakfast with Emperor Hirohito
For I am involved in no international affairs . . .

Steffen Mensching, 'World Timetable'

When the world remembers nothing else about East Germany it will remember it as the country which built a wall to keep its people in. The memory of the concrete scar through the heart of Berlin lingers as a symbol of Europe's post-war division, of the Cold War. The Wall demonstrated at once the strength and the weakness of Soviet communism.

That its German disciples could build such a monstrosity in the heart of Europe was a sign of their determination to preserve their fiefdom at all costs. That they had to resort to such a draconian measure to stave off its collapse laid bare the country's central weakness: many thousands of its own people wanted to flee it.

When, in the early-morning haze of Sunday 13 August 1961, the troops of East Germany's special civil forces, the *Kampfgruppen*, the People's Police and the army spread themselves along the sector borders and erected the first line of low barbed-wire, Berliners east and west woke to find their worst fears come true. Their city, already ideologically divided and with separate currency, transport and telephone systems, was now being physically rent in two.

In the weeks leading up to 13 August, the number of refugees streaming from the east had swollen daily. It was no secret that the East Berlin government intended to staunch the flow. That some form of heightened border control was imminent was clear to all. A wall was the simplest and most effective solution to the East's problems.

Walter Ulbricht's avowal of 15 June – 'No one has the intention of building a wall' – was the first time that the idea was publicly mentioned by the Eastern leadership. Recalling the event on the thirtieth anniversary of the Wall's construction in 1991, Willy Brandt, who had been ruling Mayor of West Berlin at the time, said that he had taken Ulbricht's words as a warning that the East was going to step up its control of the border, but had dismissed the mention of a wall as rhetoric. 'The idea of building a Wall through the city of Berlin burst the bounds of the imagination. It was simply inconceivable to us.' The determination of the communist bureaucrats of East Berlin to save their socialist experiment exceeded the wildest dreams of politicians and people alike.

The division of Berlin was the climax of a long preamble of conflict. It was at once a logical but unimaginable consequence of the tensions which had governed the city since its division into zones under the control of the four Allies in 1945. It had not taken long for the Soviet Union to regard the existence of West Berlin as a disruptive factor in its plans for the region. The attempt to force the capitulation of the western sector by means of a blockade in 1948–49 had been unsuccessful, not least because of the crassness of Stalin's approach, which made an American response inevitable. In 1958 Nikita Khrushchev tried again, this time replacing Stalin's strong arm tactic with his own favoured method of combining a carrot and a stick in one policy.

In his note to the Western Allies of 27 November, he announced that the Soviet Union intended to sever unilaterally the four-power agreement on the administration of Berlin, and proposed that the western sectors of the city be converted into a 'demilitarized free city' which would be allowed to maintain its economic and political independence. Failing agreement to this, Khrushchev threatened to transfer to the German Democratic Republic full rights over the access routes to West Berlin, effectively ending the West's free access to the city. The proposal was followed in January 1959 by the proposal of a draft peace treaty. Taken together with the Khrushchev note, the move by Moscow provided a new variation on the post-war Soviet aim of a demilitarized, neutral Germany, to prise the heart of Europe away from American protection and influence.

It was an aim followed doggedly, if latterly without hope of success, by the Kremlin, until the advent of Mikhail Gorbachev switched the focus of foreign policy. Even after that it lived on in the political sleep-talk of pro-Soviet politicians. When in February 1990 the East German Prime Minister Hans Modrow made his 'Germany One Fatherland' speech agreeing to the demands from demonstrators for unification, he proposed an initial confederation of the two states and their eventual unity as a demilitarized area, outside both NATO and the Warsaw Pact. The notion was immediately turned down by Bonn and the West, which had woken up to the fact that the decrepit East would readily fall into the arms of the West without any great struggle. In the acute difficulty in which Modrow found himself as prime minister of a collapsing state, it is doubtful whether he thought that his proposal had even the remotest chance of acceptance as a negotiating position. Rather it seemed like the last rattle of the rusty sabre of Soviet strategy for Europe. When it was ignored, Modrow seemed neither surprised nor disappointed: he had merely been following the old – and now redundant – rules of the game.

The Khrushchev ultimatum can be regarded as the last serious attempt by Moscow to prise West Berlin out of the control of the Western powers. The threat to hand over control of the access routes to East Germany was never fulfilled. Khrushchev wanted to remove what the Kremlin persisted in calling the 'anomaly' of a capitalist city surrounded by a communist state. But as he grew in political confidence and the shadow of Stalin over foreign policy faded, he attached less importance to specific local issues such as the Berlin question and more to establishing the basis for superpower relations with America. President Kennedy, who had succeeded Eisenhower in January 1961, shared the view that the interests of the USA and USSR and their bilateral relations should be separated more clearly from the interests of their respective allies. The two leaders confirmed their more relaxed approach to the Berlin question when they met in Vienna in June 1961.

Ulbricht was displeased at Khrushchev's new reserve and disorientated by the realization that Moscow no longer considered the interests of the regime it had installed in East Berlin after the war as the decisive factor in its treatment of the Berlin question.

At the Warsaw Pact summit in Moscow at the end of March he had tried to persuade his alliance colleagues of the necessity of a guarded barbed wire along the Soviet zone border. The Kremlin has yet to open its archives on the discussions which led up to the building of the Wall, but from the account of Jan Sejna, the Czechoslovak deputy defence minister who defected to the West in 1968, there was little enthusiasm for the proposal.

The Hungarian leader Janos Kadar and the Romanian leader Gheorghiu-Dej apparently rejected Ulbricht's suggestion, Kadar claiming that such a move would discredit socialism, and Gheorghiu-Dej saying that such a flagrant breach of the four-power agreement would unleash a military response from the West. An incensed Ulbricht protested that, unless something was done to prevent the 'bleeding dry' of his country, it would be unable to fulfil its economic obligations within Comecon. Khrushchev nevertheless refused to agree to the proposal, claiming that he had 'wider goals and not yet full clarity about the new Kennedy administration'. Ulbricht left Moscow without the Pact's approval for his plan.

Back home, however, he carried on with technical preparations for a fortified border. Erich Honecker, responsible in the Politburo for security questions, was put in charge of co-ordinating the project. The number of refugees fleeing to the west was growing by the month – in January 1961 10,000 had left, in July 30,000. Half the refugees were young, skilled people under twenty-five – those East Germany could least afford to lose. About 2.7 million East Germans had left for West Germany since 1949. Sometime between the end of April and the end of July Khrushchev must have dropped his opposition to the project. After 13 August he sent a message to Adenauer via the West German ambassador in Moscow, the tone of which was unusually regretful and which, in a rare departure from the front of silence about affairs within the Warsaw Pact, made it clear that the impetus had come from Ulbricht rather than him.

I know the Wall is an ugly thing. It will disappear again one day, but only when the conditions which led to its erection have fallen away. What could I have done? . . . There were two sorts of countermeasures: an air blockade or the Wall. The former had already brought us into a conflict with the USA which could have led to war. I could not and did not want to risk that. So the Wall was all that was left. I do not want to hide from you that I was the one who in the end gave the relevant command. Ulbricht had been pushing me for some time and harder and harder in the last months, but I do not wish to hide behind his back – he is far too slight a figure to conceal me.

The date and final details of the building of the Wall were approved by the Politburo at its meeting on 7 August in the coded form of a resolution confirming 'the commencement of the intended supervisory measures'. Only on 12 August did Ulbricht call together the council of ministers to inform them of the decision. The tightness of the timetable indicates that he did not want to risk dissent. Erich Honecker had planned the opera-tion with military precision and in thoroughly military style, even to the extent of setting up a special staff, with a plan of action and precise instructions for each stage of the operation.

At midnight the alarm was raised and the teams of police, army and civic troops moved into action, throwing up a barbed-wire cordon along the Soviet sector border to West Berlin. Honecker's detailed planning paid off: by 6 a.m., East Berlin was sealed off from the West. All underground and overground rail links between East and West were severed immediately, and telephone lines with West Berlin and West Germany were cut.

In the days that followed the metal fence was replaced section by section with a concrete wall 3½ metres high. Concrete had to be diverted from other building projects throughout East Germany. At the polytech-nic in Ilmenau in Thuringia, which I visited in 1984, a senior academic apologized for the half-finished look of the place: 'We were supposed to be a show-piece, but before we completed the site they came and took away the building materials in 1961. They were never replaced.'

As the building of the Wall began, Willy Brandt issued a request for help to the three Western Allies' city commandants: 'At least send patrols to the sector border to counter the feeling of insecurity and show the West Berliners that they are not in danger.' But it took twenty hours for the patrols to reach the border and three days before a protest was delivered to Moscow. If the prompt action of the Western Allies in 1948 in countering the blockade of the city had established a bond between Berlin and the USA, the failure of the West to respond more strongly to the closing of the border – a breach of the four-powers' agreement for Berlin – proved a deep and jolting shock.

Particularly in the East, where the population listened to RIAS (the radio station of the American sector) to counter the propaganda doled out by their leaders, and which had always urged them to resist and pledged its support for the restoration of their freedom, the expectation of a military response by the West was high. President Kennedy, having received the news from Berlin on board his yacht *Marlin*, had telephoned his foreign minister to ascertain whether the Russians had mobilized and whether the rail, road and air routes to West Berlin were threatened. On hearing that they were not, he carried on with his sailing trip.

President Kennedy replied to Brandt's pleas five days later in a statement which declared America's 'revulsion' at the closing of the border, but stated that there were 'no steps at our disposal which would bring about a fundamental, material change in the present situation'. Apart from the strengthening of the allied garrisons in West Berlin and the usual protests, the West did nothing to counter the move.

On 22 August the Politburo approved a catalogue of measures isolating East Germany from Western Europe. The border with the Federal Republic, demarcated with a wire fence in 1952, was fortified to the point of being completely impassable. It was announced that West Berliners would henceforth need permits to enter the East. The contribution of East Germans to West German publications was forbidden and the import of Western newspapers stopped. For the first time, there was indication of an order to shoot escapers. Honecker's speech included the words, '. . . that everyone who undertakes to contravene the laws of our German Democratic Republic be called to order: by the use of arms if necessary'. A week later a fully-organized border control was in force along the length of the country's Western frontier and the border with West Berlin. By 1964, flight from the East was only possible at the risk of death. Automatic shooting devices, installed in 1970, made escape even more hazardous.

The Wall was the dominant symbol of Europe's post-war division and the countries on either side were so estranged that they could not even agree on what it was. The West dubbed it the 'Wall of Shame' while the East's politicians referred to the 'anti-fascist protection barrier'.

A whole family of euphemisms sprang into being and a recent linguistic study points out that, in the aftermath of its construction, the East German media avoided any reference to the word 'Wall' for an entire year. Later, they talked of the 'security constructions of the border', or simply the 'State border'. Even in the eighties it was considered bad form to call the Wall a wall. When talking with officials, they would laboriously correct any mention of the four-letter word.

Latterly, Erich Honecker took to using the taboo Wall-word in speeches, but only when he was on the political offensive, such as in January 1989 when he said that it 'would still be standing in fifty or a hundred years, as long as the conditions which led to its erection pertain'. The media, caught on the hop by this sudden change, could no longer avoid the word but took instead to printing it in inverted commas – a belated tit-for-tat for the way the mighty West German Springer Press enclosed the letters DDR in quotation marks in all its newspapers. The publisher Axel Springer, a life-long opponent of the division of Germany, insisted on the measure to indicate that he did not accept the state-next-door's right to exist. The quotation marks were finally dropped in early 1989 only a few months before Springer's hated 'DDR' began its final collapse.

The Wall provided one of the greatest ingenuity tests of this century as the unwilling inmates of the fortified state resorted to improbable Heath-Robinson contraptions to cross it. There were patchwork balloons, home-made hang-gliders and light aircraft, adapted cars with fake compartments – all constructed in back rooms and garages. Others simply tunnelled, climbed and scrambled their way to freedom. Between 1961 and 1989 more than 5,000 people successfully escaped across, through or under the Wall, with another 35,000 repeating the trick at the snaking inner-German border.

Not all were successful. West Berliners saw more than 3,000 would-be escapers arrested at the Wall, and 191 people paid the ultimate price for their dream of a new life, killed at the state or city frontier. In an incident which brought the inhumanity of the fortification home to the world, Peter Fechter, a baby-faced eighteen-year-old, was left to bleed to death after being shot in no man's land near Checkpoint Charlie in 1962. West Berlin border guards responded to his fading pleas for help by risking their lives to throw him first-aid kits. Fifty minutes later their eastern counterparts carried away his lifeless body.

But in the mirrored world of the Cold War the East also had its martyrs. The fifteen border guards killed on duty at the frontier after

1961 were transformed into state heroes, 'victims of the armed attacks and provocation of imperialism'. Most were killed by armed escapers, some when people in the west opened fire during escape bids. Asked in 1990 whether he felt sorry for the nearly 200 people killed at the border, Erich Honecker would only reply: 'I am sorry for the twenty-five comrades [ten died before 1961], who were assassinated at the border.'

Two years after the Wall was completed, President Kennedy addressed his most famous speech to the people of the divided city when he declared that free peoples everywhere were honorary citizens of West Berlin and added, 'As a free man, I am proud to be able to say, "*Ich bin ein Berliner*".' But despite the rhetoric of roll-back, liberation and unification, 13 August demonstrated that the West had accepted the communist domination of East Berlin and East Germany as the price for the stability guaranteed by the pull of equal and opposite powers: the security doctrine which would dominate until 1989.

As Willy Brandt wrote twenty years later, it was the day in which Germans faced the truth that their unity was no longer of prime importance to the West. 'We shed illusions which had outlived the hopes behind them. Illusions, pinned to something which in reality had ceased to exist.' The Wall was there to stay.

Life in the Mousetrap

The River Werra winds its way through the two medieval villages of Grossburschla and Altenburschla. They are linked by a narrow hump-backed bridge which the locals cross by foot, tractor, bicycle and, now and then, car. It is a picture-postcard idyll of rural life. The air here is sweet and clean, the cornfields stretch as far as the eye can see and the only sound is the early-morning song of the curlews. Only the watchtower by the river banks reminds one that Grossburschla sat until recently on the front line between capitalism and communism, between one Germany and another.

Grossburschla lay in East Germany's former high-security zone, the 500-metre strip running alongside the border. Its 1,300 residents had to have special passes to enter, and a single road linked them to the rest of East Germany. They needed police clearance to invite their relatives from outside the zone into the village, and it was often refused. 'It was like living in a mousetrap with no way out. We were cut off from West and East alike,' says the minister, Thomas Anbau.

Long before the Wall severed Berlin, Grossburschla in Thuringia had been prised away from neighbouring Altenburschla in Hessen. In 1952 the border troops erected a barbed-wire fence along the river bank and mined the fields behind it. Families considered politically unreliable were expelled in an overnight raid entitled 'Operation Vermin'. Altenburschla only just escaped absorption into the East when the Russians arrived to take over from the Americans in May 1945. American and British troops had reached Thuringia first, but its exchange for West Berlin had already been agreed at the Yalta Conference. Hessen was to go to the Western Allies. The Russians mistakenly crossed the bridge and occupied Altenburschla. The villagers managed to persuade them that they had come a bridge too far and sent them marching the 800 metres back to Grossburschla.

Fritz and Marga Müller laugh as they tell the tale and shake their heads. 'That's how easily you can end up on the wrong side of history in this part of the world,' says Fritz. An elderly couple, they are slowly overcoming their unease at the unexpected visit. They have no telephone and it was impossible to send a message even from East Berlin. There are only a couple of telephones in the village and the mayor, Hans-Joachim Aulich, acts as the link with the outside world, referring to himself as the town crier. Even so, the line was so bad that he couldn't hear me, so there was nothing for it but to arrive unannounced, the six-hour journey from Berlin ending with the narrow, winding road from Eisenach.

'You were lucky to find us,' says the mayor. 'They've only just put the signs back up.' East Germany sought to wipe the villages in the strip from the minds of its own people. They were never officially mentioned. No investment or building was allowed, in the hope that people would gradually leave and the communities die out. They had, however, reckoned without the stubborn nature of the residents, who were prepared to live in the mousetrap rather than leave their homes.

The Müllers are unsure whether they want to tell their story. 'It just opens up the wound,' Fritz says. Ten minutes later, hospitality has conquered reserve. Marga offers lunch of home-cured sausage and garden vegetables. Both of their families have lived in Grossburschla since the sixteenth century. In 1982, they found out once again how easy it is to end up on the wrong side of history. They were expelled without warning from the village on the orders of the regional Party headquarters in Eisenach, deemed a risk to the security of the border.

Their story began in 1979 when their nineteen-year-old son Reinhardt fled to the West across the River Werra. At a dance in the village he had become embroiled in a political argument with his old civic studies teacher, who told him he was 'not a fit person to be trusted in the security zone'. It was the coded language of threat known to all East Germans, and especially ominous for those so close to the border. The Stasi was particularly alert to any signs of dissent in such a sensitive area. Gripped by panic and anger, he ran to the river, chose a blind spot where the Werra bends, and swam to the West, cutting through the wire grille in the middle of the river. He arrived at his aunt's house in Altenburschla in the early hours, a dripping, sobbing figure. His first words to her were 'my poor parents'.

Unfortunately for the Müllers, Reinhardt happened to choose the Day of the People's Police for his escape, the national day of self-congratulation the force awarded itself for its labours. Fritz recalls the outcry:

They were all sitting round at the station here and had just finished their yearly report, which included the statistic that no one had escaped in the last twelve months. In came someone from the border guards and said, 'Sorry gentlemen, but Müller's youngest has just pitched up in Altenburschla.' They were furious. It ruined their record for the whole year and probably cost them their merit money. We were visited time and time again by the police, the Party and the Stasi, and questioned on whether we had encouraged him to go. I said, 'Look, my son is an adult and what he does is his business.' The functionary said, 'Herr Müller, you are a citizen of the German Democratic Republic with all the duties that entails. If your son were forty, we would still hold you responsible for what has happened.'

The wheels of revenge ground slowly but surely. Three years later, in the early morning, a furniture van rolled up outside their house and the Müllers were ordered to leave Grossburschla immediately. They were to be resettled in the far north in Grossspiegelberg in Mecklenburg. 'It might as well have been on the moon,' says Marga. She does not mean only the distance, although the two villages are about as far away from each other as you could get in East Germany. 'They are just a different people up there. A different dialect, different manner, strangers to us. Down here, we like to stay among our own sort.'

They spent the day packing their possessions. 'A whole house, a whole life,' says Marga. Still under police guard, they pulled out of Grossburschla in the evening, forbidden to speak to anyone as they left. 'The whole village was crying,' adds Fritz, and repeats the phrase twice, as if seeking comfort in that manifestation of helpless solidarity. Under cover of darkness, they were transported across the republic to their new home. Marga sobbed all the way. Grossspiegelberg was a village comparable in size to their own, clearly selected because of its distance from Grossburschla. The similarity in the names seemed a final cruel jibe from the functionaries. 'I think those Party people thought of us as village idiots,' says Fritz. 'They just assumed they could cart us from one place to another and we wouldn't notice the difference.'

The Mecklenburg locals were told to keep their distance from the newcomers. The local Party spread the rumour that they had been expelled from their home for drug-running. A less plausible tale would have been hard to find. Their first months were spent in despair. 'We would lie in bed at night and ask God why this thing had happened to us, what sort of people were they who thought of things like this? Did they have no heart?' Fritz was worried about his wife's health. She had already suffered a collapse after the journey from Grossburschla. 'She would just sit there saying nothing, pining for home,' says Fritz. 'One day I looked at her and thought, "We have to fight this."'

Interrupt to ask why the Müllers were so intent on returning to the inconvenient, enclosed life of Grossburschla, and they look puzzled at the question. 'It's our home,' says Marga, 'a wonderful piece of earth.' There is nothing more to say.

Fritz wrote to the Party headquarters in Eisenach but received no reply. He tried to engage legal help, but no one would touch his case. A sympathetic lawyer told him that there was no provision for pursuing the case through the courts and suggested that he turn to the Church for assistance. First, however, he addressed a letter to Erich Honecker begging to be allowed to return to Grossburschla. East Germany maintained a near-feudal system of appeal in which any citizen who felt that they had been unjustly treated could put their case to the General Secretary. In practice this usually meant that the local authorities would receive a message from Honecker's office telling them to clamp down on the complainants. The result of the appeal against a miscarriage of justice was, more often than not, increased attention from the security police. The Müllers never received a reply from Honecker but they did receive one from the Eisenach Party headquarters. It was sent by a functionary in the interior affairs department identified only as 'Hartmann' and read: 'This is our final word. You will not see Grossburschla again.'

The Müllers finally found allies in the Bishop of Eisenach, Werner Leich, and Magdeburg's bishop, Christoph Demke. Demke suspected that the Müllers' case had been dealt with by vengeful functionaries under pressure from the local police chief. He also believed that their plea to return had never reached Honecker's desk, but had been diverted back to Eisenach by his underlings.

Since his ascent to office Honecker had attempted to build bridges with the Church, intent on demonstrating to the outside world that his brand of socialism could coexist with religion. The country's bishops were allowed to bring pleas for leniency before him. In return, the Protestant Church was mild in its public criticism of the system – a trade-off which displeased many senior clergy in the West but which was generally welcomed by desperate petitioners in the East, for whom the Church offered the sole way out of the tight cat's-cradle of the political and the legal system. Enlisting the help of a senior clergyman was often the only way of escaping the grip of the state apparatus.

Bishop Demke received an assurance from Honecker that the Müllers would be allowed to return on condition that no publicity was given to their case. On 15 July 1983 he met them in Erfurt. 'It was like a dream,' says Marga. 'He walked towards us and said, "The way is clear for you. Please don't ask how, but you are going home." Every single day we were away I prayed to God to let us return. I know it sounds odd but when he came to us in Erfurt that day, it seemed like the word of God to us. He answered our prayers. What happened to us was a miracle.'

This evaluation is scarcely exaggerated. Of the several thousand East Germans expelled from their homes, the Müllers were the only ones known to be allowed to return. The Party rarely admitted even tacitly that it had made a mistake, and certainly not in a matter of such symbolic importance. The Müllers' story is a rare and uplifting triumph of will over power, of the small man over the apparatus of fear. Their victory is all the more remarkable in the light of their ordinariness. Over the years I have met many East Germans who took on the system in one way or another, but none who fought from such a position of hopelessness and won. They were as far removed from the type of ready-witted, frustrated urban intellectual one imagines under the banner of 'dissident' as possible. These were uneducated, homely people whose horizons had been bound by their village not just during their own lifetime, but for centuries, at once shy and disdainful of the machinery of the state.

They were, on their own admission, terrified of writing letters and nervous in the presence of civil servants. Even after the decision from Honecker to allow their return, they were turned back by the Eisenach authorities. Fritz had to place repeated appeals with the Party headquarters which he calls 'the Kremlin' and adds, 'Even with our bishop behind us, my knees would literally knock whenever I had to go there.'

They were sustained both by a deep sense of the wrong that had been done to them, and by their instinct to return to the place where they belonged. While they are telling their story Marga is peeling a bowl of apples for jam to last the winter; Fritz is anxious that my glass should not be empty for more than a second before the next beer is on its way. Their eyes are a startling blue; the clarity of their complexions belies that they are both in their seventies. But their experiences have deprived them of their certitude and equilibrium: they may have robbed the state of its claim to infallibility, but it robbed them forever of their peace of mind.

It took two more years after Bishop Demke's message before they were able to return. They had to sell their house in Mecklenburg and by the time they found a buyer there, their old home in Grossburschla had been sold. In a gesture of resistance to the decision to ban them, none of the villagers had bought the Müllers' house after their expulsion, despite the local authority's intention of having it occupied as soon as possible so that it would not stand empty as a reminder of its inhabitants' fate. Property in the 500-metre zone was not usually offered to outsiders, but since no local family had been willing to move in, it had been sold late in 1986 to a couple from Eisenach. The Müllers were distraught at the prospect of having to return to a different house. The new owners, who heard of their fate from neighbours, promptly pulled out of the deal and offered them their home back.

On 18 May 1987 their five-year exile ended. The whole village turned out to wave and greet them as they made an emotional return. Only the door of the police station remained firmly shut.

Eberhard Töpfer remembers well the night which set in action the chain of events. As captain of the local border guards, he was carpeted the next day for allowing Reinhardt's escape. 'The day after someone had gone there was always hell to pay,' he says. It is hard to avoid the impression that he nurtures a residual resentment of the escapers for making his life difficult.

He arrived in Grossburschla as Company Chief of the border guards in 1978, in charge of eighteen men and four guard dogs. Ask him to describe his job and he recites the description drummed into him as a young soldier: 'To prevent the breaching of the border and to combat provocative measures from the Western side aimed at disturbing the peace of our republic.' Ask him why he opted for a career manning the border and he seems unable to remember. 'Someone had to do it. The border was a fact of life for us. It seemed like a necessity to me.' He grudgingly admits that the high wages and preferential place on the East's interminable waiting-lists given to border troops were factors. 'I enjoyed my job, though. It was a constant challenge. You knew exactly what your task was and you carried responsibility for it. Better than working in some factory where there were never enough materials and production was years out of date. Everything worked well on the border: it had to.'

When I had asked if it would be possible to meet the local company chief, it was in the expectation of refusal. Former border guards, like former Stasi men, are disinclined to be loquacious about their past. Herr Töpfer, however, arrived punctually and cheerfully for the assignation on the banks of the Werra where his men had once patrolled. It did not take long to figure out the reason for his openness: he was genuinely devoid of any feeling of guilt about his minor part in East Germany's unhappy past.

This stretch of the border counted as one of the most difficult to watch because of the winding course of the river and the precise geographical knowledge of the residents. 'Anyone who really wanted to go west from here managed it. These families have been around for centuries. They know every field, every dent in the river bank. I used to say to the boys, "You're up against experts with this lot."' In the early years after the border was closed, escapes across the river were frequent. Later, teams of scuba-divers were enlisted to place a metal grill in the middle of the river. 'But whatever alarm system we installed, they found a way of short-circuiting it. It was the sort of knowledge that got around.'

His flippancy about the mechanisms of incarceration, the portrayal of the border troops as players in a light-hearted cat-and-mouse game, was unnerving. Later, however, I find that the villagers largely accepted this approach. A shrug of the shoulders appears to have been the only way to deal with life cheek by jowl with the world's most fortified frontier. In the local pub the landlady serves up fresh trout from the river. 'Used to be the best protected fish in the world. Don't know what's hit them now,' she says, and adds that between you, me and the gatepost, she rather misses the guards. 'When they were here there was always life in the village. The girls are moping around without much to choose from now. I married a guard. Why not? They were only doing a job, and most of them were conscripts, poor things.'

They are patient people down here. The border remained closed for four days after the Wall had opened in Berlin. Only on 13 November did Eberhart Töpfer receive orders to dismantle the fence, a development which he recounts laconically as if it were just one more disruption to his quiet life.

It was a hell of a task. We had to call out all the soldiers and then we realized that we didn't know how to dismantle the bloody thing. It was good German handiwork, so to speak, and built to last. After the first hour of snipping here and there I gave up and sent the lads round the farms to borrow as many electric saws as they could and we just hacked it to bits – all that expensive building material gone to waste in a day.

Yes, of course he was pleased that the border was gone and all the embracing and cheering had been great . . . but his is the least enthusiastic account of the end of Germany's division I have heard. His best memory, he says, was being invited to drink schnapps with the men from the West German border guards who watched the frontier from the other side. 'Sometimes, when we were mending the fence or painting the border posts, we would walk along just a few metres from each other, but of course we were not allowed to say anything. I recognized them all – we used to watch each other through our binoculars. It was weird to meet them after all those years.' Cold War reserve, it transpires, was soon overcome by ample quantities of apple brandy. The Eastern guards arrived back from their first excursion on to enemy territory 'in no state to guard a kindergarten, never mind a country' and received a telling-off from their battalion commander. Within an hour, he too was clinking glasses with his opposite number, the two men comparing the braid on their shoulders and their pips with keen interest.

Along with many of his former colleagues, Töpfer is now employed dismantling the border fence in Thuringia and tidying up the rough strip of land along it. It is work for two years, for which he is grateful. His employer is the old West German border patrol authority, now reduced to little more than a landscaping enterprise. From the top of the hill above Grossburschla you can still see where the frontier stood. On every visit the contrast with the land around is less sharp; the wild grass is growing fast.

What about the guard dogs? 'If you were a German you would have asked me that before you asked anything else,' says Töpfer. In truth, little moved the hearts of Germans east and west in the days after the frontier fell more than the fate of East Germany's canine protectors. I can put their love of large dogs no better than did the invaluable commentator Peter Schneider, who once wrote: 'When the Lord created the first German, he gave him an Alsatian as a companion.' And when Hitler committed suicide in the Berlin bunker he first ensured that his Alsatian had been humanely put down before he dispatched himself. Five thousand dogs, mainly Alsatians, Rottweilers and rough-haired terriers did duty at the border. On 10 November the societies for the protection of animals in East and West Berlin were inundated with calls from concerned dog-lovers wanting to know what the fate of the animals would be now that their working lives had so unexpectedly ended. Undeterred by some colourful reporting in the mass-circulation *Bild Zeitung* about 'killer hounds' and 'blood-thirsty beasts', whose teeth were (falsely) reported to have been strengthened to provide a better grip, offers of homes poured in. The East German animal welfare organizations condemned the 'western media witch-hunt' against border dogs. 'All they need is a bit of love and attention,' said one spokesman.

On the principle of just division of a national treasure, it was decided that half the dogs should be placed with families in the West, half in the East. After their initial wave of concern, however, few East German families wanted to adopt one. Shortage of space in the modern apartment blocks was blamed, but Schneider discerned the real reason for the back-down: 'After forty years of anti-fascist education, the population of the GDR had switched its custom to pets which could not be abused as symbols of power and potency – to budgerigars, cats and rabbits.' The majority went west.

Töpfer defends the reputation of the guard dogs. 'They were really there for show. I never used one to bring down an escaper. The soldiers became very attached to them – a lot of them took a dog home with them after the border opened and they don't seem to have had any problems apart from the dogs' needing a lot of exercise. They were used to being outdoors all day.'

He is equally defensive on the all-too-human subject of an order to shoot. 'It was always presented to us as the last resort. Thankfully, we were never faced with the situation down here because those who jumped were usually gone long before we realized.' Töpfer claims to have been unaware of the order of Erich Honecker, delivered at a meeting of the National Defence Council in 1974, which urged border troops to make 'ruthless use of firearms' to prevent 'infringements of the border'. It is on the basis of this injunction that a warrant for Honecker's arrest for incitement to manslaughter was issued and from which he fled to the Soviet Union.

I should know, says Töpfer as we part, that he instilled into his soldiers 'the greatest hesitation' about the use of firearms. He recalls that one new recruit had pressed him for advice on what to do if he had an escaper in his sights on top of the final fence. 'I said to him, "Let him jump."' It is yet another East German anecdote intended to clear the speaker's name from the annals of the guilty. It may be true; it may not. The only way that the new Germany can live with itself is to give the thousands of Töpfers who perpetrated repression for a living the benefit of the doubt. He is a lucky man, and he knows it.

Post-Script

Lined up in the dock of Alt-Moabit criminal court were four less fortunate young men. They are all in their twenties, former conscript border guards in Berlin, who went on trial for manslaughter in September 1991. Their shots killed Chris Gueffroy in February 1989, the last of nearly 200 people who died trying to flee East Germany. The case was brought after the campaign by his mother Karin Gueffroy for trials of those responsible for issuing and carrying out the shooting orders. On the day the trial opened she said, 'I do not want revenge on these young men. I lived in East Germany and I understand the pressure under which they acted. I want the whole chain of command to be opened to scrutiny and the people who directed the killings to be punished. I regret that it is they and not Honecker who are first in line.'

Chris Gueffroy was twenty when he died. Together with a friend, Christian Gaudian, he tried to cross the border between the eastern district of Treptow and West Berlin's Neukölln. On their way to the border Gueffroy told his friend, 'Just imagine, I'll soon be standing on the Ku'damm saying, "Hi Mum, guess where I am."' He never made it. As they tried to scale the second of the two walls (Berlin was doubly fortified), a hail of fire rang out. Guadian was hit in the foot. Gueffroy turned round and was shot through the heart. He bled to death in the no man's land between the walls. The medical report in the police hospital recorded 'death due to non-natural causes'.

The four guards, three of whom had fired, were rewarded with a buffet meal, extra holiday and a merit payment. Asked in court what he had felt after the killing, one of them said, 'I felt bad, of course, because a human being had been killed before my eyes. But the commander told us not to lose sleep, that we had done the right thing.' They were all redirected to another posting.

The case was brought as a precedent for prosecuting other guards and their commanders. Senior East German officers, the former Minister of

Defence Heinz Kessler and the Interior Minister Friedrich Dieckel, have also been charged. Further cases have since opened, despite the defence's plea that no western court was entitled to pass a verdict of guilty on crimes committed in the old East Germany and with the sanction of that state.

How great the pressure on the guards was to shoot to hit an escaper is difficult to ascertain with certainty. The troops always patrolled in pairs so that one could watch the other. It is none the less accepted that many aimed off target. The problem is that an inexperienced marksman shooting to miss often hits. The prosecution argues that the guards were not under such duress that they were unable to resist the order to shoot, although such a refusal may well have resulted in a prison sentence. The defence counters that the men, indoctrinated by the state, believed in the absolute authority of the command.

The sight of the defendants, all young, all working-class, constrained by unfamiliar ties and mumbling answers in the echoing court-room, was unnerving. One cannot avoid the thought that they could never have imagined when they joined the *Grenztruppen* that they would end up on manslaughter charges before the court of a country they were taught from childhood to regard as the enemy. Perhaps they did not have to shoot that night. The tragedy is that they probably thought they did.

A group of their superiors, including the former defence minister, delivered a deposition to the court appealing for clemency on their behalf and reiterating that they were acting under orders. The defence played this down. In the second half of the twentieth century every German knows that acting under orders is not a permissible defence, nor one inclined to elicit much sympathy. Other mitigations must be sought. It was not a normal court case. The judge had to evaluate the environment in which the guards lived, a world unfamiliar to west Germans. He had to weigh up the effect on a person's moral sense of life under a dictatorship. He looked confused at some of the answers he received, replies instantly comprehensible to the east Germans in the room.

The first to give evidence was Andreas Kühnpast, an unemployed twenty-seven-year-old from Dresden with pale, adolescent features. He told of Gueffroy's killing in a rapid, halting voice. The judge asks what he thought about life in East Germany. 'I was a member of the Young Pioneers as a child,' he said. 'I was proud of my country. I believed in the regime up there.' The last phrase sounds equally odd in German, but one could see his point. The system was up there, he was down here: down on the rough ground of the death-strip, wielding a rifle when he saw two figures running in the dark towards the Wall, and the command came from behind, 'Fire!'.

Surely, the judge countered, he must have had doubts about some aspects of the regime, some reason to doubt its ethical basis? Kühnpast was silent. Eventually he said: 'I knew nothing else. I was happy there.' Opposite, in the gallery, Karin Gueffroy began to cry.

The trial lasted four months. Ingo Heinrich, the guard whose shots killed Chris Gueffroy, received a three-and-a-half-year prison sentence, Andreas Kühnpast a two-year suspended sentence. The other two guards were acquitted. It was a jumble of verdicts, the result of an attempt to establish a scale of culpability from the confused and tragic events of the death strip. The trial predictably left behind a feeling of dissatisfaction at its conclusion and confusion over its implications.

In his summing up, the judge identified the court's quandary in the question 'Is everything to be considered right which a state declares as law?' and concluded that the shooting of escapers was 'a law which did not deserve to be obeyed'. The ruthlessness with which Heinrich fired at Chris Gueffroy's chest from a 37-metre range made the shooting 'akin to an execution', he said. Kühnpast, by contrast, had profited from 'the good fortune of having missed'. The third guard who had shot at Gueffroy's feet and the fourth who had shouted the order could not be held responsible for the victim's death, he decided.

It was the first attempt of a German court to come to terms with crimes committed under the old East German system, which made the legal and moral questions intractable from the start. The trial and the verdicts amply demonstrated the inadequacy of a western legal system to deal with the outrages of an eastern dictatorship. It went some way towards meeting the demands of those who had suffered, by showing that the crimes of the East could be punished in the West, but it failed to place the offence in the context of a command structure, and to apportion guilt along a chain of responsibility. Asked whether she was satisfied with the outcome, Karin Gueffroy said that she was relieved to see 'guilt made visible'. Outside the court, Andreas Kühnpast's mother apologized to her and said that mothers should dissuade their sons from doing military service.

7
Writing on the Wall

Bertolt Brecht: Communism's Wayward Apologist

> After getting myself into the bad books of the FDJ (Free German Youth) by spelling Honecker's name on a telegram with two 'g's instead of a 'ck', I have to be doubly careful. I really must try to keep a few friends.
>
> Bertolt Brecht, letter to Friedrich Wolf, July 1952

The British do not know much about Brecht but they know that they do not like him. The West Germans know their Brecht well and still dislike him, while the East Germans knew a lot less Brecht than they thought, but knew that they ought to like him. By now, his reputation has come to say more about the societies which hold these opinions than about the man himself.

The division of Germany proved a hindrance in the study of Brecht's work and life. The battlelines drawn between East and West, Marxist and capitalist, are unsatisfactory orientations for discussing any literary output, let alone that of the man who turned modern dramatic theory on its head and whose work ranged from wily, if not always wise, Agitprop to some of the century's most haunting poetry of love and exile.

One of the worst things that history has done to Brecht is to make him a litmus paper for political tastes. While in the seventies it was *de rigeur* to adore Brecht and puzzle endlessly over the implications of the alienation effect, it is equally imperative these days to consider him a didactic bore, a fraud and a fellow-traveller.

Perhaps only now that the Friedrichstrasse station – where theatre-goers arrive for performances of *Mother Courage* and the *Threepenny Opera* at the nearby Berliner Ensemble – no longer carries the unofficial appellation, 'Temple of Tears' (because it was the point at which Western visitors disappeared through clanging doors into the forbidden half-city beyond), will the uninhibited reception of his work begin. The West was never going to take kindly to a playwright who, with an Austrian passport and a Swiss bank account under his belt, volunteered to go to Ulbricht's East Berlin (taking with him his BMW sports car – *ça s'entend*). For its part, the East laid unrelenting emphasis on Brecht's rejection of Adenauer and of America's policies towards Germany, and on his horror of rearmament, but chose to suppress his equally scorching comments on the local interpretation of the dictatorship of the proletariat. 'This place gives me the creeps,' he wrote in his diary soon after his arrival.

It was the casual discovery of that entry that set me wondering what Brecht had really thought of the country where he ended his life, and of its claim to embody the aims to which he had pledged his work as a young Marxist. When he set up his theatre by the Spree, one month before the founding of the East German state, he was considered the greatest cultural prize of post-war Germany, an early spoil of the Cold War carried off by the East. The other great literary emigrant, Thomas Mann, dissatisfied with both Germanies, moved to California and finally settled in Switzerland.

During its early years the German Democratic Republic held a strong attraction for writers and intellectuals, who were impressed by the new state's commitment to anti-fascism at a time when the West was beginning the rehabilitation of Nazi officials, judges, teachers and doctors. Newsreels recorded the arrival of many of the great names of German culture in East Berlin: Louis Fürnberg, Arnold Zweig, Anna Seghers. Bertolt Brecht joined them, after some dithering, with his actress wife Helene Weigel and his usual coterie of helpers and lovers. Their numbers were soon swelled by dozens of students who flocked from all over Germany and beyond to study at the master's feet.

Brecht lies buried in the Chaussee Strasse graveyard, in the exclusive company of dead German poets, philosophers and Huguenot generals. Alongside him repose the musicians Paul Dessau and Hanns Eisler, his wife Helene Weigel, the philosophers Hegel and Fichte (whose graves had to be replaced after the cemetery was bombed during the war) and the author Heinrich Mann. In death, at least, things are just as he would have wished: he lies surrounded by his co-workers and great German thinkers, a category in which he would have included himself. Even here he has not lost his tendency to attract trouble. In 1990 his grave and that of Weigel were desecrated and smeared with the words 'Jewish Swine' (Weigel was Jewish, Brecht was not, but when branded by the Nazis as a Jew he promptly offered to become one, and added with an unhappily prophetic touch, 'Perhaps they will take me. The way things are going they will need some volunteers.').

What he would have thought of the fate of his theatre is less easy to guess. Over the years the Berliner Ensemble took on the role of the unofficial East German state theatre, and it is proving difficult to shed. It became a conservative, risk-free establishment, dominated by directors in thrall to the master's theory, but too often bereft of his talent: a theatrical mausoleum. The dead hand of the executors has weighed heavily upon the theatre since the death of Brecht, while Weigel proved an autocratic successor and alienated many of Brecht's students. The rights to his plays are now held jointly by the playwright's son Stefan Brecht and his daughter Barbara Brecht-Schall. While Stefan chose to remain in America and pursue a modest career as a poet rather than brave the imbroglio of East Berlin and the Berliner Ensemble, the formidable Frau Brecht-Schall is on the theatre's board of management and personally oversees what rights are granted to which theatres.

She is over sixty now, brash, funny, and with an excruciating Hollywood accent picked up as a child during her parents' exile there. When I visited her in 1989 the GDR was still intact, although the stress cracks in the state artifice were becoming increasingly evident to everyone except her. I asked her how she viewed the uncomfortable political situation. 'Like my father, I can only say, "I live here, don't I?" He made a decision which Germany he wanted to live in, and so have I. If you ask what he would have thought of things today, I think he would have been for them.' It was disconcerting to find Brecht's daughter, more than three decades later, supporting her choice of Germany with arguments that could well have been her father's when he arrived in 1950. It was as if her interpretation of her role as her father's keeper extended to reproducing his enthusiasm for the new state, regardless of how dust-coated and neglected his ideals of a freely creative socialist society had become.

Her ideological constructs were a zany mixture of extreme libertarianism and Cloud-cuckooland. In the manner of Lewis Carroll's Humpty Dumpty, when she used a word, it meant what she wanted it to mean, neither more nor less.

'Communism for me is when everyone has exactly what they want. It doesn't mean that people can't be rich, as long as they don't harm others by it. I am well off, but whom do I harm by my wealth? No one. Barbara Hutton liked playing with diamonds all day. What's wrong with that?' In the next breath she is attacking western defence policies and defending –

a touch self-consciously as she sits in her elegant chandeliered apartment – East Berlin's hideous housing estates. 'I don't feel guilty about living here. No one wants these big places any more: they just gather dust.' She was the self-styled First Lady of East Berlin and revelled in her social position in a country whose élite was otherwise distinctly frumpy. Margot Honecker reputedly could not stand her because her clothes bore the stamp of the international design salons, while she as the leader's wife had to make do with the well-tailored but distinctly provincial offerings of her private dressmaker.

The two-storey apartment Frau Brecht-Schall shares with her husband, the actor Ekkehard Schall, is a temple to her father's work, the walls hung with Caspar Neher's stage designs and the Japanese Noh masks he employed in *He Who Said No*. There is even a small wardrobe with her favourite costumes: Edward II's crown, Coriolanus's leather cloak. And then there are her Venetian chandeliers and plaster angels, 'twiddly bits' she has picked up on her travels. 'I love the Alexandra Palace flea market,' she said, her eyes twinkling with excitement.

For a woman whose behaviour as her father's heir has set her alongside Winifred Wagner and the Strauss family as domineering epigone, she can be disarmingly charming. The apartment, stuffed with superior clutter, is like the fulfilment of a child's dream: when I'm rich . . .

'Come and look at my Hollywood bathroom,' she says. I gape. It is cavernous, pink, and multi-mirrored. The bath tub is of proportions which would have sufficed for the famed East German swimmers to practise lengths. 'We all got three wishes when we moved here, and this was mine,' she says happily. The iron lady of the German theatre takes such pleasure in her bathroom that it would seem churlish to begrudge her it.

Her name inspires an involuntary wince in theatres across Europe. 'You'd think she'd written the damn plays herself,' said one British director whose rehearsals were interrupted when an unannounced voice boomed from the darkened stalls, 'Papa would not have liked that bit'. She has always had the final say on casting and even on points of interpretation in the Berliner Ensemble, and her influence was felt far beyond it. She once banned a West Berlin company from playing *Fear and Misery of the Third Reich* in a way which suggested that many of the repressions of that period could be found again under East German socialism.

She has refused to have *The Measure Taken*, Brecht's look at the moral consequences of revolutionary thinking, played at all. 'It always ends up anti-communist. Later in his life, my father only used it for rehearsals because he said he didn't want it used as propaganda against the socialists. I see no reason to change that. There are still a lot of anti-communists around.' As long as East Germany still existed, no one challenged Frau Brecht-Schall's right to single-handed control of the Brecht heritage. But, as his 'Song of the Moldau' has it: 'Times change / The ambitious plans of the mighty / Grind to a halt.'

The theatre's funding of £10 million a year now comes not from Honecker's boon, but from the Berlin Senate, which in 1991 decided to join battle against the house of Brecht and its restrictive practices. Frau Brecht-Schall threatened to withdraw all rights to her father's plays if the Senate imposed a director and terms without her approval, and announced that she was prepared to entertain the idea of no more Brecht plays being performed at the theatre he founded rather than give up her control over the works.

It turned into an interchange of sophisticated snarls as the city's cultural senator promptly responded by threatening to seek a boycott of the plays in other theatres in the city too. The Senate declared that the new general director must have absolute freedom to cast and produce as he or she saw fit. The old incumbent, Manfred Wekwerth, a former member of the East German Central Committee who had been a pupil of Brecht, was ousted as 'politically burdened'.

What should have been one of the most sought-after posts in European theatre went unfilled for over half a year. Unable to find a general director who (a) was prepared to risk his or her career by venturing into the Ensemble under such complicated conditions, (b) didn't run a mile from Frau Brecht-Schall and (c) was acceptable to her, it was announced, in autumn 1991, that Wekwerth would be replaced by a team of five artistic directors, including Thomas Langhoff, Peter Palitzsch and Heiner Müller. Respectable names all, but like the Council of the Gods in *The Good Person of Sechzuan*, they are faced with the task of staying true to their own aims and principles in the less than ideal setting of a theatre still firmly under the influence of its founder's daughter.

Her autarchy is the result of the GDR's breathless worship of its most famous *émigré*. The state commemorated its most prized sceptic by doing with his legacy what he would have hated most: institutionalizing his drama and mummifying his memory. The cult was carefully tended. Selected quotes were plucked out of poems and letters and strung up as banners to advertise the regime's peaceful intentions. My fellow students at Humboldt University in the mid-eighties wore their hair shorn tight, round glasses and shapeless smocks, and cultivated the unwashed look which had made their mentor appear as if he had collected the grime of every country he passed through during his long exile. While other personality cults were strongly discouraged by this stage, adoration of Brecht was considered acceptable.

Those communists who considered themselves a cut above the pedestrian recycling of Marx-and-Lenin quotes sought legitimation in Brecht's elegant, evasive definitions of the ideology as described in his poem 'In Praise of Communism': 'It is the easy thing / Which is difficult to do'. Long after they discovered, to their own and their country's cost, just how difficult, it has remained an internationally valid rule of thumb that dim communists bang on about class struggle while clever ones blind with dialectical materialism.

Perhaps it was the singular lack of charisma exhibited by its leading political figures that made East Germany look elsewhere for heroes, even if that meant a good deal of primping and trimming to get them to fit the required criteria.

In the selective folk memory of the GDR the ferocious Helene Weigel was reduced to a mumsy figure, whisking up an omelette for her husband while learning the lines of Mother Courage. At the 'Brecht-Keller' in the Chaussee Strasse, in a pub with the sort of manicured cosiness he would have despised, you can still indulge in 'Helene Weigel's Viennese Cooking', and during the guided tour of the house there is a nauseating eulogy of her skills as a wife and mother. In this reduction of *die Weigel*, hard-line ideologist and actress, to homely Mrs Brecht, you can glimpse communism's patriarchal unease with strong women. The Party has always preferred them as handmaidens, standing by their men in the tradition of subservient medieval female saints.

In fact, Weigel was a far more conventional communist than her husband – he never joined the Party despite the energetic efforts of President Wilhelm Pieck to recruit him – and though both were capable of devastating cynicism, he never quite matched her comment on learning that several Ensemble members were going West, appalled and frightened by the spread of Stalin's purges to eastern Europe. 'When you plane wood,' she said sagely, 'shavings will fall.' (It is to the credit of the actor to whom she issued this dismissal of the terror that he replied, 'Yes, but it's just that I'm scared of becoming one of the shavings.')

Brecht's *bête noire* was Walter Ulbricht, who is said to have remarked to his prime minister Otto Grotewohl, after watching *Mother Courage*,

'And this is supposed to be art?' (Admittedly, this puts him in line with a number of western critics of the time.)

Despite his dislike of the leader, Brecht crawled shamelessly to him during his first years in East Berlin. The letters to Ulbricht and other communist functionaries are little more than devious pleadings to have his work performed, and he was prepared to resort to absurd flattery and scarcely disguised trade-offs of benefit to achieve this goal.

While Ulbricht and his cohorts realized the propaganda value of having Brecht on their side of the demarcation line, they also treated him with scant respect, and did not hesitate to intervene in his work when they thought it deviated from the Party line, grumbling like theatre-goers who hadn't had their money's worth.

When it came to the absurd formalism debate – the fall-out from Stalin's artistic henchman Zhdanov's declaration of the binding necessity of socialist realism and positive example – everyone had their say, regardless of whether they knew what they were talking about. Fred Oelssner, the Party's economics and propaganda expert, announced in 1952 with the unshakeable conviction of the clueless, 'If a man as gifted as Brecht were to write a cogent and composed piece of theatre, what a powerful work of art we would have.' The young Erich Honecker in his role as leader of the Free German Youth also turned his hand to literary criticism, asking Brecht to amend the *Herrnburger Bericht* cycle he had written on the organization's commission. As it turned out, the work was embarrassingly bad anyway: 'You see what happens when I have to make shoes to fit the wearer,' Brecht wrote dolefully to a friend afterwards.

The 17 June uprising came as a shock to Brecht, probably because it made him realize for the first time how remote he had become from the working classes in Germany. For his initial response he relied on the testimony of fellow theatre-workers and friends in the Party and accepted their version of the events as a counter-revolution. On the day itself he called Ulbricht's chief architect Hermann Henselmann for guidance on what to think. Henselmann told him that the intervention of tanks would be welcomed by the mass of the populace. Armed with this misinformation he went for a walk to the Brandenburg Gate and encountered the Soviet tanks rolling down Unter den Linden, headed by the Soviet Commandant in an open jeep, waving to the bystanders. 'Brecht,' recalls his student Manfred Wekwerth, 'was one of the few who waved back.'

He went on to swear his support to the Party in a letter, the last line of which was printed in *Neues Deutschland*: 'I feel the need at this hour to express my solidarity with the Socialist Unity Party of Germany.' This brought him hefty criticism in the West and from his Frankfurt publisher Peter Suhrkamp.

The rest of the text, which came to light in the seventies, provides a more differentiated picture as Brecht, under the guise of praising the Party for its 'revolutionary impatience', made clear his condemnation of the straight-to-hell course of the early fifties and recommended that, in future consideration of the tempo of the development towards socialism, the Party would do well to consult the populace first. This is typical Brecht: the bite of criticism lurking in the blurb of praise, the sting in the tail. But the Party was wise enough to his ways not to print the entire letter, and Brecht could not have been unaware by now of this tendency to selective quotation when he sent it.

His initial faith in the leadership's competence quickly paled: he was so irritated by its abrogation of responsibility for what had happened, and the schoolmasterly attitudes of several writers (notably Kurt Bartel, secretary of the Writers' Association) that he wrote the poem 'The Solution', with its memorable suggestion that the leadership should deselect the populace and replace it with another.

Only in the aftermath of the uprising did Brecht come to appreciate its full significance. He withdrew to the country to write his *Buckower Elegies*, reflective and melancholic verse at odds with the predominantly combative work he had produced since his return to Germany. The first poem bears the title 'Changing the Wheel', and depicts the poet as a traveller between two stages of history, ill at ease with the past, apprehensive of the future, but impatient with the present:

> I sit by the roadside
> The driver changes the wheel
> I do not like the place I have come from
> I do not like the place I am going to
> Why with impatience do I
> Watch him changing the wheel?

The early *Elegies* point to confusion and uncertainty. While much of Brecht's behaviour in East Berlin was cynical and opportunist, and while he declared himself a materialist, he was unable to shake off the Christian demons of doubt and guilt: the 'weaknesses' which probably saved him from being completely intolerable. The poem 'Nasty Morning' presents a scene of rebuke and self-loathing reminiscent of a biblical revelation:

Last night in a dream I saw fingers pointing at me
As at a leper. They were worn with toil and
They were broken.

You don't know! I shrieked,
Conscience-stricken.

When he, in his dream, berates those who 'don't know', the workers, he is simultaneously aware of the dreamer's position as their intellectual superior, prescribing from his desk a socialist Utopia for those whose hands bear the stamp of manual work. The gap between the constructs of communist intellectuals and the reality of working-class existence pre-occupied him. While he could not bring himself to accept that the uprising was a justified challenge to the communists' claim to power, it shook his faith in the Party's declaration that a revolution without shots had taken place in 1949 (this spurious theory was pulled out of the ideological hat to make the import of Soviet socialism into Germany conform with the revolutionary teachings of Lenin); and it made him realize that the position of the working class under socialism was not significantly different from that of the masses under capitalism: both were disaffected, ill-organized, and heartily hostile to Marxism.

In his work journal, he entered the line, '17 June has alienated my whole existence.'

Towards the end of his life Brecht became increasingly preoccupied with the relationships of the strained triangle of power, the masses, the state and the Party, in socialist society. He was exercised by the question of how the Party should determine the will of the people and how it should react if it did not like what it found. He was posing the question that was to exercise socialist intellectuals again in Hungary, Czecho-slovakia and Poland in the years to come: how should they react when the People's Army turn their tanks or fire on the people?

Janos Kadar, the Hungarian leader, had no such qualms when he spoke to the Budapest National Assembly a year after the uprising there:

The task of the leaders is not to put into effect the wishes and will of the masses
. . . the task of the leaders is to accomplish the interests of the masses. Why do I differentiate between the will and the interests of the masses? Because in the recent past we have encountered the phenomenon of certain categories of workers acting against their own interests.

If Brecht had been tempted to believe in this perverted recipe for patriarchal repression when he arrived in East Berlin, he could no longer do so after 17 June, and the distance between himself and the Party rapidly widened. By the summer of 1956 the political stagnation of the East was so advanced that none but the most blinkered could hope for change within the Ulbricht regime. Brecht convened a meeting of fellow-intellectuals and writers and declared that he considered Ulbricht an 'orthodox dictator, alienated from the people, through whose policies the humanist content of socialism was being destroyed and degenerate circumstances were being created in the GDR'.

Walter Janka, a challenger to Ulbricht who as head of Aufbau Verlag was responsible for publishing Brecht in East Germany, maintains that by the time of his death that year (1956), the writer was considering leaving the country or at least spending more time outside it. 'He chose a sanatorium in Munich and told me he wanted to see his home patch of Bavaria again and that he wanted a break from what he called "the nonsense" here. I was left with the impression that he might well not return.' But whether or not he planned to turn his back on East Germany, he remained more convinced of the injurious nature of capitalism than the inherent weakness of communism.

As things turned out he did not even travel. He died of a heart attack, brought on by exhaustion, on 14 August 1956. His colleagues, hoping to find a final political pronouncement among his documents, were disappointed. True to form, he was more interested in the fate of Bertolt Brecht. He left detailed instructions that his aorta be opened to eradicate the danger of his being buried alive, and insisted on being encased in a steel-lined coffin. In his will he divided his possessions between Helene Weigel and his mistresses, leaving his entire literary estate to Weigel. He had ordered that no speeches be made at his grave and that the funeral should take place with a small circle of family, literary friends and a small selection of his many lovers from the Ensemble, where his *droit de seigneur* was a house tradition.

His son-in-law and former student, the Berliner Ensemble actor Ekkehard Schall, remembers him as 'shamelessly old-fashioned' in his attitude to women. 'In that respect he was a product of his generation – an old-fashioned cavalier, God knows what he would have thought of the feminist movements of the seventies and eighties. Actually, I can guess: he would have admired their revolutionary, challenging aspects, but it would not have altered his own behaviour one jot.'

While Western commentators and Hollywood made much of Brecht as a womanizer, the East treated this side of his nature coyly. When Werner Mittenzwei (a musicologist and producer who worked with

Brecht) insisted on dealing with it in his thorough biography published in 1986, he was cold-shouldered by a large section of the socialist establishment, who feared that it could have an adverse affect on the nation's young – a belated, fitting retribution for their insistence on turning an erratic political thinker and *bon viveur* into a sanitized role-model of socialist ethics.

Brecht is an equally poor patron for sexual and political moralists. He was too unreliable, too paradoxical, and far too egoistic for that. Rather he was, as he himself admitted, '*Ein Mensch in seinem Widerspruch*' – a human being in all his contradiction. Moreover, he was frequently wrong in his political prophesies. He, who embodied the necessity for the co-operation of theory and practice in the theatre, relied almost exclusively on the former in politics. He died with his private and public utterances on the state of socialism at odds.

During the last months of his life he wrote four damning anti-Stalin poems, the best of which calls him 'The honoured murderer of the people', and he told the young dramatist Peter Hacks that it would be the task of the coming generation to deal with Stalin's crimes, as his had been exercised by Hitler's

Here, belatedly and inadequately, he put his record of vacillation, cowardice and self-deception towards Stalin straight – only to blur it again when, asked by the dramatist Hacks what he thought of the dictator, he replied with the following poem:

> I have a horse
> The horse squints, limps and is raddled.
> Along comes a man and says: the horse squints. It is lame and look,
> It is raddled too.
> He is right, but what good is that
> To me?
> I have no other horse.
> So it is for the best that I think
> As little as possible about its weaknesses.

Stalin, the 'great genius leader' in the official prose of the GDR, was for him no better than a worm-raddled horse. Yet it is harder to forgive this calculated tolerance of a recognized evil than the unthinking admiration of the robotic functionaries he despised.

Brecht's moral and political error was to think that a society built on the injustice, violence and disrespect for the human soul endemic in Stalinism could ever recover from these roots. He wanted to construct a new truth on the basis of an old lie, and failed. He was punished for his self-deception by having to witness the revelations of Stalin's crimes in 1956. In 1930 Brecht had taken the bull by the horns in his unsparing analysis of Leninist mores, *The Measure Taken*, when he wrote the famous lines:

> What baseness would you not commit to
> Stamp out baseness?
> If you could change the world at least, what
> Would you be too good for?
> Who are you? Sink in the mire,
> Embrace the butcher, but
> Change the world: it needs it!

You can read these words, hear them on the radio but to this day you cannot, on the orders of his daughter, see the play performed. When the play does return to the stage, the words will be heard less as an injunction than as a warning. For the theory they contain was that the Party, the materialist's ersatz for the Almighty, could control the process of destruction, that the humane end would proceed from inhumane means, a peaceful society from violent beginnings.

It could only work as long as one carried on believing in the correctness of the prescription despite the devastation it caused. Unlike the Party's truly faithful sons and daughters, the Kuczynskis, Werners and Jankas, Brecht was unable to make that leap of faith. Despite valiant attempts he could not avert his eyes from the mess. In the end, communism's wayward apologist was left, saddened and weary, with a simpler clutch of truths. If you embrace the butcher, you end up bloodied. When you sink in the mire, it is the dirt which sticks, and not the inspiration. And no spoon is long enough to sup with the devil.

Useful Fools or Agents of Change?

My dear, that is the division of labour
This one speaks softly and that one screams
When those such as yourselves never go far enough
Those like myself must go too far.

Wolf Biermann, *The Division of Labour*

I lean my head against the grey wall
Of the monument to the victims of fascism
More than I wish to leave here, I wish
For a reason to say.

Steffen Mensching

East Germany's literary production was prodigious: books were one of the state's best exports. Its authors brought the country what its politicians never could: respect and membership of the international community. In the founding years, many of the best German authors returning from exile had chosen to make the East their home and became the country's first alumni. The Soviet cultural officers who established arts policy in the Eastern zone were the first to realize that the new state would gain legitimacy more quickly if it was seen to have the support of artists and writers whose protest against the Third Reich had lent them moral authority in a time when few other groups could claim it.

They took on the role traditionally ascribed to the German aristocracy and grande-bourgeoisie as *staatstragend* (state-bearing), lending credibility to politics and institutions, and occupying prominent roles in the ministries, media and politics. It was an uneasy marriage from the start. The German Communist Party had always been a battlefield between intelligentsia and proletariat and the two had a poor history of co-existence, even before the war. Moreover, many of the Party's Jewish intellectuals had perished in Hitler's camps or in Soviet exile. With the effective loss of Ernst Thälmann as leader in 1933 (he died in Buchenwald concentration camp in 1944), the Party lost its main unifying figure. Pieck, initially acceptable to intellectuals, soon became Ulbricht's lapdog.

On reaching Germany in May 1945, Ulbricht showed little interest in the fate of German intellectuals until prompted by the Soviets to encourage their return. While few were impressed with the dour, unyielding Ulbricht, they saw in the new state a clearer departure from fascism than in the emerging Federal Republic. In the 1945–49 period the country developed a magnetic pull for writers, many inspired by the presence of the impressive duo of Seghers and Brecht in East Berlin.

Bonn failed to counter this adequately. Even those such as Thomas Mann, Heinrich Böll, and Wolfgang Borchert, who were not to be persuaded to go East, kept their distance from the Adenauer state. In truth, Adenauer and his successor Ludwig Erhard cared little about whether writers did or did not support West Germany. Erhard infamously compared German writers to pinscher dogs – snapping, bad-tempered inconsequents who understood little of the real nature of power and its problems. Later, the Bavarian premier Franz Josef Strauss referred to West Germany's critical writers as 'rats and dung-flies'.

Between 1945–69 West Germany tolerated its literati but did not enjoy them, notably because the dominant theme of post-war writing had been the failure of the state to come to terms with the Third Reich – a fact of which older politicians, striving for world acceptance, were never keen to be reminded. As time passed, West Germany came to accept both its past and its writers. East Germany coped with both only with the aid of extreme selectivity.

One of the descriptions the East used of itself with the greatest self-satisfaction was *Leseland DDR* (the GDR: land of reading). There was much truth in this, although not for the reasons the politicians and cultural functionaries hoped. They fondly imagined that authors liked living there because their creativity was encouraged by their socialist surroundings, and that the public read so avidly because its taste was more sensitive and thoughtful than that of its western brethren.

In fact, the majority of (good) writers stayed because they thrived on the creative tension of the gap between the official state doctrine and the reality of daily life. The readers meanwhile, trapped in the confines of a socialist state, scanned the literary output as a substitute for the foreign travel they were denied, and for the critical interpretation of their situation which should have appeared in the newspapers but didn't.

When, in 1985, Volker Braun published the *Hinze-Kunze Roman*, a satire on the mores of communist power based on the relationship between a Party functionary and his driver in the early eighties, it became a talking-point in universities, pubs and factories, read and discussed with the critical enthusiasm which would in the West accompany a Sunday newspaper's well-researched investigation into corruption in parliament. One simply put real names to the fictional characters. Authors, not journalists, had grown to be the scourge of pretence in the east. When there is no one left alive to describe what sort of place it was, students will learn much more from the literature of 1949–89 than from the newspapers or, come to that, from much of the hopelessly inaccurate or tendentious academic work on the country which appeared in the West. (In the Federal Republic, in particular, academics were divided into two hostile camps: those who had come from the east in the fifties and had been prophesying its collapse ever since, and the younger ones who believed so firmly in the desirability of dual statehood in Germany that their wishful thinking obscured a clear perception of the east's economic and political plight.)

Towards the end of 1958, Ulbricht came to the conclusion that the greatest hindrance to the development of a productive socialist economy was the lack of enthusiasm among the work-force for his grand economic ambitions. A seven-year plan for the chemical industry was hatched, intended to kick-start industrial expansion. It was to be accompanied by a major propaganda effort and a literary experiment launched at a meeting of workers and authors at the Bitterfeld chemical plant in April 1959, christened the Bitterfeld Way.

Poets, playwrights and novelists were invited into the factories to observe the workers and glorify their deeds by celebrating them in their literary output. Anxious to break down the old barriers between the creative and the working classes, Ulbricht did not stop there but encouraged the workers to write about their own experiences. As far as he was concerned, the nation's literature should ideally come from the workers themselves. His only criterion for good art was its usefulness as propaganda. 'Let us be honest,' he announced at a meeting of aghast writers and artists. 'It is not about aesthetics. It is about the workers' and peasants' power and the victory of socialism.' As one might have expected, this attempt to functionalize literature produced some absorbing first-person accounts which otherwise would not have come to light. It also produced a lot of semi-literate drivel, and after Ulbricht's death, it was admitted that 'socialist art and literature must be encouraged which does not have its primary source amongst the workers themselves' (*Literary History of the GDR*, 1976).

The experiment failed to heighten the work-force's interest in the scientific-technological revolution, but it paid off in a more subtle way, by introducing authors to the grim reality of life in the outdated industrial plants of the East. (Many were still working with machinery built between the wars when they closed in 1990–1.)

The problem was that authors who wrote too honestly about what they saw became a problem for the censors. Christa Wolf's *Divided Heavens* portrayed the frayed labour relations and the political tensions in a coach factory in the run-up to 13 August 1961. Erwin Strittmatter's *Ole Bienkopp* described the conflict between a gifted individual and an inert farm collective, and was thus a conscious continuation of a theme dominant in the nineteenth-century German novel – some elements of *Ole Bienkopp* seem to parody Theodor Storm's *The Rider on the White Horse* (1888). These were successful works but failed dismally to provide the optimistic driving force the politicians had hoped for.

The experiment was quietly abandoned in 1964. A year later, at the notorious Eleventh Party Plenum, came the clamp-down, with many authors being punished for writing about the very subjects the Bitterfeld Way had recommended to them only a couple of years earlier. Werner Bräunig, who had spent the previous two years working on his novel *Fairground* (set in the Wismuth mines on the naturalist model ostensibly favoured), found it damned on the eve of publication because of its 'obscene details'. His faithful reproduction of the language of the miners was deemed an 'insult to the working classes'. Half of that year's DEFA film production was banned, and critical Marxists such as the poet Wolf Biermann, author Stefan Heym, and philosopher Robert Havemann, were attacked as 'inimical to the progress of socialism'. Beat music was attacked as being a ploy by the West 'to drive our young people to dangerous excesses'.

The sterile cultural policies which dominated the second half of the sixties mirrored the general decline in the late Ulbricht years. His successor, Erich Honecker, came to power promising to make East Germany a more relaxed, modern society, free of the Wilhelminian structures Ulbricht had never escaped. Almost overnight the schoolmasterly tone in which the Party addressed artists and writers changed. The talk was no longer of duty, watchfulness and partisanship but of variety, imagination and tolerance.

At the Central Committee conference of December 1971 Honecker delivered the following promise to the intelligentsia: 'If one proceeds from the firm position of socialism there can, in my opinion, be no taboos in the area of art and literature.' In the glow which followed Ulbricht's demise this was interpreted by the artistic community as a major liberalization: the words 'no taboos' stood out as a beacon amidst the standard language of cultural policy which for the last two decades had been occupying itself with forbidding this, limiting that, discouraging the other. Publication was approved of critical authors such as Stefan Heym, Hermann Kant and Volker Braun, who had previously been available only in the West. Humanist West German writers such as Heinrich Böll were printed in the

East for the first time. The damned jazz, blues, and blue jeans were rehabilitated. It would take another ten years before the regime would accept the place of rock music in its culture. As the crisis of confidence in the government grew with the eighties, concerts and records were made more freely available in the hope of placating grumbling youth. Towards the end Honecker even accepted the gift of a fedora hat from its other noted wearer, the West German singer Udo Lindenberg, and sent him an autograph in return. In 1986 I had the dubious honour of acting as interpreter to the first punk-rock group allowed to play in the East: The Neurotics from Harlow New Town, who caused fervent excitement in Leipzig and Dresden but received a cooler reception from an audience of horrified middle-aged functionaries at the Party Institute in Mittweida, summoned to see for themselves the musical product of alienated capitalist youth.

In their enthusiasm for the early changes East German intellectuals paid scant attention to the ambiguous nature of Honecker's promise. 'When one proceeds from the firm position of socialism . . .' was still a catch-all which could be turned at will on those authors who, in the Party's eyes, were not proceeding from the required basis. The distinction between what ranked as permissible criticism of the socialist system and rejection of it was still drawn by the authorities. Moreover, they overlooked Honecker's basic lack of interest in the arts as anything other than a conduit for socialist ideas, coupled with a streak of puritanism inherited from the Ulbricht era.

The thaw ended abruptly in November 1976 when the troublesome poet and songwriter Wolf Biermann was, without warning, stripped of his citizenship: effectively locked out of his country by its leaders while on a tour of West Germany for which they had given him permission. After moving East from Hamburg at the height of the Cold War in the fifties, Biermann had built up a cult following with his repertoire of acid political songs and excoriating attacks on the *Bonzen*, or Party big-wigs. This was particularly wounding to the regime as Biermann came from a communist family and his parents had perished for their beliefs in Auschwitz. Forbidden to perform in public, he had carried on playing for small social circles, and made records in his flat in the Chaussee Strasse, where he had installed himself as a symbolic continuation of the Brechtian tradition of critical, politically conscious writing.

Biermann himself described the consequences of the expulsion succinctly when he remarked, 'They wanted to get rid of me the quiet way. Instead they kicked off an avalanche with their fat feet.' Within days of the action twelve leading writers and artists, including Christa Wolf, Stefan Heym, Stephan Hermlin and Heiner Müller, all of whom were widely enough known in the West and valued enough in the East for their dissent to be embarrassing to the regime, had sent a letter of protest to the government, calling for Biermann's citizenship to be reinstated. Hundreds of others followed, many pointing out that the Nazis had also made use of the instrument of forced exile to rid itself of its opponents.

Honecker's honeymoon period with the intelligentsia was over. He regarded the protest as a betrayal by those whom he thought he had won over with his limited relaxation. He was particularly irritated by the wording of the petition, which quoted Marx back at the communist government. It read:

Wolf Biermann is an uncomfortable poet, a characteristic he shares with many poets of the past. Our socialist state, in line with the words of Marx's *Eighteenth Brumaire*, should criticize itself constantly and must, in contrast to anachronistic forms of society, be able to bear such discomfort calmly and in a spirit of reflection.

This was just what the government could not do. Instead it reacted by accusing the petitioners of ingratitude and instigated a wave of purges in the Party, Writers' Association, and Theatre Union. It turned into an undignified race, with the Party unable to issue 'disciplinary procedures' as fast as the writers sought to leave the state's organizations of their own accord. In the years that followed hundreds of intellectuals left the country. Anxious not to repeat the débâcle of the Biermann affair, Honecker instructed that they be allowed to leave without hindrance. When, towards the end of the seventies, the haemorrhage became so severe that it was joked that there were more East German writers living in Hamburg (where Biermann had established a sort of unofficial exiles' colony) than there were living in East Germany, the government agreed to the unusual compromise that leading writers could retain their citizenship while being allowed to live and work in the West. That way, it could take the credit for their work while not being troubled with the destabilizing effects of turbulent public figures on its doorstep.

The latter development had the – not accidental – accompanying effect of deepening divisions between the workers and the intelligentsia, a policy for which Kurt Hager, in charge of culture in the Politburo, was responsible. In a snide attack on writers who published in the West, he accused them of turning to the enemy to line their pockets with hard currency. For the mass of the population, embittered by their own lack of hard currency, the jibe rang true. The fact that artists and writers were given visas to travel

more freely than other citizens was also a source of resentment. The
boons given to the intelligentsia in periods of leniency were inevitably
used as evidence of its corruption when it suited the rulers to do so.
Despite its attempts to unite workers and intellectuals in its ranks after
1945, the Party never entirely shed the divisive anti-intellectualism which
had dogged the old Communist Party of Germany (KPD) from 1918 to
1933. When it realized that large numbers of intellectuals were still
against it, it simply made a virtue of necessity by denouncing them before
an envious and wider public.

The Biermann affair did however teach the wiser heads in the
leadership the lesson that, faced with a clutch of 'difficult authors' with
good contacts in the West German media, it was better to ignore them
than create martyrs. Biermann, a prickly, arrogant character, received
more sympathy and attention because of his expulsion than he would
ever have managed without it.

Policy towards authors was, by the mid-eighties, so chaotic as to be no
policy at all, veering between caution and liberalism. And yet there was
no great flowering of opposition literature, mainly because authors, wise
to the whims of the censor, saved him the work by censoring themselves
first. Now and then a book 'came through' which caused consternation
(usually less because of its content than because of the fact that it had
been published at all).

The younger generation of lyricists, Steffen Mensching and Hans-
Eckardt Wenzel (to name but two fashionable poets of the young 'Prenzlauer Berg school') mixed Dada-derived, random wordplay with neural-
gic sensibility and love poems which expressed both erotic and, by
analogy, political longings. By now, readers were so familiar with imagery
and analogy that they naturally read beneath the first level of meaning. It
was an approach which bemused the censors to the extent that they
couldn't find anything wrong with it.

Looking at the workings of censorship, one comes to two main conclusions. The first is that there is a kind of writing which always defeats the
censor. It is the polite, tentative tone of aching introspection and it grows with
the dominance of the censor. In 1968 – at the height of the late-Ulbricht
deep-freeze – Christa Wolf published *Reflections on Christa T.*, a novel which
expresses the sadness of a generation primed under National Socialism,
enthused and relieved as young adults by the advent of a system which
described itself as anti-fascist, but which, as a result of the creeping effects of
Stalinism and stagnation, realized that the constraints of the early years were
not mere teething troubles but a condition of life under communism.

To the amazement of the German literary establishment, and not least of its author, the novel passed the censor, although after publication it incurred the wrath of orthodox critics for its pessimism, and Heinz Sachs, its publisher, was induced, in a comical attempt at damage limitation, to write a crawling piece of self-criticism about how he had been wrong to publish the book. It was a case which exemplified the difficulty the censor faces when confronted with the sophisticated, often elusively formulated literature that his very presence encourages: he does not know what to cross out, nor can he justify banning the whole. A censor, unless he employs rough 'positive censorship' in which he only allows material which glorifies the regime, and where the merest hint of pessimism becomes grounds for withdrawal, runs into problems with the finer shades of feeling and the hues of despair. The problem for a censor is that often he doesn't know much about art, but he knows what he doesn't like.

Not that there was censorship in the GDR, said Klaus Höpke, pouring me a cup of tea in his office in Karl Liebknecht House, the historical home of the German Communist Party and the focus of brutal street fights after Hitler's accession to power. He clearly enjoys starting interviews with this line, to watch the outrage flicker across the features of Western guests. 'There were,' he pronounces after a pause, 'certain phenomena in evidence similar to censorship. Please observe the difference.'

Höpke is an elegant middle-aged man with a quirky sense of humour. As deputy minister for culture 1973–89, he went by the unofficial titles of minister for books to his friends or chief censor to his enemies. To be fair to the elusive Herr Höpke, he was widely regarded as 'not one of the worst', which was about the best that could be said of a senior functionary.

He is also one of the despised *Wendehälse* (turncoats) who managed, just in time, to proclaim doubts about the Honecker regime and made a smooth passage into the reformed Communist Party. Nowadays he is one of their handful of MPs in the Bonn Parliament. He admits that he was 'trapped in a thought system which proscribed independent thinking or judgement', but his basic line is still defensive. 'I enjoyed my job. Every problematic book that I got through was a victory for me. I was not a hinderer to the passage of literature, I was a promoter of it.'

With his neat phrases, ready wit and wide range of cultural reference, he has off to a fine and fascinating art the post-collapse defence of the old élite, a nippy sleight of hand which turns an active role in propagating the old system into a passive one, and whose parrot cries are, 'I was a medium for policy drawn up at a higher level,' or 'I always resisted within the range of possibilities open to me,' or 'I fought to get things past my boss and you wouldn't believe the problems I had keeping my job.'

Hermann Kant, who as President of the Writers' Association in 1979 carried out a mass purge of undesired writers, thus making it impossible for them to earn a literary living in the East, now complains of the ingratitude of his members, who ousted him at the first opportunity. This is sophistry verging on intellectual self-immolation. Kant and many like him desire credit for 'defending' authors against the regime whose senior *apparatchiks* they were. Matters such as the expulsion are presented as a regrettable failure to stave off the worst rather than what they were: a craven espousal of the ritual demands for intellectual blood-letting.

A vital part of this retrospective strategy entails the former functionary convincing the listener that he did not really do his old job well at all. Censors start to boast that they let through critical texts; officers in the border troops say that they always told their men 'in so many words' to shoot to miss; regional Party secretaries insist that they repeatedly ignored East Berlin's orders; and the regime's former press spokesman at the United Nations recently boasted to me that he hadn't passed on half 'the propaganda crap' he was supposed to. If only the exercisers of power had really been so lax, the country would have fallen apart long ago. The truth is that they all did their jobs far more conscientiously than they now admit.

East Germany's censorship was less direct than that employed in Poland or Czechoslovakia, but that does not mean that it was less effective. 'There was never a red pencil: there was no crossing out,' Höpke says. Instead there was, as he describes it 'an agonizing, drawn-out, to-and-fro process aimed at reaching a consensus'. This is typical Höpke-speak, in which a half-admission of guilt is quickly covered over with a mitigation. You have to be quick to spot them though, before he is on to the next point. 'Hold on,' I say, a good five sentences down the line, 'what do you mean by consensus?'

Consensus, it emerges, is when the author's and publisher's will was sufficiently worn down and their despair at ever seeing the work appear so advanced, that they simply gave in and let the censors – no, wait, 'the colleagues at the ministry of culture' – take out the offending passages. The wheels of East Germany's publishing houses ground exceeding slow even for 'unproblematic' works. One acquaintance waited three years between delivering a manuscript and its publication. Any political question hanging over the enterprise could extend the delay still further.

The wilier ones thought of ways around the inevitable delay before it happened. Volker Braun told me that he took to including 'china bulls' in his work – references to politicians or criticisms so obvious that they were spotted on the first reading and marked down as unacceptable. 'I would to and fro a bit, say that they were ruining the artistic integrity of the work and that I couldn't possibly lose that passage, and then eventually I would say, "OK then. It's my final offer. That bit goes, but the rest stays."'

Reiner Kunze was driven out of the country by the Stasi after the appearance in the seventies of his scathing novel about being young in the East, *The Wonderful Years*. He points out that the culpability of East German writers lay not in what they wrote, but in what they didn't. 'The constant presence of the Stasi, the destruction of the environment, the nepotism which pervaded society, are not to be found in East German literature – even in critical works, the reality which was being criticized was subject to cosmetic improvement.'

His colleague Günter Kunert sees the very 'gentleness' of East German censorship as its most insidious aspect:

As authors, we were always trying to be ahead of the censor, to second-guess his instinct about what was 'on' and what was 'off'. That meant that we put ourselves in the position of the censor, we composed our texts with an eye on this super-ego. After a couple of decades doing this, we got so used to this second opinion lurking in our own heads that we considered it our own. We believed that we were writing in freedom and under no one's influence, but we weren't. That was the most odious aspect of this system – it allowed us to believe we were free, and we wanted to believe in our liberty too. So we played along with our own oppression.

Certain themes were, however, so taboo that no amount of fast-footwork and bargaining could get them through. I asked Höpke what subjects used to make him blanch when the manuscripts were put on his desk. 'Well, fleeing the Republic was very touchy. The rule of thumb was that it could be indicated, but it was not allowed to be presented as the norm, even though in real life every East German knew someone who had done it. Then there were certain planks of social policy which were untouchable. You couldn't say that many pensioners lived badly here, or that lots of hospitals were outdated. And you couldn't really touch the army, the state security or relations with the Soviet Union.'

Nowadays, East German authors are having to learn to live without the censor, but it has proved to be more than merely a process of liberation. Many, perversely, had come to rely on the presence of a censor to provide intellectual challenge, in a dependency recognized by Heinrich

Heine's ironic declaration when he fled conservative Prussia for Paris in 1831: 'How shall a man write without the censor who has lived only with the censor? It will be the end of good style ... I feel helpless. I hope it isn't true at all and the censor continues.'

Absolute freedom of expression (coupled with the difficulties posed by the more competitive Western publishing world) has led to not a few writers' blocks. Where nothing is forbidden, where the prickle of fear is missing and the attention of the reading public is sated with other stimuli, they complain that writing for a living is not as fulfilling as it was. Several East German authors have thus assumed a rather tearful tone about their lot and the fate of their country. Kunert compares the mood among the intelligentsia with that of the Weimar Republic: 'When inflation began to bite, people looked back to the good old days of the Kaiser. Now a lot of our writers look back at the GDR as a disappeared homeland – something that was stolen from them.'

Writers had always busied themselves more industriously than any other group with the question of East German identity. Their belief in the separateness of the country from its western neighbour and their fascination with its internal contradictions outweighed by far those of the majority of citizens. To be fair, they were often pushed into the task of representing the elusive quality of East German-ness by virtue of the failure of its national image to cut much of a dash outside the country. It is no exaggeration to say that while the majority of working-class East Germans found their feelings of national identity awakened by sport and the satisfaction of watching the country rise up the Olympic medal tables, the intelligentsia were gratified by the news that Christa Wolf had received the Büchner Prize in West Germany or that Heiner Müller (the rake dramatist) had a new hit in London. Even the Party faithful knew that the country enjoyed a low standing abroad and there was a constant hankering for this to be compensated by an outstanding performance in spheres outside politics.

The literary past has become the focus of an acrid post-unification debate about the role of East Germany's writers in the dictatorship, and whether their readiness to work within the system contributed to the strengthening of it. It is an argument which, once begun in the arts pages of west German newspapers, provided the first flash of a moral storm over the apportioning of guilt and responsibility for the disaster of East Germany's socialist experiment.

It began with the publication in early 1990 of a slight volume by Christa Wolf entitled *What Remains*, a book that she had written ten years before and which recounts her fear and disillusionment at the discovery that she, who considered herself a critical socialist, was judged a fit target for observation by the Stasi. Naturally, it could not have been published at home (one imagines the genial Herr Höpke undergoing a silent implosion had it landed on his desk); nor in the case of such a sensitive subject did she have the half-way option of publishing it in the West. Had it appeared there, it would have provided its author with a one-way ticket out, on the model of allowing an offending author to keep citizenship but not to continue to work in the country. Christa Wolf had always made it clear that she believed her place as an East German writer was in East Germany.

If the work had been that of a lesser author, it is doubtful whether anyone would have concluded anything other than that it was an interesting if now obsolete description of life under the cold eye of Big Brother. But the fact that it came from the pen of Christa Wolf, the east's leading writer and as such the main symbol of its literary production, elevated a minor work into a major row which has filled pages of the better German newspapers and soured the intellectual aspects of the post-unity debate. Wolf is widely read throughout the German-speaking world and enjoys near-cult status in Italy, France and Japan (why the latter's readers find such satisfaction in her finely-wrought excursions into the German soul remains mystifying). She is less well-appreciated in Britain, due mainly to appalling translations.

The critic Ulrich Greiner sounded the call to arms in the pages of the influential weekly *Die Zeit* when he accused Wolf of cowardice, of having ducked conflict with the regime, of indulging in the 'Christa-Wolf Sound', which he defined as 'this limp melody of the non-committal, cast in finely formulated language, the typically blurred relation between the real world, which shimmers as a distant presentiment, and the poetical world of her texts'.

This is a fair description of her writing style, which is marked by the self-imposed exile of the private sphere, the flight from the language of exhortation into that of lyricism, where quiet despair is the basic tone. It is far from new in the history of Germany's political extremes and the reaction of its writers to this. The approach traditionally takes the form of retreat from participation in political life. Under Hitler, it was known as 'inner emigration' and under Honecker as the '*Nischengesellschaft*' or 'niche-society'. The inner emigration that Christa Wolf practised is part of a tradition which stretches back to the Weimar circle of the eighteenth century. When Goethe found himself unbearably annoyed by the petty warrings of the principalities, he would flee to the woods of Ilmenau and fling himself to the earth. It is fitting that the Thuringian town of Ilmenau ended up in East Germany.

What has now become institutionalized as the 'Christa Wolf Debate' dominates discussion of East Germany's contribution to European literature. It also shields a much more thorny problem – that of the relative ease with which Germans adapted to living with dictatorship twice in one century, and the retrospective urge to find individuals to blame for this phenomenon.

The heart of the matter is how we who have lived in free societies in the post-war period expect writers to behave under a dictatorship. There has always been a suspicion of authors who chose to stay in their own countries and thus lent legitimacy to the regimes, and the West German literary establishment has traditionally been much keener on those who left the East than those who stayed behind. In the East, the judgements are reversed. There was a strong feeling that writers who 'went over' (excluding those for whom life had truly been made intolerable) had left their readers in the lurch. East Germans, bounded by the barbed wire of the border and the less tangible but equally inhibiting constraints of their system, had a deep fear of being deserted by the remnants of the humanitarian European tradition, in short of being left alone with their rulers. One of the reasons that Christa Wolf enjoyed such high standing at home was that she had pledged to stay, although her dissatisfaction with the development of her country was evident from 1968 onwards.

A further expectation is that authors will take on the system, go to prison for their ideals, publish their work in *samizdat* and eventually enjoy the triumph of right – the fairy-tale scenario embodied by Czechoslovakia's Václav Havel. Havel was a much braver writer than Christa Wolf, a writer who raged in word and deed against the tyranny around him and eventually defeated and supplanted it. That is why it is fitting that he now holds an office of state and she does not. Whether it is sensible or useful to judge writers solely according to personal bravery is, however, another question.

Biermann was one of the reckless ragers whose tone was far from gentle and who could legitimately claim to have paid a high personal price for his art. But it was he who first pointed out the necessity of push-and-pull opposition in the seventies when he dedicated the lines to Christa Wolf asserting that the softly-spoken word and the cry of anger were part of the 'division of labour' amongst intellectuals under communism. Nowadays he springs to her defence: 'However fearful, hesitant

159

and torn she was, she never played the heroine. We should judge an apple tree by its fruit and not complain when it doesn't produce staves of oak.' Between the craven apologist for the state and the courageous dissident there is a broad spectrum which we ignore at the risk of misunderstanding the cultural make-up of eastern Europe – before and after the fall of its regimes.

Totalitarian systems do not produce only total dissidence or total obedience. Particularly in East Germany, where the project of socialism was less alien to intellectuals because of its Nazi past than to other countries in the bloc, there was a hybrid of acceptance and protest. Wolf stayed a Party member until the very end, but was a staunch helper of young writers in trouble at home and a campaigner for the release from prison of Havel and other writers in trouble abroad.

We should have no illusions. The majority of critical writers and intellectuals in Eastern Europe did not rage against the *status quo*, and balked at offering themselves as martyrs. Much of their work is cast in moderate, muted tones: the Christa Wolf Sound was by no means limited to Christa Wolf. They reflected the wary, tentative voices of their readers, and the half-resigned, half-hopeful heartache of their lands. The history of the intellectual behind the Iron Curtain is not one of storm and stress, but of hesitation and doubt.

So far, there is little result from the critical wrangle, apart from the unhelpful strengthening of old divisions and loyalties. Almost every East German I have asked for a response to the debate said that they considered it a 'witch-hunt' against their authors, and a moral attack by arrogant *Wessis* sitting in judgement on a past they had not experienced. It is an understandable but faulty line of defence. On the contrary, it is time for a thorough reassessment of East German literature and even a good shake-up of the old pieties. Many works will survive only as document-ations of life in the disappeared state, others will survive as works of literature, and this is the time to begin discussing which belongs on which pile. The East too must learn to live with criticism. Brought up in a system where denunciation in the columns of a national newspaper meant the end of a career or worse, its authors have come to fear scrutiny and are appalled at the rough manner of intellectual discourse in the west.

There is, in truth, no reason why the west should be particularly nice to eastern writers. For too long, the inmates of the 'other Germany' were given patronizing intellectual approval from across the border, as if the landscape between the Elbe and the Oder were a sort of cultural nature reserve. But there is every reason for us to prod our dozing memories about the way things really were and recall the context of East Germany's culture. A work that seems harmless now, a tone of writing which strikes us as cautious or evasive, were minor bombshells in their time. There are few classics, but many fascinating runes of the society which produced them. There is also a prophylactic record of authors dwelling in the grey area between Lenin's useful fool, who unwittingly serves the cause of power, and Shakespeare's critical, disobedient fool, who demonstrates the vulnerability of that power.

It will be a fascinating debate, when Germany gets round to holding it. For now, it is drowned out by the harsher cries of recrimination. The *Schuldfrage* (question of guilt) which sustained West German writers after the war is back on the agenda. This time it is turned on their eastern brethren and the spectacle is an undignified, depressing sight.

The fact that West Germany has prior experience of the phenomenon seems however to have made it no more probing, but a whole lot more retributive. It appears that there is nothing more lacking in compassion and discriminating judgement than an establishment, force-fed in its youth on a diet of guilt, when its turn comes to sit in judgement on another's culpability. This may prove to be the harshest lesson of the post-war period in Germany.

8

Know Your Enemy

Four Legs Good . . .

We are turning to you in great distress. We are finding enormous difficulty in accustoming ourselves to life here, especially the children. Andreas has almost no contact at all with other children. In his earlier kindergarten he was an open and sociable child. The problems connected with the change we have made are also affecting Heiko badly. His school performance has now diminished so drastically that he wasn't able to move up into the 9th class. We ignored all the warnings of the authorities in the GDR but now we realize that there is no secure future for us and our children here and regret most deeply the step we have taken.

Belated insights. Too late. This petition from citizens wishing to return and many others are being carefully examined by the responsible authorities of the German Democratic Republic.

From *How and Why: Information, Arguments and Summaries for the Agitator*
SED Publication, February 1989

One of the most entertaining publications in East Germany was *How and Why*, the propaganda booklet distributed monthly to Party members. Its purpose was the defence of the indefensible, the protection of SED members from the embarrassment of being confronted by awkward realities without a theory to hand to explain them away. The agony column of letters, from East Germans who had fled to the clutches of capitalism and now wanted to return, was intended as a collection of cautionary tales. They were as coarse and colourful as the contents of the Western tabloids the regime affected to despise. There were children who couldn't settle in their new environment and children who settled rather too well. 'My son is a neo-Nazi' was a favourite horror story. There was unemployment, homelessness, drug abuse and always, a declaration of regret, a petition to return to the East.

To be fair, there were isolated cases of East Germans who had fled and wished to return – usually for private reasons (those who departed by illegal routes were barred from ever returning, even to visit dying relatives). The trick was that the letters were not spontaneous. They were the price the authorities demanded for allowing the penitents to hop back over the Wall, and the menu of outrage and disappointment was prescribed to them by the East German Representation in Bonn (the two countries never exchanged embassies) before their applications were even considered.

East Germany's propaganda machine was a smoothly oiled if antiquated model. Its whirring and clanking accompanied life in the country from the cradle to the grave. Absurd, chilling, at times hilarious, it aimed to make clear to its citizens that they were living in the secular Eden of 'actually existing socialism' while on the other side of the 'anti-fascist protection barrier' lurked the realm of exploitation where imperialist forces gathered their strength for a cataclysmic final battle. Yet neither was this propaganda as widely disbelieved as the West hoped. Even sceptical East Germans laboured under exaggerated views of the harshness of daily life across the border, and held equally inflated notions of their own country's success and stability.

The existence of West Germany, the economic giant next door, was the single biggest concern of the East German regime and it is little wonder that its propaganda was tilted at the Federal Republic. One cannot deny a certain desperate pluck on the part of the rulers. Which Western marketing company would have taken on the task of telling a population which waited ten years for a car, thirteen for a telephone, and whose holiday destination read like a journey on the Eastern bloc's Central Line (Berlin-Prague-Budapest-Sofia-Berlin), that it had a higher level of social development than the most economically successful nation in Europe, whose energetic wanderlust was the terror of holidaymakers from Florida to Phuket?

The fear that the GDR, if destabilized, would be subsumed by its more powerful and appealing neighbour was the motor behind the propaganda effort. This concern proved prophetic as protests against the regime in 1989 turned rapidly to demands for unity. Until the collapse on their doorstep was upon them, most West Germans believed that unification was unlikely in their lifetime. In the East, even venturing the opinion that it was likely to occur at all was seen as seditious.

Erich Honecker declared at the Eighth Party Congress in 1971 that the national question had been 'decided by history' and that the German

Democratic Republic was not only a separate state but had its own nationality. He even went so far as to claim that there were 'two German nations: one socialist, one bourgeois'. East Germans were to accept that the division was final. True, the Party did not specifically exclude eventual unification, but it phrased its philosophy in terms so vague and on conditions so unlikely as to quench any hope of it. Ten years later, at the ninth Party Congress, Honecker hitched German unity to a revolution in the capitalist world, saying: 'When the day comes that the working people of the FRG turn towards the socialist reconstitution of the Federal Republic of Germany, the question of the unification of the two German states will take on new meaning.' No one held his breath.

Propaganda was an inevitable feature of life throughout the Eastern bloc, but as a half-country struggling against the bonds of common language and history, East Germany had the additional task of separating its culture from that of West Germany, of making of a single country the borderline between capitalism and communism. Of course, this also gave the proponents of the regime a clear and close enemy to portray: not just the 'imperialists', 'warmongers' and 'exploiters' of Soviet political lore but a specific rival – the foe next door.

Young men arriving for national service were confronted on the first day with their Officer for Political Tasks bearing a placard which read '*Die BRD – Dein Feind*' ('The FRG – Your Enemy'). If, they were told, the peaceful aims of the GDR were ever to be subverted by the bellicose Bonn government, they would be fighting Germans, not Americans. Even during the relative *détente* of the eighties, when contact with Western foreigners, if still unwise for those intent on a safe career or political preferment, was no longer punishable, communications with the Federal Republic and its citizens remained particularly frowned upon.

Post from West Germany was opened as a matter of course or did not arrive at all (the Stasi was notorious for helping itself to Christmas presents intended for estranged relatives), whereas letters I sent from England, even those containing forbidden cuttings from Western newspapers, usually reached the addressee. It was relatively easy, I found, to put through a telephone call to England and even to file critical reports, although in May 1989, after the blatantly falsified elections, I read over a piece describing the opposition attempts to have them declared void, only to find six Stasi men waiting patiently outside the post office to confiscate my notebook. The incident was intended as a warning and to remind me that I was observed. But ultimately, the regime cared little what *The Times* printed as it was unlikely to fall into East German hands. It clamped down far more strongly on West German correspondents, for whom expulsion was a constant threat.

Roughly half the propaganda produced in the country was devoted to glorifying the achievements of the Workers' and Peasants' State in unlikely and often absurd forms. A couple of collectors' items from the eighties include the headline in an annual report of the Berlin Party Congress: 'The Revolutionary Elan of our Building-Site Youth', and a *Neues Deutschland* front-page splash: 'Workers Gather Crops Tirelessly until the Early Evening'.

The other half was dedicated to countering the effects of western television and the widespread envy of West Germany's prosperity by presenting the misery of life under capitalism. When it became clear, in the seventies, that no one really believed that the Federal Republic was on the verge of economic and social collapse as Honecker's predecessor Walter Ulbricht had ritually prophesied, the propagandists switched arguments to concentrate on the inequalities of capitalism and convey to its people that while many lived well over the border, a substantial proportion did not.

Language was the primary tool in the process known as *Abgrenzung*. The word literally means demarcation, but came to stand for the East German policy of detaching itself from West German culture and traditions, a move which was seen as an essential component in establishing a separate GDR identity. Walter Ulbricht, who in his later years abandoned his adoration of the Soviet Union for fierce East German patriotism, declared in 1970 that 'the traditional German language of Goethe, Schiller, Lessing, Marx and Engels, filled with humanism, differs sharply from the language of the West German Federal Republic which has been polluted by imperialism and the capitalist monopoly publishing houses'. He went on to explain how the classical language of the great poets thrived in the GDR – a statement of dubious probity, even if it were restricted to the last two of his cited authors. As usual, the argument was tailored to the ideologically convenient conclusion.

But he was right about one thing: the language spoken in East and West had diverged. Despite the fact that the two Germanies spoke the same language, they often did not speak the same German. This conundrum exercises linguistics experts to this day as, with the benefit of hindsight, they try to establish how far fears that the East was – by intent or accident – developing a separate language were justified, and what the effects of forty years of linguistic as well as geographical separation have been.

One of the most eminent researchers in the field, Wolfgang Fleischer, produced the now widely-accepted theory that while there was not a 'GDR language', there was a 'German language of the GDR' distinct from that used in the West. Since the opening of the border, whole comedy sketches have been written about the difficulties in communication between Germans divided by a common language. One featured an East German family explaining their daily woes to visiting cousins in a string of abbreviations as impenetrable to West Germans as to British readers:

Peter spends most of his time active in the FDJ, which could be an advantage if he's to have a chance of visiting an NSW country one day. He could do with a flat of his own but the KWV can't come up with anything. Georg has been promoted to an ABV and Fritz is on an LPG. There's nothing in the *Centrum* these days but thank heavens for the *Delikat* and the *Ex*.

From this one could deduce that Peter was an active youth functionary who was hoping to get permission to visit the West (coyly euphemized as a 'non-socialist economy') and that the housing authorities had no state flat free for him, that Georg must be a policeman, now responsible for a residential area, and Fritz worked on a farm. The *Delikat* and *Ex* were the highly-priced food and clothing shops which offered a wider choice than the miserable selection of the *Centrum* (state department stores), in an attempt to give high earners something on which to spend their surplus of *Aluchips*, the tinny East Marks.

The East had a separate political vocabulary based on the precepts of Marxist-Leninism with touches of Old German thrown in for authenticity and local colour on the socialist canvas. The frequent use of the words *Volk* (people) and *Heimat* (homeland), considered suspect in the West because of their National Socialist connotations, thrived in the East. Only with the advent of Helmut Kohl as Chancellor, intent on sweeping away the dustier remnants of guilt-culture and on strengthening the Federal Republic's self-confidence, did such emotive words return to the political vocabulary, and even then were used far more infrequently than in the East.

Other traditions unthinkable in the West were carried on in the East without demur. There was the *Fahnenappell* (saluting the flag) and the *Fackelzug* (torchlight processions), and the use of a uniform colour as an expression of political identity. The critical theorist Walter Benjamin had defined fascism as the 'aesthetization of political culture'. The East German experience indicates that this process was not restricted to the Nazis, but was recognized by the successor regime as a means of establishing swift identification with a political direction for the benefit of the masses. The brown shirts of Hitler's SA gave way to the blue shirts of the Free German Youth, and the footage of massed youths marching in the FDJ parades of the fifties and singing, 'Those who oppose us, show yourselves', and 'This world must belong to us', is barely distinguishable from that of Hitler Youth gatherings a decade earlier. A friend told me of his dismay when as a young communist he visited his grandmother in his new FDJ uniform. 'Oh dear,' she said coolly, 'Marching and singing again are we?' The similarities in aesthetics and language were disquieting indications of the subliminal links between the two systems, both of which appealed to the power of collective consciousness and the draw of mass activity.

While West Germany took the denazification of language to a sometimes absurd extent, replacing for instance the innocent word *Bürgersteig* (pavement) with the invented *Gehweg* (walkway) because the word *Bürger* (citizen) was considered to be negatively charged in the early post-war years, many areas of East German language in use until the collapse of 1989 were inherited from the Nazi period, not least the bestowing of military titles on the police, state security and customs forces. Even the Five-Year Plan, most commonly associated with the Soviet influence, was for the citizens of the Eastern zone a mere continuation of the Four-Year Plan which had been the focus of Hitler's centralized economy. The progress of the SED to simply *die Partei* (the Party) was familiar from the political monopoly of the Nazis. Louis Fürnberg's hymn of praise would have been perfectly serviceable under the previous regime too:

> It has given us everything
> Sun and wind unstinted
> And where it was, was life itself.
> The mother of the masses led us
> Borne on her sturdy arm
> The Party, the Party, it is always right
> Comrades, that's the way it will stay.

Its imagery of the Party as earth mother, a subconscious return to the notion of the pagan goddess of the Nietzschean-Wagnerian variety, nourishing and dominating the nation with her eternal power, was far from new.

Yet despite the Communist Party's penetration of the adult population – one in every six, the highest proportion in any communist country, were

Party members – daily life was not spent discussing the Five-Year Plan or Lenin. It is here that the development of a separate language is a more lasting vestige of the division. The German spoken in the East remains to this day more old-fashioned than that in the West, where Anglo-American influence is dominant.

In the East, one did the shopping in a *Kaufhalle* (buying hall) and never a *Supermarkt*. The only shop was the *Intershop* where only those blessed with generous relatives or other sources of *Valuta* (hard currency) could buy western goods. The word 'secretary' was avoided as smacking of the boss-worker relationship and also being uncomfortably close to the elevated Party post of *Sekretär*, so thousands of women gloried in the title 'skilled worker for writing technology'. Because restaurants could never guarantee a delivery of specific foodstuffs, menus often contained the intriguing offer of 'supplementary fillers' with which one took pot-luck.

East Berlin was never *Ost-Berlin* – or quickly corrected if it slipped from the tongue as such – but for officials and roadsigns 'Berlin, Capital of the GDR', and for the rest simply 'the Capital' or 'Berlin'. West Berlin was run together as a single word *Westberlin* to avoid the conclusion that its other half must be East Berlin. In the West, the diehard proponents of unification still referred to East Berlin as 'the eastern part of the city' and 'the eastern sector' to the end. Although Berlin now refers to the whole city, the linguistic division remains. We still announce that we will do our shopping in 'west Berlin' or go out for the evening in 'the east', while *drüben* (over there) is used in both parts of the city to refer to the other side.

The man in charge of the chiselling of language and information to the leadership's requirements was Joachim Herrmann, responsible for agitation and propaganda in the Politburo 1978–89. A former editor of the Central Committee paper *Neues Deutschland*, he issued his instructions to newspaper, TV and radio editors in regular bulletins which left no room for dissent. In the office of all news media stood a red telephone via which Herrmann and his coterie of media functionaries gave daily orders about what the populace was and was not to discover. Günter Schabowski, who succeeded him as *Neues Deutschland* editor in the late seventies, later revealed that this was decided at a daily meeting with Erich Honecker, who took time off from running the country to correct the proofs of pages one and two of the paper, often changing the layout and the size of the pictures – notably his own. Honecker's personal interest in the Party daily led to a minor personality cult, and after his appearance at the Leipzig Fair in spring 1989, the paper printed forty-six pictures of the leader in a single edition.

Herrmann was a thorough if plodding functionary who was to wail after the collapse of the regime that his task had merely been to pre-empt Honecker's views and issue his master's orders to editors. A sample of his instructions during the summer of 1989, when the exodus of East Germans was in full flood and the economy faltering, makes illuminating reading:

– There is no reason for us to hold back in rebuffing the aggressive attacks of the Federal Republic's media. Our task is the propagation of the values of socialism and the effective revelation of the crimes of capitalism.
– Please do not publish material on conflicts with foreigners in the country.
– We will deny ourselves any comment on shortages in our newspapers.
– We will report more sparsely on the visits of ministers from the Federal Republic. Not every visit needs to be commented on.
– The theme of 'exodus' should not dominate daily conversation in the GDR. The events are damaging our image. With the aid of the western media, the unignorable successes of forty years of socialist policies in the GDR are being disputed because the GDR does not fit into the picture of communism in crisis. We will not let ourselves be provoked.
– We will report nothing of those returning from the west to the GDR.

The final instruction on 7 October 1989 was a particularly desperate volte-face from the traditional propaganda line of exploiting the return of East Germans who fled to the West and then changed their minds. The simple reason was that there were too few penitents. The camps for those returning from West Germany remained almost empty. A week later, Honecker fell, and with him, in the first wave of ousted hardliners, his chief of propaganda and agitation.

The Party directly controlled 70 per cent of the country's publications, the rest being produced by the so-called mass organizations, such as the youth movement and trade unions, and the minor parties, which also adhered to the communist line. Those in search of a critical edge turned instead to specialized publications such as the Church's journals and the Culture Association's weekly *Sonntag*. *Sinn und Form*, the literary magazine, also provided the odd modest departure from the expected line in the post-1985 period. These were allowed a measure of critical comment so long as this was robed in the language of academic discourse, so that only intellectuals, who were reckoned to be a dissatisfied puling bunch anyway, could understand and partake.

Herrmann's directives apart, few written rules governed the activities of journalists: the restrictions and prescriptions were so firmly imbued that they needed no confirmation. The shaky status of the GDR as the most westerly communist outpost, practising Soviet socialism in half a country whose counterpart was the thriving, confident Federal Republic, produced parochialism to an absurd extent. Even its socialism, constructed with blind faithfulness on the Soviet model, came to be described with the phrase 'in the colours of the GDR'.

In the early years of East Germany's existence, Western linguistics experts feared that the language was becoming so sovietized that a hybrid of German-Russian was taking the place of High German. Certainly, the Soviet occupation and the close political ties with Moscow did produce an odd mixture of usage. Functionaries such as Ulbricht, who had spent their exile from Nazism in the Soviet Union and for whom that country was a cultural model, spoke a Russianized German (although in Ulbricht's case this attempt to imitate his idols was often drowned by a clobbering Saxon accent).

Naturally enough, individual words, particularly from the vocabulary of Bolshevik organization, were taken over to reflect the transition from a capitalist to a socialist order: *Kollektiv* (collective), *Brigade* (workers' brigade) and *Objekt* (building). Of greater concern to the purists was the perversion of German syntax by the widespread introduction of genitive chains, which work perfectly well in Russian, where the case is expressed by word-endings, but are a grammatical nightmare in German. This tendency resulted in one newspaper announcing the appointment of 'The President of the discharge-committee of the city-soviets of the delegates of the working people'.

Russian was the first foreign language in all schools, and proficiency in it was deemed no less than the meeting of a debt to the Soviet Union. 'Learn the language of our friends!' was a frequent slogan throughout the country's schools. The unspoken converse, 'Don't bother too much about the language of our enemies', resulted in careful neglect of English and French, standards of which were low, even at university level. It was considered dubious to be too proficient in the languages of capitalism: how had you earned your fluency if not by those frowned-on Western contacts?

This accounts for the rush of East Germans of all ages now trying to learn these languages in over-filled evening-classes, while the glut of unemployed Russian teachers grows daily. One of them is the redoubtable Frau Simonova, who taught me Russian in an evening-class full of unwilling East German mechanics throughout 1986. She invested even the most pedestrian exercises with fierce political energy and took her class's mediocrity as 'an insult to those Soviet citizens who fell fighting Hitler'. One routine entailed us all parroting our daily activities. 'At what time do you have your Party meeting?' 'I have my Party meeting at . . .' When it came to my turn, I confessed that I did not have any Party meetings, ever. 'Well, you should have,' she replied. She also kept an attendance record and would complain to her students' Party boss in their factory or office if they failed to turn up for their voluntarily-compulsory lessons in the friendliest of languages. Confounded by the absence of a works' functionary to report me when I missed a couple of classes, she promptly phoned up the British Embassy in East Berlin and harangued an unsuspecting diplomat about the unreliability of British students.

East Germany's propagandists faced their main challenge in the avail-ability of Western television, which could be received across most of the country and whose faces were as familiar in the east as those of their own. The sterling work done by the East's 7.30 p.m. news programme in convincing viewers that all was well in the socialist kingdom was under-mined by the pincer attack of less positive interpretations from the West's ZDF news at 7 p.m. and its ARD broadcast at 8 p.m.

Nothing reflected the schizophrenia of Germany's division more comically than the sight of two newsreaders on separate channels being beamed into German living-rooms East and West, delivering opposing interpretations of German reality in the same language. Even the weather forecasts were different, with the East preferring a relentlessly optimistic approach. A warning of heavy smog in West Berlin would be rendered 'heavy cloud' in the eastern version – the East never admitted to the existence of smog, fearing that this would draw attention to the dire pollution levels.

For the western reporters covering the East, the peculiarity provided a challenge which many now miss. Michael Schmitz, the East Berlin correspondent of the ZDF channel recalls, 'Our work had an extra dimension which no other posting carried. We had two audiences in mind: the western one for whom the GDR was more or less a foreign country which needed to be explained, and the eastern one, who needed news to correct the picture they were given by their own media.'

The East Berlin leadership feared the power of western news broad-casts and always included the 'capitalist mass media' in its list of evils. Its response was a mixture of paranoia and a determination not to look too closely at its own shortcomings. But to a certain extent its concern was justified. No one should underestimate the role of Western television in the 1989 revolution. Given that the home media studiously avoided reporting the exodus and the demonstrations, it was the only way of confirming the state of affairs in the country.

'I don't believe that television can start a mass movement,' says Schmitz. 'But it can be essential in giving people confidence. I think we had a great effect on the Leipzig demonstrations. People would come up to us and say, "Thank God you're here." They considered the fact that we were reporting what they were doing a protection against a violent put-down and a confirmation that the risk they were taking was worthwhile.'

The East's journalists, meanwhile, were a mixed bunch. Many were hardened propagandists who identified with the definition of their profession recorded in the *Dictionary of Socialist Journalism*:

The socialist journalist is a functionary of the party of the working class. He helps to strengthen the relation of trust between the people and their state. He differs from the bourgeois journalist in that the latter's basic task is to spread bourgeois ideology, defend the capitalist social order, manipulate people for the goals and purposes of monopoly capitalism and fight socialism without respite.

However, there were others, not heroes or even dissidents, but more aware and sympathetic than they are often given credit for. Reiner Oschmann has worked on *Neues Deutschland* since 1971 and remains there to this day, struggling to reform it from a government mouthpiece to a socialist paper of independent temper with, he admits, only modest success. 'I am no longer ashamed of the overall product but we have a dreadful legacy to contend with,' he says. 'In the old days we were less a newspaper than a welfare organization for those with a clean security file. Many of our so-called journalists never wrote a thing. It is still a mystery to me what they did at their desks every day.' When the old guard were sacked, he and his colleagues were faced with the bewildering task of sorting out who was fit to continue as a journalist and who were merely functionaries behind typewriters.

Oschmann was sent to London as British correspondent in 1981, one of the greatest honours in East German journalism. He recalls:

The brief of a foreign correspondent for *Neues Deutschland* was unlike any other, even in the socialist world. On the one hand we were expected to deliver socially critical reports about life under a capitalist system; on the other, the GDR had a massive inferiority complex about its standing in the diplomatic community and a belated, grudging recognition that any targetted criticism of the other country's rulers was taboo. I was in Britain throughout the early Thatcher years and the miners' strike, when there was a lot to be written about the social effects of her policies, but the message from the office was always to go carefully, to be discreet in case our criticism rocked the diplomatic boat. We were doubly censored: first by our prevailing ideology and second by being required to be bland about that of our hosts.

Rather like Nicolae Ceaucescu who, on his state visit to London in 1978, took dawn walks with his aides in Buckingham Palace's gardens because he automatically assumed it was normal to bug the bedrooms of foreign guests, Honecker, who refused to allow even the mildest criticism of his persona or policies in the East German press, assumed it was bad form to criticize other governments – even those of the class enemy.

A posting as a correspondent to the West was seen as a representative function, allied more closely to diplomacy than to journalism. Oschmann and his wife were installed in style in the swish diplomatic quarter of London's Hyde Park Crescent, in surroundings to which even the best-remunerated West German correspondents could not have aspired. 'It was wickedly extravagant, albeit very simple on the inside: a ghastly mixture of British and East German decor. The main thing was that we could hold our heads high in the international community even if we had hardly a penny to rub together.' His wages were paid in East German Marks with only a scanty living allowance in pounds.

The East German government was one of the most paranoid in the bloc about its emissaries' links with Westerners. The rest of the world was presented through the narrow prism of internal interests and conditions. *Neues Deutschland* for years carried an international cookery slot in which correspondents would present recipes for local dishes. The ingredients, however, had to be those which an East German housewife could find locally. 'It rather narrowed the spectrum,' Oschmann remembers. 'Whether you had a recipe from Timbuktu or the Himalayas, it had to be one you could prepare with East German ingredients – a tough challenge at the best of times.' A feature he wrote for the paper on the Scots' whisky-drinking habits was turned down because it was feared that the mention of what was a luxury item, available only for hard currency, would prompt people to notice what they were missing.

Despite these restrictions he became a commentator on British affairs, author of a book entitled *Die Feine Englische* (That Certain English Touch) and a member of the tiny band of journalists one could talk to, and more important trust, under the old regime. I had met him when I was a student – my hellish hostel overlooked the grim façade of *Neues Deutschland* – in 1986. He walked into the café, extended a hand and said: 'Please, don't tell me what you think of our newspapers, I already know and I agree. It will change.' Neither of us could have guessed how soon and how completely.

But there were questions one avoided then, for fear of placing friends in awkward positions: unwritten rules as binding as those at *Neues Deutschland*. It was well over a year after the fall of the regime that I plucked up courage to ask the inevitable Westerner's question: did he ever consider staying in the West when he had his chance?

Oh yes. It was the guilty secret in my heart, and my wife's. Though we told no one, we often thought about it. Every time we came back to East Germany it felt stranger to us. Landing at Schönefeld airport, you couldn't mistake that you were back: the dirt, the incompetence, the awful clash of those metal doors while they looked at your documents.

What stopped him?

It was always a Western mistake to assume that East Germans only stayed because they were locked in behind the Wall. Staying here certainly didn't mean that one was in agreement with what was going on. It was a question of solidarity with one's people. Loyalty not to the state but to those left behind, to one's country, however awful one knew some of its aspects to be. This loyalty sounds sentimental, but perhaps more understandable to British people than others – to our West German neighbours, for instance.

Ironically, the incident that finally made up his mind was when he was approached by a British agent. An acquaintance from the East German trade mission had gone over and, just before he took the decision, made a call to Oschmann.

That call was evidently picked up – I'm afraid we weren't the only ones who bugged phones. I was approached, discreetly, in a very British way. I turned up for an interview in the City and, at lunch afterwards, we were joined by another man. My interview partner suddenly discovered that he had to dash and I was left with the stranger, who asked me some polite questions about my views and pushed over an envelope, saying that if I ever needed help, here was an address. It was quite clear what was meant.

At that moment, I realized that to go over would be a defection, something governed by the quiet war between the systems, rather than my own decision. I would have felt grubby. Now, I admit, I sometimes look back and think, 'If only I'd taken the envelope'.

'Our Goebbels'

By birth and personal development I stand on the forefront of the conflict
between two systems. Ever since I changed both my class and my allegiance, I
have felt particularly bound to the organs of power which, on our side, were in
the right hands, the people's hands: the border troops – who I regarded as my
political godchildren – people's police, army, *Tscheka* and the *Dzierzynskis* [élite
state security troops]. My task is to establish in the minds of our citizens the truth
about the enemy.

Karl Eduard von Schnitzler, *My Castles or How I Found my Fatherland*

He was, quite simply, the most hated man in East Germany: not Erich
Honecker, who had supervized the building of the Wall, nor Erich
Mielke, whose Stasi secret police kept the nation in a state of permanent
distrust and fear. The hatred of them has been largely retrospective,
fuelled by revelations of corruption and the laying bare of unpleasant
truths many suspected but few wanted to believe. No, the one they hated
all along was Karl Eduard von Schnitzler, dubbed, *Sudel Ede* (debauched
Eddy), the most unpopular face on the nation's TV screens.

His aristocratic name could not have been less well matched to his
leanings and function. Von Schnitzler was the country's chief TV propagandist for thirty years, and his weekly slot *Der Schwarze Kanal* (The
Black Channel) presented the West, and the Federal Republic in particular, through the twisted prism of his perceptions, using illustrations
cleverly culled from West German television overlayed with a commentary of iodine mixed with bile.

His bulky figure would appear after the news each Monday, lounging
in a chair, his small eyes glittering with malice behind thick spectacles.
He spat out the words 'Bundesrepublik Deutschland' with venom and a
curl of the upper lip, developing a vocabulary which made the standard
Cold War rhetoric sound like pillow talk. West Germany was rechristened, 'the Land of Wolves'; Konrad Adenauer was simply 'Hitler's
heir'; Western Europe 'the World of Yesterday'; America 'the Herald of
World War Three'. One could not deny his perverse style, his opening
line a fluted variation on a single theme: 'Poverty, unemployment,
breached human rights, lies and state-sanctioned murder,' he would
intone mournfully. 'The Federal Republic of Germany today. A cordial
good evening, ladies and gentlemen.' East Germans claimed that they
never watched it. 'What,' ran the joke, 'is a "Schni?"' Answer: 'The unit
of time it takes to leap up from the armchair and press the TV off-
switch.' But watch they did, aghast and addicted at the same time.

When the mass demonstrations began in East Berlin and Leipzig in November 1989 there were as many placards calling for the removal of von Schnitzler as of Honecker's short-lived successor Egon Krenz. (He was particularly outraged by a recurring slogan exhorting 'Schnitzler for the Muppet Show' and still more furious when the intellectual magazine *Die Weltbühne* remarked that his commentary on life in the west had been so crassly unbelievable as to have actually encouraged the exodus.)

He remains cordially loathed, for his cynicism rather than for his ideology. Even Lothar de Maizière, the first and last freely elected prime minister of East Germany, who otherwise preached forgiveness towards the old guard, drew the line at a *rapprochement* with him. When von Schnitzler turned up as a somewhat ill-conceived 'surprise guest' on a television show with de Maizière, the quietly-spoken premier promptly rose from his studio chair, claiming that he would not appear on the same podium with him. Von Schnitzler, who could not be accused of lacking sheer brass neck, stayed put for the whole programme despite rough treatment from his hosts, while the prime minister hung around in the wings.

The memory fills von Schnitzler with glee, his mouth contorting to something between a grin and a grimace which I had always assumed was reserved for the camera. 'I have always stood by the maxim that one should use the platforms that the enemy offers for the good of one's own cause. Lenin said, "Learn to use the enemy's weapons so you can turn them on the enemy one day!"'

We were talking in his bungalow in the village of Zeuthen, south of Berlin, an area favoured by the beneficiaries of the communist regime, with secluded detached houses and spacious gardens. Deprived of his status as the regime's mouthpiece, stripped of the confidence publicity brings, he is simply a prolix, rather corpulent old man slouched in his armchair ready for a good grumble.

'I know the gossip. They used to say I lived in a luxury villa with a swimming-pool. Now you can see for yourself, I live like any other East German citizen.' The living-room was small and over-filled with books and ornaments from the Eastern bloc and Arab countries: he had a 'special relationship' with Iraq, he added indicating an embroidered wall-map. There was Western furniture and the awful giant leather suite which passes for good décor in both parts of Germany. It was not luxury, rather the over-heated, crammed and cage-like prosperity to which better-off East Germans aspired.

His Hungarian wife, Marta Rafael, a newsreader on Budapest television in the fifties and defender of the Soviet invasion of 1956, snapped vindictive interjections now and then. Papagena to his Papageno, she is the perfect match for her husband, managing by a minor miracle to be even more hardline than he. 'Now Marta, let us be charitable,' he said as she suggested that Helmut Kohl had earned the death penalty for betraying the East German people. When we reached the topic of the 200 deaths on the old border, she enquired icily if I knew how many people the West Germans shot each year on the Dutch border 'for smuggling butter'. He and his wife hate in stereo, inexhaustibly, sustained by endless cups of coffee. It appears to be their main pastime.

There is the inevitable *dacha* in the country too, but I doubt that it is any more extravagant than the house. Rather like the case of the Romanian dictator's son Nicu Ceaucescu, the rumours are less a reflection of the facts of his life than a measure of public contempt, their pale beginnings magnified and strengthened with the passing of the years and the accumulation of resentments. In the GDR there was little gossip about Honecker but reams about his oleaginous crown prince Egon Krenz (that he was diabetic and an alcoholic, neither of them true, but spread with such consistency that they became folklore which passed into Western newspaper profiles as fact).

Of von Schnitzler, even wilder tales circulated: that he had been a Nazi and a womanizer with a taste for orgies; that he owned a house in the West and had his shopping done for him in West Berlin by a chauffeur driving a black Mercedes; that his wife had been caught stealing tights from the West Berlin luxury store Kaufhaus des Westens (this was true and he proceeded to base a broadcast on it, claiming that she had done it to draw attention to the evils of imperialism). His nickname 'Debauched Eddy' reflected the view that he was not only an offensive cold warrior, but afflicted with moral turpitude. For the outsider, his broadcasts were the best comedy on German TV, rooted in the Cold War, the frenzied driving of a verbal bayonet into a straw doll. But for East Germans, they were distressing, shameful reminders of what their country was built upon, a chilling *aide-mémoire*, recalling the days of Nazi disinformation. Even the language was the same: 'vermin', 'agents of evil', 'filth' were frequent appellations for the foe. 'I cannot laugh,' said one acquaintance quietly, after a particularly baroque commentary shortly before his enforced departure. 'Every week they beam Goebbels into our living-rooms. It makes me shiver to see the similarity.'

Von Schnitzler was the first victim of Egon Krenz's brief attempt to introduce cosmetic reforms. After almost three decades of berating

Western imperialism and the 'Nazi heirs of the Federal Republic', he arrived for his broadcast with his usual scripted tirade and was promptly told to discard it and bid a five-minute farewell. This he did with dignity, although it was impossible to miss the trembling of the hand and the brittle edge to the usually sovereign voice. The rest was vintage von Schnitzler: 'I have been criticized for adhering to a Cold War picture of the world. I have only ever had one criterion for friendship or enmity and it is this: for or against humanity, for its freedoms, its rights, its life, or against it.' He finished, as ever, with a veiled threat and a flourish: 'Many will cheer at my departure. But I shall not give up. I shall serve socialism in other ways.' As his face faded from the screen for the last time, corks popped in living-rooms across the republic. *Sudel Ede* was gone: the first concrete sign of reform. It was not only the end of a broadcasting era, it was the symbolic switching-off of East Germany's central propaganda machine. The rumbles which emanated from it under the Krenz government, and even under the last reform administration of Hans Modrow, were merely a drawn-out death-rattle and impressed no one. With von Schnitzler gone, the state's grip on information went limp and its claim to absolute truth crumbled.

Karl Eduard Richard Arthur Gerhard von Schnitzler was born in 1918 into a leading Rhineland family, although his parents had moved to Berlin by the time he was born. His father was a diplomat under the Hohenzollerns and at the turn of the century the Kaiser's most senior representative in Shanghai. Konrad Adenauer, who was to become the Federal Republic's first Chancellor, was a family friend and according to family lore bounced the infant Karl Eduard on his knee. Later, he probably wished he had bounced that bit harder.

He made an early break with family tradition, joining the *Sozialistische Arbeiterjugend* where his heritage earned him the unflattering nickname 'Blue-Arse'. Later, when he arrived in the Soviet zone, he asked Walter Ulbricht whether he could drop his tell-tale aristocratic 'von'. 'Don't be stupid,' the proletarian Ulbricht said in his guttural Saxon accent, 'people should know what sort of people are coming over on to our side.'

He built a career out of his hatred of his unprepossessing relations. The signature of his Uncle Georg, sales director of the chemical concern IG Farben, can be seen on deliveries of Zyclon B, the gas used in the Nazi extermination chambers. The family banking house I. H. Stein was one of Hitler's major financiers: his cousin Baron Kurt von Schröder was one of the initiators of the Hartsburg Front Fund in which five pfennigs per ton of Ruhr coal mined were donated to the coalition of right-wing parties, with the lion's share going to the German National People's Party (DNVP), but a sizeable chunk received by the National Socialists. Von Schröder arranged the reconciliation of Hitler and President Hindenburg in early January 1933, which smoothed Hitler's way to the chancellorship on 30 January.

Von Schnitzler's war is still a subject of debate, with large chapters apparently unaccounted for. He says he was injured, worked in intelligence and was later transferred to the notorious Strafbataillon 999 in Africa, where disgraced soldiers were sent for brutal punishment. If this were true he would be one of only a handful to return to active duty.

At any rate, he was captured by the Canadians in Normandy in 1944 and takes up his own story:

I was taken to Britain, to Kempton Park racecourse, which was being used as an interrogation camp for German prisoners of war. The interrogator was clearly well prepared for me. His first question was:
'Who is Georg von Schnitzler?'
'The sales director of IG Farben, supporter of Hitler and my cousin,' I said.
'Who is Kurt von Schröder?'
'Banker in Cologne, financier of Hitler. Also my cousin.'
'Who is Herbert von Dircksen?'
'Cousin and Hitler's ambassador in Tokyo, Moscow and London.'
'Who is Diego von Bergen?'
'A cousin and ambassador to the Vatican.'
'Hm,' he said. 'And don't tell us, you're an anti-fascist now, right?'
'No,' I said. 'I was against Hitler when your industrialists granted him loans, when your government accepted the remilitarization of the Ruhr without resistance, when you sacrificed Czechoslovakia to Hitler so that he would continue to march east and not attack you.'

Here, at least, von Schnitzler's account tallies with British evidence. He was sent to a meeting in Brondesbury attended by leading German anti-fascists and the Labour MP and later Foreign Secretary Gordon Walker. The plan to create a BBC radio programme in which German prisoners-of-war addressed audiences at home was hatched under the auspices of Hugh Carleton-Greene, later Director-General of the BBC and brother of Graham, and Lindley Fraser, head of the German Service. It is one of the weirder ironies of East German history that the country's leading propagandist learned his craft in Bush House. He still praises the organization fulsomely, but it is a tribute which the Corporation would probably rather not use to advertise its virtues.

'It was the only journalistic training I received but the best, I believe:

thorough, objective and professional. I have the BBC to thank for my training.' Carleton Greene was impressed by von Schnitzler's sharp microphone style and sent him as political commentator to the British Sector's North-West German Radio (NWDR) in Hamburg and in 1946 as acting Director-General and head of political coverage at the NWDR.

It is difficult to imagine how Carleton-Greene could have failed to notice that his protégé's left-wing tendencies went way beyond democratic socialist sympathies. He was not alone in his error of judgement however: Rudolf Augstein, publisher of the influential weekly *Der Spiegel*, also offered him a job when he was setting up the weekly magazine. Von Schnitzler denies to this day that he was working for the Russians at this time, but admits that in 1945–46 he made frequent crossings of the Berlin zone frontier at the clandestine Oebisfelde crossing-point and fondly recalls meetings with Colonel Sergei Tulpanov, chief political adviser in the Soviet sector.

He was dismissed when his communist sympathies began to penetrate his reports too blatantly, and promptly disappeared, only to turn up shortly afterwards broadcasting on the *Berliner Rundfunk*, the mouthpiece of the Soviet administration, then based in the western sector of the city. His colleagues were amazed. 'He loved the good life and was one of the leading traders on the black market,' said Hans Starke, who worked at NWDR with him. 'We assumed that there must be something in it for him financially – he was not one of those people motivated by a cause unless it suited his own comfort.' The suspicion grew that von Schnitzler had been enticed by the Russians by a mixture of bribery and blackmail.

In a TV interview in 1985 marking the twenty-fifth anniversary of *The Black Channel*, Carleton-Greene claimed that von Schnitzler tried to defect back to the West in 1949, and that a meeting with a middle-man was arranged in the Western sector to fly him to Hamburg. 'I had everything prepared for him, including a slot for him to broadcast to the East on why he had left,' Greene said. Von Schnitzler appears to have got cold feet at the last moment – perhaps he had also heard that the BBC intended to fire him for 'lacking character' after the broadcast – and failed to show up for the assignation.

He covered the Nuremberg trials for Soviet sector radio – 'half of my family was in the dock' – together with a younger colleague, newly returned from Moscow in Walter Ulbricht's entourage and working under the name Michael Storm. Storm left *Berliner Rundfunk* shortly afterwards, having been delegated to a different task: under his real name, Markus Wolf was to be head of the East German espionage service for thirty years.

Besieged by British troops in 1952, the radio station moved into the Eastern sector. Von Schnitzler began to expand into film and television and quickly gained currency as Ulbricht's chief propagandist. When in 1960 he had the idea of a weekly programme attacking the western media (by then attracting droves of viewers from the stultifying GDR service), it was warmly welcomed, and *The Black Channel* was born. Where East German politicians and functionaries gradually shied away from the harsher facts of the division of Germany, mumbling instead about peaceful coexistence, von Schnitzler never stopped battering. As an enemy of *détente*, he suffered during brief political thaws, being sacked as director of East German radio in 1958, and removed from his job as political director of a major television discussion show in 1967. He even disappeared for several weeks from the screen after the military build-down in 1988. But he was prepared to do the dirty work which others shied away from, and his programme was frequently used to send coded messages and threats to the Western security services.

'If there is such a thing as a *Schreibtischtäter* [a desk-bound criminal] von Schnitzler is it,' says Gero Gandert, who shudders involuntarily at the name. The phrase is commonly used in Germany to describe those bureaucrats who were essential to the workings of the Nazi terror without ever bloodying their own hands. Their instruments were the signature and the stamp of approval. The violence was carried out by others. Now the united Germany has to live with a second generation of desk-bound criminals.

As a young West German film critic, with a special interest in the East German DEFA studio's output of the fifties, Gandert had criticized the 'Stalinization' of Eastern bloc productions. One night, returning from a colleague's house in the East, he was snatched by the Stasi and later tried and sentenced to four years in prison for 'sedition endangering the socialist state'. He was finally rehabilitated in 1991 at a symbolic rehearing of his case. The judge ended the proceedings by saying that Gandert had been 'an innocent civilian caught between the fronts of a silent war'.

For over a week after his disappearance in 1958 the GDR refused to answer West German enquiries about his whereabouts. His parents' first news of their son came in a von Schnitzler broadcast on 2 September 1958:

To divert attention from his shameful, barbarous practices, a hue and cry has been organized by Herr Lemmer [then minister for intra-German affairs] about a certain Herr Gandert whom he appears to have mislaid. Well then, he should take better care of his agents. To be on the safe side, he should avoid recruiting them in the first place. That way, there will be no accidents in the workplace.

Over three decades later, I showed the transcript to von Schnitzler. He clearly did not remember who Gero Gandert was. 'If I said this on the radio, I must have had the relevant information to support it from our security forces,' he said. 'There were hundreds of *provocateurs* sent over here by the West to interfere with our socialism. Do you expect me to remember all of their names?'

If his dirty work for the regime was contemptible, his talent for abuse was beyond doubt. The West German media had no one to match him for sheer poisonous stamina, even at the height of Cold War rhetoric. Although most of their leading commentators tilted at him over the years, he outlasted all of them. Here he is, for instance, commenting on the West German news reporting with dead-pan accuracy: 'A microphone rammed into the car window, the meaningless sentence of a minister. An equally meaningless shot of the rear view of another minister arriving. Journalism, ladies and gentlemen?'

But if his system had all been so beneficial, why had it collapsed? 'I admit we should have presented the benefits of our system more clearly to the public,' he said. 'Perhaps a more liberal policy on travel would have helped, but of course, the Wall was necessary; no, more than necessary, it preserved peace, protected us from attack.'

By now he was in a trance, wafted by the power of his own words, quoting verbatim from his broadcasts and writings, with only Lenin granted a second opinion. As he talked on about imperialism and the class struggle, in the museum language of confrontation, my mind wandered to something Hans Modrow, the country's leading reform communist (and thus 'traitor' in von Schnitzler's vocabulary) had said when asked what he considered the worst aspect of the forty-year history of East Germany. He replied, 'The deformation of personality by ideology.'

The obfuscation, fake parallels and vindictiveness were beginning to be stifling. At last I began to understand why East Germans could not laugh at him. 'I want you to know one thing before you leave me,' he said. 'I never lied. Not once. Tell people that. I was the one who told them the truth. Our people lived in better social conditions than they live in now in this larger Germany. It was a battle, and when we faltered the imperialists took their advantage and won. Soon we communists will be in the underground. Already they spy on us, tap our telephones, read our post. Like 1933.'

But not, apparently, like the Stasi-dominated East Germany of the last four decades?

'More citizens are spied on by the security services in the west than here.'

Would he return to broadcasting if he could?

'Only if I had the same freedom I had under the Communist Party. Your censor is more powerful than ours ever was.'

We had reached the point where further conversation was impossible. 'I am sorry that you have still not grasped the fundamental fact,' he said. 'Everything that the socialists did here was for the good of the people, for humanity. What capitalists do is always motivated by profit, by the desire to force working people to accept the continuation of their power. That is why we are more moral than you will ever be.'

He rose unsteadily and remarked that it was growing late. The interview was over. '*Auf wiedersehen, junge Frau,*' he said. 'A safe journey home.'

'Ah, von Schnitzler,' said an old communist acquaintance. 'A sad man. He never really escaped his class, his past: you can't. In the beginning, he was a figure of fun for us. The Red Baron Mark Two, we used to call him. An aristocrat who wanted to be a revolutionary, who exaggerated everything because he believed in nothing. In the end he was just despised, you know, even in the Party.'

In 1990, he was stripped of his membership of the reform-Communist Party of Democratic Socialism.

9
The Fall

Drowning Not Waving

Only then, when the lower classes will no longer tolerate the old ways and the upper classes are no longer capable of continuing in the old ways, only then will the revolution be victorious.

Lenin, *Collected Works*, Vol. 31

All in all, the balance of the GDR over forty years shows that great things have been achieved through the work of the people and for the people. In the future too, great efforts will be required. New challenges demand new solutions and we will find an answer to every question together with the people as we stride onwards on the path of socialism.

Erich Honecker, speech on the 40th anniversary of East Germany's foundation, 7 October 1989

On 5 September 1986 I arrived in East Berlin, entrusted with the mission of strengthening friendship and solidarity between the peoples of Great Britain and the German Democratic Republic. This, at least, is what the League of People's Solidarity declared in their letter of welcome. It seemed a small favour to perform in exchange for that most precious of commodities, a long-stay visa.

At Oxford my undergraduate contemporaries were set up to spend the third year abroad with cushy-sounding jobs as assistants in posh Viennese schools or still cushier grants for a year's sojourn at one of the more elegant West German universities. All I wanted, I would moan to my tutor, was a year in the East. Eventually he grew sick of my moping and we combined forces on a begging letter to the East German Embassy in Belgrave Square, recommending me as a passionate lover of GDR literature with a burning need to consult arcane research volumes not available in the West.

Back came a letter from the London-based Britain-GDR Society requesting more details. It was not difficult to work out what sort of outfit the society was. Based in ramshackle premises in the Seven Sisters Road, it was run by those British communists who had lost the battle between the hardliners and the Euro-communists in the Party, and saw its main function as providing slide-shows, meetings and outings for Stalinists of a certain age. It was run by a man called Jack Berlin who believed that the only trouble with the GDR – he shook his head regretfully – was that it had lost its revolutionary purpose. It had been different under Walter Ulbricht, he sighed.

Despite a cultural agreement between Britain and East Berlin, the promised exchange of undergraduates had never thrived. I suspect that the incumbents of Seven Sisters Road had delegated a clutch of trusted youngsters in the early years and then run out of candidates. They seemed quite pleased to have a volunteer. They even arranged a grant – in Eastern currency of course.

Ferried to the sixteen-storey students' hotel on the Franz Mehring Platz by a desperate-to-please functionary of the East Berlin Friendship Society, we found that I was marked down to share quarters the size of a student's bedroom in England with three Polish students, who spent most of their free time working in the nearby Narva light-bulb factory in order to afford the relatively luxurious offers of East Berlin's shop windows. There were rickety bunk-beds, no carpet on the floor, no curtains, and a kitchen to be shared between fifty students but more frequently inhabited by cockroaches.

Matriculation at Humboldt University, the grand neo-classical building on the Unter den Linden, was an altogether more ceremonious affair, conducted by the Rector, whose perk it evidently was to have the longest academic title at the university: Prof. Dr Päd. habil. Dr. phil. h.c. Klein. All foreigners were gathered together for a lecture which began, 'We, the anti-fascist Germans', and continued with a recital of the country's successes. The vast majority of those gathered were from Third World Marxist countries and clearly hadn't a clue what he was talking about. The man on my left was a Cuban who spoke pidgin German and was training to be a doctor; on my right was a young Ethiopian whose eyes shone as he told me about Mengistu and the revolution. When I asked him about the country's civil war and its recurrent famines, he replied that he was here 'to learn the answers from the German Democratic Republic'.

For the majority of Marxist countries, East Germany was the place

with all the answers. There was an astounding array of food and consumer goods in comparison with their homelands. The universities, too
few and under-appointed by Western standards, were high-tech para-
dises for the Soviets, Cubans, Africans and Vietnamese who clamoured
to study there. It was left to the North Koreans to preserve a chilly
distance from their hosts, mixing only with each other and outraging the
Free German Youth functionaries by distributing glossy multi-lingual
literature explaining why Kim Il Sung's communism was more highly
developed than the European Marxist variety.

In the hostel, I was stranded in an amiable Warsaw Pact ghetto: an
agreeable Bulgarian neighbour with her black-haired baby on one side, a
stoical quartet of Czechs on the other, and the sombre duo of Heide and
Katrin, East German teacher-training students, opposite. It didn't take a
particularly highly developed antennae to detect the latters' heavy-
handed interests in my movements and opinions. Down the hall lived
Roland, the Free German Youth (FDJ) secretary. His ideological conviction was so fierce as to be deterrent. A system which demands a twenty-
four-hours-a-day zeal from its adherents has to be suspect somewhere. I
once asked him what his tasks as FDJ functionary were. 'Motivating
other students towards collective living and making sure the cleaning rota
is adhered to,' he replied.

The other native students were curious as to why a British student of
German and philosophy should want to study there. One popular theory
was that I had failed to reach the academic and financial standards
required for a study year in West Germany, the other was that I was a
staunch communist. I was invited to give a talk to explain and said that,
when I had been given the visa application to complete in London, I had
been tempted to answer the question, 'Purpose of the journey?' with the
honest response, 'Satisfaction of curiosity'.

Afterwards a grave young history student called Steffan came up to
me. He had never imagined, he said, that someone from the West could
be curious about the East: curiosity, for him, was simply a product of
living behind a closed border. That said, it strikes me that he was right
about the lack of interest of West Germans about the East. 'They care as
little what our lives are really like as our political bosses do,' he added.

I had given no thought to West Berlin for the first few weeks. Given
that the realm of experience of my co-students was bounded by the Wall,
there was little reason to. And then one day I got a sudden itch to read a
British newspaper. It became rapidly intolerable. I would go to the West
and buy one. Only then did it occur to me that my visa was marked

Einreise – einmalig (Entry: single). There was no mention of an exit, let alone a re-entry. I sought out the secretary at Humboldt's international relations department.

They were unenthusiastic about the project. 'Visits to Westberlin' – she ran the words together in the official East German pronunciation – 'are for emergencies only. We can't really allow Western students to go over when our own can't.' Put like that, it seemed a reasonable argument. But the desire, once planted, would not be suppressed. Next I hankered to visit British friends working in West Berlin. Then I developed a craving for tinned tomatoes and fresh oranges. And finally I was overcome by cold anger that anyone should dare not to let me out if I wanted to go.

After three months the tension was palpable in the small lobby of Western students (overwhelmingly Italian and French) or, as our woeful official description had it, 'Guests from the non-socialist countries'. Having tried and failed alone, we banded together and stormed the international relations department in a gaggle of thirty to demand the right to breathe the air of capitalism once in a while. Overpowered by number and volume, the director gave up and unlocked a cupboard in which was a metal box. He unlocked the box to reveal a smaller box. He unlocked that to reveal a stamp. With the new label 'eligible for multiple visa' on our identity cards, we were dispatched to the police for – what else – another stamp, and begged to be discreet about our cross-border comings and goings for fear of 'awakening needs we are not in a position to satisfy'.

Getting oneself out of the East was, however, simplicity itself compared with getting a visitor in. I invited a friend to stay for a week, arranging invitation letter, visa and currency exchange. We decided to spend the first evening at Humboldt's student club and I approached the students who ran it for an extra ticket. 'Is it for a citizen of the German Democratic Republic?' they wanted to know. When I announced it was an English visitor, they huddled together in the corner for a lengthy discussion of the relevant protocol before turning down the request for a ticket. 'We cannot allow Western citizens into our social events,' explained the Free German Youth secretary solemnly. 'The proximity of our university to Westberlin means that there is a danger of *provocateurs* infiltrating the campus here. The world is still divided into two hostile camps, you see.'

It was little wonder that the authorities were jumpy that year. The economy had been growing steadily worse throughout the early eighties,

the political scene was stagnant and the numbers of *Ausreisewillige* –
(would-be emigrants) was growing steadily. East German students, carefully selected on the basis of 'political maturity' as well as, or sometimes
in place of, academic performance, were a well-behaved group with no
substantial links to the emerging opposition, but even they were aware of
the lack of progress.

Soon I was barely making a trip over Checkpoint Charlie without a
shopping list from fellow-students, who received the occasional bounty
of Western currency from relatives but could not, even with it, get the
things they hankered for in the East. There was, for instance, Katharina's wedding dress. We had met while working as volunteer inter-
preters for the yearly Festival of Political Song, where my task was to
translate English punk lyrics to an uncomprehending but enthusiastic
audience while she tried to do the same for a Filipino band. While our
respective charges bellowed and strummed in praise of socialism, we
would absent ourselves for long conversations about life under the real
thing.

Her one ambition was to marry her sports teacher fiancé in a white
dress of Plauen lace. This should not have been unduly difficult, as she
came from the town where the lace was made. But not a stitch of it
reached the townspeople. Like the majority of East Germany's quality
products, it was exported to the West for hard currency. From the acres
of the stuff in the *Kaufhaus des Westens* in West Berlin, I carted five
metres back over the border, from where they were sent back to their
town of origin to be made into that longed-for dress. Another friend
asked me to bring back a book of essays on Marx not published in the
East. The customs man stared at it thoughtfully, called over his super-
visor, and seemed on the brink of confiscating it. I asked what was wrong
with Marx. 'It's not our Marx,' he growled. 'It's Marx from over there.
That's what's wrong with it.'

Mikhail Gorbachev made his first visit since taking office in April
1986, while I was visiting friends in East Berlin. The route of his car
from a reception to the Communist Party headquarters was swept clear
of pedestrians. When I asked if I could stand behind the cordon to catch
a glimpse of the Soviet leader, the policeman looked back irritably. 'Are
you mad?' he said. The guest's presence was kept as low-key as possible,
but the curiosity of the East Berliners was awakened. A friend arrived
with a 'secret' to show me. It was a badge bearing a blurred photograph
and overlaid with the letters 'Gorbi'. 'Shhhh,' he said.

A clamp-down was under way on gestures and fashions which could be interpreted as expressions of dissent. In the West, it was by now fashionable for rock bands and their fans to wear Soviet badges: Lenin heads and minor orders. The authorities in the East were unsure how to deal with this when it came their way. How, in a country which declares its absolute faith in Marxism-Leninism and the leading role of the Party, can you legitimately object to young people wearing badges declaring precisely that?

Then there were the ribbons and 'A' plates. The ranks of those who had applied to leave the country but still not received permission to do so had begun to break their silence with symbols. They would stick 'A' signs of exaggerated proportions in the rear windows of their car (A standing for *Anfänger* (learner) but also for *Ausreisewillige*). The police were again powerless to act against this sudden swell in the numbers of learner drivers. Encouraged by this, people began to seek more overt signs of dissent. I found the most moving and sad one was the long white satin ribbon, tied to a car aerial. Its message was surrender. It became the symbol of those hopeful emigrants who did not just want to leave the east, they wanted people to know that they had been driven to it.

The popular East German musician Gerhard Schöne captured the impact of the symbol in a song about his shame and anger on seeing the fluttering ribbons, 'a reproach in the wind' to the system and to those quiet dissidents like himself:

> Perhaps we are to blame,
> Too patient, too lame
> Instead of blooming wild and tall
> Even our dreams cower small.

It is intriguing to ask why East Germany's opposition was so belated, why people living in one of the most repressive states of the Eastern bloc gave the broad impression of grudging acceptance rather than of burgeoning opposition. To the end, no Václav Havel, no Lech Walesa appeared. East Germany's opposition was a timid child. It whispered its objections, tiptoed to peace vigils in the sanctuary of churches. It did not impinge on the lives of most other East Germans other than in the phrase '*Andersdenkende*', literally 'those who think differently', who were treated among the general population with tolerant disregard, rather as one might view a harmless, irrelevant sect.

There were several reasons for this. One was the pervasive effect of the 'singularization theory', in which opposition to communism was held to be akin to support for fascism or at least for right-wing capitalism.

This sophistry, which stemmed from the anti-Hitler propaganda of the twenties and thirties, was no longer declared explicitly, but it continued to be suggested by the media and it lingered in the minds of many.

Another was the export of dissidents to the West. Honecker had come to realize that harassing or imprisoning opposition figures was bad for the country's reputation abroad and that it often strengthened the very challenge it sought to dispel. He was also fortunate in having next door a country willing to accept immigrants from East Germany and even pay the communists in hard currency and goods for allowing their release. It became common practice for East Berlin to offer one-way tickets to the West. Honecker could thereby thin out the numbers of dissidents, bleeding the opposition of potential leaders and at the same time buck up the economy – a deal other eastern European dictators could only dream about.

Despite the repression which they suffered at home, intellectual circles retained an attachment to Marxism far deeper than that in other Eastern European countries. Czech and Polish dissidents, whose agenda was the removal of communism, were frustrated and uncomprehending that their East German peers wanted to keep it, albeit in a vaguely conceived 'Third Way' form. The banned authors and thinkers who found most favour among the opposition public in East Germany were not polemical anti-communists, but polemical reform communists: Wolf Biermann, Rudolf Bahro, Ernst Bloch, to name but three.

Like almost all other aspects of life in the country, the opposition was unconsciously influenced by the fascist past. This is the salient point of difference from the other opposition movements. As the self-appointed 'anti-fascist state', built by those who had risked opposition to Hitler in their youth, the GDR's political élite was perceived as having a moral claim to power long after it had sacrificed this through stupidity, intolerance and perpetual disregard for democratic legitimation.

Among rank and file members of the Communist Party one frequently found dissatisfaction with the nonsense spoken by the leaders: but apathy ruled. The desire to keep the country as orderly and regular as a carefully-tended patch of lawn was not restricted to the top politicians. To suggest that a little upheaval might be healthy almost always brought forth baleful stares. The hardliners said that things were just fine as they were. The progressives said it would all sort itself out in the course of time. The reliance on gradual change, preferably without anyone having to get up and actually take part in it, was East Germany's gospel in the mid-eighties. The five hours I spent as a guest at a student Party gathering are the nearest I have come to witnessing true futility.

Across East Germany I sought debate with Party members, intent on discovering whether it was mere self-interest which led them to spend long evenings approving motions from above which would be implemented whether or not they objected. The simple question, 'Why are you in the Party?' produced a range of replies I had not expected. A middle-aged doctor in the Harz mountains replied, 'It goes with the job.' Reiner, a cheerful engineer and a member for twenty years, said that he was a Comrade because the only true democracy was collectivism. We would argue for hours; nothing shook his good nature or his faith. Once he admitted that the nationalized state enterprises were not as successful as the published plan figures suggested, 'But it's the people's fault,' he cried. 'They haven't realized yet that the economy belongs to them.' Sonja, a gentle-natured nurse from the children's clinic next door, was in it 'because the aims are right even if the path we're taking looks a bit crazy'.

There were hundreds of bad reasons. But there was also more genuine belief in the rightness of socialism than I had expected. For some of the older and middle generation, the creed's strictness and emphasis on discipline appealed to the instincts National Socialism had awakened. At the same time, it defined itself as the enemy of fascism and based its claim to moral superiority on this role. For the young, socialism was not about Germany or the Soviet bloc at all, but about faraway battles for justice. Arguments begun about the shortcomings of Honecker would inevitably slide into attacks on American policy in Nicaragua. They had long since ceased to be interested in moribund domestic politics.

The central paradox of East Germany is that although it finally shook off its existence with no hesitation and little regret, it was until very shortly before its collapse a proud country. The relative strength of the economy – or at least its ability to provide more consumer goods than its communist neighbours – gave people a sense of superiority. The efficiency of East German industry was wildly over-estimated, but when one takes into account that the range of comparison was that of the communist world, it is easy to see how people fell into the trap of believing that the country was thriving.

The mixture of subservience and competition which hallmarked East Germany's relations with the Soviet Union peaked in absurdity when Honecker responded to Soviet encouragement to introduce *perestroika* with the argument that the East's industry did not need restructuring. Even Honecker's experts had been telling him for some years that industry and much of the infrastructure needed a thorough overhaul, so he could not have been totally unaware of its plight. He simply took comfort in the fact that it was not in such a bad way as the industry of the Soviet Union, and used that modest comfort as grounds for boasting to the international community and not introducing reforms.

West Germany's *Deutschlandpolitik* in the eighties was a lazy and largely aimless affair which, apart from a steady increase in cross-border visits, achieved little. The East German regime profited from the recognition brought by Honecker's 1987 Bonn visit, and from hidden trade subsidies, while not coming under undue pressure to deliver much in the way of concessions in return. Honecker instinctively understood and played on domestic desires to be regarded by the outside world. In the period of decline between 1986 and 1989, a cross-questioning of economists, factory managers and journalists in the East would often end up with their admitting that the government's stubborn policy of high spending and low investment was disastrous, but concluding: 'But it can't be that bad because we are a significant trading partner for West Germany.' German-German co-operation had become self-evident. Relations had been normalized to the point where few still noticed their basic abnormality. The principal aims of *Ostpolitik*, placing reform pressure on the east with a view to keeping the goal of unification open, no longer impinged on East Berlin. Sometimes, one had the impression that they had been forgotten in Bonn as well.

Tracing the quiet revolution of 1989 back to its source and inspiration, one arrives at an unlikely starting-point: an official commemoration in honour of an approved socialist, the Rosa Luxemburg demonstration, held annually on the anniversary of her assassination in 1919.

Rosa Luxemburg was at once a useful and threatening figure for East Germany's communists. Her lively writings and her humanism made her attractive to young people and women who were less attracted to Marx and Lenin. On the other hand, her late writings are peppered with criticisms of the dictatorship, terror, and suppression of individual rights that the Russian Revolution had brought. Her support for free elections and a free press, and her warnings against 'blind belief in authority', made her works potentially explosive. Her most famous declaration, 'True freedom is always the freedom of the non-conformists' was, in the East German edition of her collected works, relegated to a footnote.

At the Rosa Luxemburg demonstration of January 1988 a group of dissidents led by Bärbel Bohley, Vera Wollenberger and Werner Fischer unfurled a banner bearing the offending quotation. East Germans were treated to the absurd spectacle of plain-clothes Stasi men tearing down the offending words of a German socialist. The trio were arrested for disturbing the peace and given the highly unusual choice of a spell in prison or a spell abroad. They chose the latter, finding sanctuary with the Church of England under the auspices of the Archbishop of Canterbury, Robert Runcie, who took a strong interest in the fate of the Church in the east.

News of the decision spread fast on the bush telegraph. It was greeted as the first minor triumph for the modern nonconformists: the state was losing its nerve. Instead of simply sentencing the offenders in a show-trial or stripping them of their citizenship, the authorities had ducked conflict, clearly fearing that public punishment of the demonstrators would – as in the case of Wolf Biermann twelve years earlier – unleash a wave of protests it was no longer in a position to contain.

From England, the three campaigned tirelessly to return to the East. 'Thousands of East Germans were aching for the chance to travel, and here we were, being offered a long holiday in the West by the regime,' Bärbel Bohley recalled later.

Six months later, they were allowed back on condition that they kept a low profile and that their home-coming was not publicly celebrated. In an attempt to avoid the West drawing attention to the event, they were flown to Prague and brought over the border at dead of night. Only in the churches of the East, rapidly developing into a forum for opposition debate on the future of the country, was their story discussed and courage drawn from it.

At the Nikolaikirche in Leipzig more and more people were attending the weekly 'Prayers for Peace' services initiated by the minister there, Christian Führer, whose sermons and discussions offered an outlet for growing frustrations. Increasingly dissatisfied with being confined to their pews, the congregation began to conclude the Monday services with silent marches through the town. Unnerved, the authorities began to arrest the participants of these informal promenades, at first by the handful, then by the dozen. But still they continued.

The Church had come of age – albeit rather late. It had not, as in Poland, galvanized latent dissent into opposition in the early eighties. Indeed, the Protestant bishops had struck a pact with Honecker, agreeing to his doctrine of the co-existence of Church and Socialism, and had allowed its role to be restricted to quiet human rights work and making life bearable for conscientious objectors.

But its role in the events which swept East Germany in 1989 was more honourable. Along with the rest, many brave ministers and bishops risked their own safety to give the burgeoning opposition what the state denied them and what they needed most: a roof under which to gather. Church journals were the first to bring into the open demands for discussion of the country's plight. Clergy such as Bishop Christoph Demke in Magdeburg frequently acted as intercessors on behalf of people hounded by the Stasi who had no other way of protesting against their persecution. Rainer Eppelman at the Samaritans parish in East Berlin made his church into a combined discussion centre, concert hall, and refuge for conscientious objectors.

A side-effect of this role was that many young men who in other societies would have become politicians, became ministers instead. After the fall of the regime they reverted to the roles they had often sub-consciously wanted all along. Eppelmann became minister of defence in the first democratic government elected in March 1990; Joachim Gauck from Mecklenburg is to this day the head of the committee dealing with the legacy of the Stasi; Matthias Gehler became a government spokes-man and admitted that his conscience sometimes struggled with the compromises that this job entailed, even in an emerging democracy. So many clergy, feeling that their job had been done, left the church when the system was defeated that the east is now short of ministers and has to import them from western Germany.

It was unfortunate for the regime that the five-yearly local elections fell in May 1989. Voting in the East was a carefully organized farce in which a list of approved candidates from the Communist Party, the supporting minor parties, and the aligned mass-movements (trade unions and Free German Youth), was presented to the voters for approval. This year, in a response to the restlessness even the pachyderm Party organization could no longer ignore, it was decided to offer mandates to that beacon of political challenge, the Association of Small Allotment Holders and Animal Breeders, an initiative which produced no other response than mirthful mockery.

Even at the usually well-behaved *Distel* (Thistle) cabaret in East Berlin the elections were parodied with the lack of respect they deserved. In the favourite sketch of the season entitled 'The Unemployed Delegate', a newly-elected local politician holds his first surgery only to find that no one knows who he is or what he is there for. 'But you voted for me,' he wailed, to gales of laughter from the audience. 'All ninety-nine comma nine percent of you, and you don't know who I am?'

It was a major challenge not to vote for the official candidates in an

East German election. Those who failed to turn up at the polling booths would receive visits from local functionaries as the day went on, 'reminding' them of their duty. While a 'yes' vote entailed simply picking up a voting slip and placing it in the ballot box, a 'no' vote meant taking the form into a booth, under the disapproving stare of the polling station supervisors, and crossing out every single name on the lengthy list of candidates. Pens were not provided. A single name left undeleted meant that the slip counted as a 'yes' vote; so did defaced voting slips.

Even under these conditions the 1989 elections produced unsatisfactory results for the regime: a mere 98.85 'yes' vote for the official list nation-wide, and loud calls of 'foul' from opposition teams who had monitored the electoral process. Over one hundred were arrested when they sought to take a petition calling for an enquiry into the result to the Party headquarters in East Berlin.

We will never know the true result, as the figures were clearly manipulated. The regime, however, practised a strange form of honesty by fiddling the figures in proportion to the dissent in each of the regions, so that those skilled in the art of reading between the fractions could deduce a fairly accurate picture of the degree of potential rebellion from region to region. The Stasi also pored over the figures of non-voters to gauge dissent. In its report after the May elections it noted 'a generally rising tendency towards non-participation' and indulged in painstaking analyses of which ages and professional and geographical groups were not voting and whether they lived in old or new apartment blocks (the regime was unshakeable in its belief that if everyone had indoor lavatories there would be an end to all political turbulence).

In my local area of Pankow they even broke down the figures on a street-to-street basis and revealed what they really thought of us: 'Prenzlauer Promenade, Thule and Florastrasse, concentration of ex-convicts and persons tending towards anti-social activity and criminality'.

In Leipzig the Stasi report spoke of 'concern-arousing indifference and growing hostile-negative views' in the city. When these documents were released, at the end of 1989, it was astonishing how accurately the Stasi's picture of the decline in morale had been. It was admitted that 'only' a 97.67 'yes' vote had been recorded in the city, the lowest since the immediate post-war years. 'What do you think of that?' said Burkhardt, a student at Karl Marx University and skilled interpreter of the tiniest deviance in the media arcana, as we poured over the tables in *Neues Deutschland*. He lapsed into broad Leipzig dialect to evoke the dismay of a local functionary discovering an unexpected truth in his morning paper: 2.33 per cent against!' Leipzig is becoming the cradle of the counter-revolution.' His words were to prove prophetic.

East Germans had until now been free to travel without complication to Czechoslovakia and Hungary, although after the rise of Solidarity only those with relatives there, or with invitations, could visit Poland.

On 2 May 1989 Hungary began to dismantle its fortified border with Austria. Politburo member Günter Schabowski recalls that an envoy from the foreign minister was dispatched to Budapest with a formal request from East Berlin not to allow its citizens to pass the border.

He came back with the reply that Budapest was not prepared to undertake any restrictions on behalf of our government and that this sort of co-operation between Hungary and the GDR would be concluded at the end of the summer. The reaction on our part was one of utter helplessness. Honecker was incapable of any reaction at all. It was simply impossible for him to come to terms with what he saw as the Hungarians' treachery, so he did nothing at all. The subject was barely mentioned after that.

The reform communist government in Budapest was well aware of the effect of its decision on East Germany, but canny enough to place western favour ahead of old bloc loyalties.

As spring turned to summer there was a sudden leap in the number of departures. The 'Gorby factor' was beginning to work against the regime, as the population realized that their leaders had no intention of copying the Soviet reforms and that no changes to the moribund system were in sight. Many of those who had drawn hope and energy from the Soviet leader's accession in 1985, and who had hoped to promote *perestroika* in East Germany, simply gave up the thankless tussle with the hostility and indifference at the top.

The economy was also in an unhealthy state, with much of the infrastructure close to collapse. The government could no longer, as in past years, simply resort to flushing out dissatisfaction with a surge of goods into the shops. The regime's damning response to the opening of the Hungarian frontier left many East Germans fearing that their leaders would complete their isolation by closing the eastern borders as well, turning them into a second Albania.

From July, thousands of East Germans sought refuge in the West German embassies in Budapest, Prague and Warsaw, and in its representation in East Berlin. This unusual escape route, which had in the past been the subject of occasional embarrassments to the East

German government, was rapidly growing into a national habit. The Federal Republic had to close the gates of all four offices in August and September due to overcrowding. On 19 August, 600 East Germans broke through the Hungarian border into Austria. No attempt was made by the Hungarian guards to stop them. Two weeks later, Hungary threw open its borders and tens of thousands rushed out. By now, the haemorrhage was unstoppable and both Hungary and, more significantly, Czechoslovakia, which had until now acted as a hardline ally, were pressuring Honecker to let the people leave without tramping through their countries first.

With an eye on the approaching festivities for the fortieth anniversary of the founding of East Germany, the government agreed to let the would-be emigrants holed up in Prague and Warsaw leave for West Germany directly. On 30 September special trains were laid on, carrying over 6,000 people to West Germany in a single day.

For those left behind, whether because of personal and work commitments or because they wanted to reform their country rather than desert it, these were the most bitter, fearful days in the country's history. On 4 October security police fought with 2,000 people who stormed Dresden station trying to spring aboard the 'freedom train' to the West. The fighting was hand-to-hand and brutal, the windowpanes of the giant station shattered in the mêlée. The events were poorly reported, as the foreign ministry had forbidden journalists to travel to the city.

I received the following letter from a minister in Dresden. It was sent to him by a young man from his congregation doing his compulsory military service and who had been called out as part of the reserve police force on the night of 4 October. Perhaps it seems odd to choose the account of someone fighting against the demonstrators, but its evocation of the terror felt not only by those facing the might of the state, but of the men pressed into duty behind the riot shields, has haunted me ever since:

They put us right at the front, where it was most dangerous. We were very scared. Stones and bottles rained down on us. Then the commander came and told us to charge the crowd. At that moment, for the first time ever, I was seized by fear for my life. We were completely untrained; many of us fainted. We were fighting for our lives. Before us stood the masses, high on fear and anger, behind us, screaming their commands, our officers and the Stasi. We were used as battering-rams against our own people and I am ashamed to say that we followed these orders. Please forgive us and pray for us if you can. Read this to the young people in church so that they will know what faces them as conscripts in our so-called socialist army. Tell them to think carefully about answering the call-up, even if the only alternative is prison. I fear with all my heart the uses to which our army and security forces may be put in the coming months.

The exodus was primarily of young skilled people, and soon hospitals were reporting acute staffing shortages. The opposition began to appeal for those whose presence was essential for reform to stay, under the motto: 'Writers, ministers and doctors, your place is here with us.'

Erich Honecker found no such words of encouragement, declaring that there would be 'no tears shed' for those who left their socialist fatherland, but even he appeared to be expecting the worst, commissioning a study from a tame professor at Leipzig University which came up with the unbelievable reassurance that East Germany could manage fine, even if a third of the adult population was to desert it.

In the period from the beginning of September to the end of December, 292,000 East Germans left the country: scarcely anyone did not have a close relative or friend who had gone west. The effect on morale was crushing, even if people joked that the new national greeting was, 'Still here then?'. The government was powerless to respond. In September, Honecker was admitted to hospital for a gall-bladder operation. 'Suddenly there was a power vacuum,' remembers Jens Reich, a professor of molecular biology and one of East Berlin's most prominent dissidents. 'Throughout that summer it became clear that something had to give. In our homes, around kitchen tables, we began to talk of reform; in the work-place even those who were usually indifferent began to mutter that this couldn't go on.'

Similar mutterings were also beginning to gather volume even within the Politburo. Honecker's crown prince Egon Krenz and the Berlin chief Günter Schabowski began to plot Honecker's downfall. During a Politburo meeting in the leader's absence, Schabowski uttered the first criticism of Honecker's lack of response to the crisis in an attempt to gauge support for his removal. To his satisfaction, he found he was not alone in his concern.

One date loomed on the horizon: 7 October 1989, East Germany's fortieth birthday. No one except the miraculously recovered Honecker was in celebratory mood. Many people had hoped that he would use his illness as an excuse to resign. Those who knew him better did not share this optimism, as Egon Krenz later told me:

There was no way that Erich Honecker would ever have voluntarily resigned from power in these conditions. The fortieth anniversary of the GDR was desperately important to him. It was intended as a major symbol of our success and our stability and of his contribution. All the Eastern bloc leaders were to be present, including Mikhail Gorbachev to whom he was particularly anxious to show how well things were going here. Our hands were tied. We could do nothing until the celebrations were over.

Perhaps due to a plant of false information, perhaps due to wishful thinking, the mass-circulation West German *Bild Zeitung* ran a splash story that Honecker was close to death. The next day East Germans were treated to a rare practical joke: a leading article in *Neues Deutschland* signed E.H. and mocking *Bild*'s story. Even this caused little merriment among people who were watching their friends and relatives leave their country for the West in a steady, debilitating stream.

By the anniversary itself, relations between Honecker and Gorbachev, the guest of honour, had deteriorated to barely-concealed enmity. The Soviet leader looked grim from the moment he stepped off the plane while Honecker, to the amazement of all who witnessed him at the airport, was jovial and spry. Crowds lined the route of the motorcade shouting, 'Gorby, rescue us.' Honecker, as if oblivious to the chaos around him, described East Germany forty years on as a 'pillar of stability'. At the military procession in the Karl-Marx-Allee, Honecker excitedly pointed out his new tank and artillery acquisitions. His guest drummed his fingers on the rail in front of him.

By now the opposition movement could no longer be ignored, although its self-effacing caution was reflected in the personalities and strategies of those dissidents who did eventually emerge to challenge the regime. Even with the country paralysed, it was comically difficult to extract fighting talk from them. I remember visiting New Forum's Jens Reich in the pleasant surroundings of his Pankow flat. He had just applied for permission to register New Forum as an organization and spent half an hour elaborating on whether the ruling communists would allow it.

Only, one suspects, in East Germany, could an opposition on the verge of a major breakthrough worry about not being officially approved by its opponents. Instead of demanding the dismissal of the regime they requested 'dialogue' with it. 'We were true children of the GDR,' says Jens Reich, looking back. 'We wanted change, but we didn't believe our own strength. We were polite revolutionaries and we wasted a lot of time.'

The breaking-point came in East Berlin on the evening of 7 October when police and security forces, anxious to prevent people disrupting the politicians' celebration of forty years of East Germany, clamped down, arresting and manhandling hundreds of demonstrators. Honecker described the protest as a 'counter-revolution' and ordered a reinforced security presence for the following Monday's demonstration in Leipzig.

On 9 October, in preparation for the Monday demonstration, hundreds of armed police were deployed around the city together with the civilian *Kampfgruppen* units, an unofficial territorial army called into existence by Walter Ulbricht after 17 June 1953 as a prophylactic against any future uprising. Tanks were stationed around the city; the hospitals told to prepare blood supplies and body bags.

The Minister of Defence Heinz Kessler has since insisted that he did not give orders for any troops to mobilize in preparation for a violent conflict in Leipzig. But anecdotal evidence, including that from a former paratrooper and one of the four senior 'officers with political tasks', confirms that the military was on alert that night. The two men I spoke to had been dispatched from East Berlin to the outskirts of the city. The paratrooper, fearing that he might be used in an offensive against civilians, had absented himself pleading a family emergency.

On condition of anonymity, the political officer confirms that all orders that night came from the ministry of defence in Berlin, and that the regional command in Leipzig had been told not to issue any instructions. The usual chain of orders and hierarchy was severed. The officers had direct communication with the ministry in Strausberg. He admits that the preparations were 'highly unusual' and that the officers had been told to prepare to deal with 'counter-revolutionary violence'.

The 50,000 Leipzigers who joined the demonstration that night knew that they were possibly walking into a massacre, and their courage brought the grimy metropolis the soubriquet of 'the city of heroes'. It is referred to as the 'miracle of Leipzig' that there was no shooting that night. It is also not entirely clear why there was none, with various people still competing for the credit.

Kurt Masur, the conductor of the prestigious Leipzig Gewandhaus orchestra, claims that he prevailed upon the Party command in Leipzig to ask Berlin to pull back the troops. Masur and three district party secretaries issued an appeal for calm and for a refrain from violence on both sides – the first time that local functionaries had spoken out against the use of force to quell the demonstrations. Of course, this alone could not have stopped an assault by the security forces, but the combination of declared resistance within the Party and the voice of Masur appears to have been taken seriously in East Berlin.

As the truth of the night's events became rapidly lost in popular folklore, rumours abounded that the troops had been issued with an order to shoot if necessary. Egon Krenz, responsible for security questions in the Politburo, denied to me that such an order existed:

There was no such thing. The preparations for that night were made by Honecker and although I expected the worst, he never came up with an order to the forces to go on to the offensive. If there had been one, it would have gone through me. Don't ask me why he held back. Perhaps he lost his nerve; perhaps he thought better of it.

Krenz's deputy was Wolfgang Herger, charged with the day-to-day organization of security liaison with the provinces. He is thus a more reliable witness than Krenz himself on the events of that night. He also has less to gain by the promotion of a retrospective mythology about the heroic reserve of the regime. Over the last two years I have come to distrust the memories of those functionaries whose self-esteem is bound up in projecting a positive picture of their own actions in October 1989 – Krenz, Schabowski and Hans Modrow all come into this category.

I sought out Herger because he had not given a single interview since then, nor (unlike the three aforementioned) had he written his memoirs. He would at least not be intent on sticking to or elaborating on a previous account, the single most frequent factor in political myth-making. As an underling, albeit a powerful one, he also saw the events in a colder light than the Politburo members, for whom the events were linked with their personal strivings for power:

There is one overriding reason why there was not a massacre in Leipzig and that was that Honecker knew that he would not have got the order through even if he had given it. It was too late to unite the leadership behind such action. Remember, he was toppled the following week. That means that by 9 October Krenz was prepared to strike for the leadership and that he was assured of the backing of the majority of his colleagues in the Politburo, including Erich Mielke (the minister of state security). Honecker probably knew that something was in the air, but he was too weak to confront Krenz or his other colleagues. He took the easy way out by having the security forces put on alert in Leipzig, but without an order on what they were to do.

What resulted was the setting for a military assault without the event. The city's hospitals were told to prepare blood reserves and body bags. Willing to wound, but afraid to strike, Honecker left the fate of the evening to the demonstrators themselves. Whether he secretly hoped for a showdown remains his secret. In spring 1992, his minister of state security Erich Mielke broke his silence to claim it was he who enjoined Honecker to hold back the troops.

Christian Führer had hung a huge white banner outside his church bearing the words 'raise no stone against them', a plea to both the marchers and the security forces for restraint. By the time the demonstrators had completed their route, the police and security presence had melted away to its 'normal' proportions. There were cheers of 'We won' and shouts to the remaining, uncomfortable policeman of 'Come back next week – but join our side'.

It now seems clear that there was never an official order to shoot, despite the elaborate preparations for violence in Leipzig. But the leadership's hesitant approach provided all the ingredients for a bloody clash, especially against the background of the political fighting talk about counter-revolution. In the command vacuum which ensued that night, it was probably just good fortune which prevented disaster.

There is one other factor which deserves mention, and that is the Soviet Union. Two senior officials at the East Berlin embassy, one political diplomat and one KGB liaison man, maintain that the reason Honecker lost his nerve was that he was told by Moscow that he would receive no help from the Soviet forces if he used violence against the demonstrators. There is no record of any request for help, so whether or not Moscow's representatives told Honecker verbally that this time their tanks would not be at his disposal is unproven. But it is worth considering the tight timetable of events in the days 4–9 October. Honecker's threats to 'deal with the counter-revolution' were most pronounced after the Dresden incident on 4 October, and his orders to place the security forces and the army on alert were issued the next day. On 7–8 October Mikhail Gorbachev was in East Berlin firmly urging a change of course. Then, at the latest, Honecker must have realized that there would be no assistance from the Soviet troops in East Germany in quelling an uprising.

Emboldened by the success of 9 October and with fears of a Tiananmen solution now fading, 150,000 marched the following Monday demanding the removal of the regime. For the first time, there were isolated calls for unification.

Krenz, urged on by the more decisive Günter Schabowski (one of those who had his own eye on power should Krenz prove a Chernenko-style transition figure), decided to make his move against

Honecker. Assured of the backing of the chief 'Old Guard' figure, Prime Minister Willi Stoph, and armed with the go-ahead from Moscow, channelled through the USSR's powerful East Berlin embassy, he made his challenge to the leader at the Tuesday Politburo meeting of 17 October. Schabowski recalls the event thus:

Even before we came to the agenda, Stoph stood up and said, quite abruptly, 'I propose to the Politburo that Comrade Honecker be relieved of his position as General Secretary.' Honecker took it without even the slightest change of expression, then he cleared his throat and as if nothing had happened, said, 'Let's get on with the agenda.' We protested at this and he said, 'Alright then, let everyone have their say,' and called on people to speak whom he thought would take his side. One by one they all turned against him, not a single one spoke for him and when the vote came it was unanimous.

The procedures of the Communist Party demanded that a dismissed leader should also vote against himself. Ever the loyal adherent to Party rules, Honecker raised his hand and ended his seventeen-year rule, then stood up and left the room. Krenz, the grinning crown prince, had finally taken the throne, although not in the circumstances he must have envisaged as he climbed his way up the greasy pole.

Known as the 'professional youth' because he had remained at the head of the youth movement until his forties, and as 'horse-features' because of his prominent teeth, Krenz was widely disliked. By a delicious irony, the television programme interrupted to bring the news of his accession was a children's drama called *Everyone Dreams of a Horse*. In the evening Krenz gave a broadcast calling for East Germans to stay, and promising reforms.

'The night he took over there were about fifty people from New Forum crammed into my flat for a meeting,' says Jens Reich. 'He reminded us of a Brecht character: the arch-villain trying to look appealing and with his Janus head turning from one direction to another. Some of us were reminded of the wolf in the Little Red Riding Hood story.'

A few days later the new leader took on the three-in-one roles of chairman of the council of state and chairman of the defence council to add to his general secretaryship. On paper, he held full power in the state. In reality, his grip on it was already lost. As head of the electoral commission he had appeared on television in May to announce the results of the patently falsified elections, and after the Tiannanmen Square incident he had travelled to China and shaken hands with Deng

Xiaoping. These memories persisted, and his brief tenure in office was a slide into helplessness, his popularity falling by the day. No sooner had he been appointed than there were tens of thousands on the streets of Berlin calling for his resignation, hundreds of thousands in Leipzig.

Had he not spent the previous thirty years of his life contributing to the calamity which befell him, one would have felt heartily sorry for Krenz. I met him frequently throughout those weeks and had known his children for many years. He was a devoted family man, prone to sentimentality and with a genuine liking for young people. When away from the cameras he was morosely humorous and human. But for the people he was, in the exiled singer Wolf Biermann's memorable description, 'a walking invitation to flee the republic'. And he failed utterly to convince with his promises of reform.

His language was the stilted vocabulary of the functionary, dismissed by the masses as 'Party Chinese', which could make even the most passionate declaration of renewal sound like an extract from the Five-Year Plan. Within hours of his appointment, the first joke was doing the rounds: 'What is the difference between Krenz and Honecker?' 'Krenz's gall bladder is still working.'

For me, the pleasure of those days consisted in watching the fear, reserve and resignation of friends and acquaintances melt away. Impressive as the demonstrations were, I was more overwhelmed by the former impossibilities which had suddenly become part of everyday life. Like Katharina, for instance, by now happily married in Plauen lace. Frightened for her job, she had begged me not to write from England in case her post was read by the Stasi. One day she strolled unannounced into the Palast Hotel, which was crawling with agents and treated by the public as off-limits, and asked to see me. I bundled her quickly into the room. 'Don't be so paranoid,' she said, neatly turning the tables. 'Who gives a damn any more?'

On 4 November the largest single protest against the regime took place in Berlin, with 700,000 people putting to good use the vast concrete monstrosity of Alexanderplatz, a square designed in the fifties with an eye to future official demonstrations. These crowds, however, had something very different in mind than fawning support for their leaders. The mood was one of triumphant defiance. Along the route, past the parliament and the council of ministers' building, stood actors from the city's theatres, stiffly raising and lowering their hands in a grotesque parody of the yearly processions presided over by Erich Honecker. The banners imitated the official exhortations of a set-piece communist display, but with witty alterations of the old slogans, and cartoons mocking the leadership.

To the surprise and not entire delight of the crowd, Markus Wolf, head of East Germany's formidable espionage service until 1987, joined the speakers calling for reform, intent on installing his protégé, the Dresden Party chief Hans Modrow, as leader.

Modrow had a rare aura for an East German *apparatchik*, and his reputation as a potential challenger to Honecker had been built up by careful leaks to the West German press. He was photographed in his modest three-room flat, an anomaly in a state where even the lowliest of regional functionaries appointed themselves generous villas. He was also known to have stood his corner for Dresden, refusing to transfer funds and building materials to Berlin for the 750th anniversary celebrations in 1987. His quiet, unstuffy manner had brought him more support in the south than the despised 'Berlin big-wigs'. Best of all, he had not been in the old Politburo and so could claim distance from its recent errors.

It is impossible to speak of a politician's popularity in a system which does not allow the public the means to voice its opinions, but Modrow was distinctly less unpopular than the rest. His attraction was strengthened by the wish of the country, Party and non-Party members alike, to be rid of Krenz.

On the day of the demonstration Krenz re-opened the border to Czechoslovakia, and 23,000 people voted against him with their feet by promptly flooding out. With no hope now of staunching the exodus with promises, the government resigned on 7 November. The following day a new Politburo was announced with Modrow as prime minister. Krenz, still clinging tenaciously to the leadership, admitted 'serious errors' in the handling of the crisis. The Party's Central Committee convened for an emergency session.

Life Ends at Forty

Wir sind das Volk (We are the people)
  Leipzig demonstrators' chant, October 1989

Wir sind ein Volk (We are one people)
  Leipzig demonstrators' chant, December 1989

On the evening of 9 November Günter Schabowski gave a press conference to announce the findings of the central committee meeting. For an hour he produced the by now routine promises of renewal, dialogue and economic reform. *'Immer dieselbe Scheisse'* ('same old crap again'), sighed the East German journalist next to me. At two minutes to seven Schabowski took out a piece of paper, perched his glasses on the end of his nose, and dropped a bombshell. The country's borders, sealed for twenty-eight years, were to be opened. Visas would be issued to those wanting to leave.

The quarter of an hour which followed was sheer pandemonium. Did the announcement apply only to those who wanted to leave for good? No, said Schabowski, as if announcing a minor detail of scant importance, it applied to everyone. When did this unthinkable, buried, but never-forgotten freedom to travel come into practice? For the first time, the Berlin chief looked uncertain and looked desperately at his notes for assistance. 'From this moment,' he said.

I ran to Checkpoint Charlie with the wings of good news on my feet. It was deserted. Peter Brinkman, the formidable correspondent from the tabloid *Bild Zeitung*, lumbered in pursuit. Soon, the media scourge of the East was trying to persuade two teenage girls to cheer for a photograph. Clearly suspecting a trick, they steadfastly refused and carried on up the Leipziger Strasse, looking idly into the shop windows.

At the barrier outside the Checkpoint, I shouted to the guards that the border was open. They laughed hysterically. 'That one hasn't got all her cups in the cupboard,' said one. So I tried the German crossing-point, the Invalidenstrasse. 'I suppose you think we're just standing here to be decorative,' mocked another. A few hours later, after the news had hit evening television, he stood shaking his head beside me as East Berliners, many still in their night-clothes, streamed past him into the West.

By midnight, the trickle of pedestrians had swelled into a cavalcade of Trabants, whooping their horns. On the other side, West Berliners thrust bottles of sparkling wine through the windows. It was pointless asking anyone how they felt. *'Wahnsinn'* ('madness'), they screamed in unison. There was hysterical laughter, hysterical tears and hysterical embracing. West Berliners who had rushed down to the Invalidenstrasse to greet the first arrivals drummed on the roofs of the Trabants which spluttered into the unknown territory.

Enlivened by several swigs from the bottles being passed around, the surly border guard of a few hours earlier wobbled over to me, planted a kiss on my cheek and swirled me round in an impromptu jig. A dancing border guard is a picture which stays in the mind as fresh as the moment it happened, to brighten up gloomy moods for the rest of your life.

Later, I asked Schabowski's Russian wife Irina what the country's rulers had been thinking that night, holed up in their Wandlitz compound while the people celebrated on the streets of Berlin. 'Nothing,' she said grimly. 'They were all in bed. Günter had gone down to the border to see what was going on and I was desperate for a chat. I thought maybe Frau Krenz might still be about, but no, every single light was out.' Her elderly mother, who speaks only Russian, emerged to ask what the fuss was about. Told that the border was open, she considered and said. 'Does that mean we will live in capitalism now?' Yes, said Frau Schabowski, downcast, it probably did. 'Well in that case,' announced the old lady, 'I think I'll hang about for a few more years and see what it's like.'

The Politburo did not intend 9 November to happen as it did. The sheet of paper that Schabowski brought with him was an announcement, prepared that afternoon by Krenz, that the people were free to travel and that visas could be registered the next morning. What was intended – and how could a functionary as traditional as Krenz have dreamt of anything else – was an orderly, bureaucratic process in which visas would be issued and the people, preferably in single file, would obediently and gradually take advantage of their new freedom. The problem was that Schabowski, the bearer of the glad tidings, was over-tired and under stress and had, as he admitted to me, 'only read the damn thing through once and diagonally at that'.

Asked when the border would be opened, he was caught off-balance and uttered the fatally marvellous words 'From this moment'. Later, the rumour spread that the border had been opened by accident. 'Nonsense,' says Schabowski. 'Of course we intended to open the border. We had no choice. There would have been dreadful civic unrest if we hadn't. What we didn't expect was the rush, the emotional drive. We thought we had a grip on things. We hadn't.' Nowadays, unemployed and ensconced in uncosy proximity to his former colleagues in an apartment block overlooking the old death strip, he is the most wholehearted penitent of the lot. Asked why he had only thought to announce the opening of the Wall after reeling off decisions which interested the population far less, he thumps the table violently and says, 'The people were always interested in completely different things from us. It was our downfall that we never realized it until then.'

Faced with the first arrivals of intrepid East Berliners at the border crossings, the guards had no idea what to do with them. They asked their commanders, who didn't know either. By the time this helplessness had been conveyed far enough up the chain to reach someone senior enough to have Krenz's telephone number, the lowly guards had lost patience and let the people through anyway. Trailing behind events as ever, Krenz told them to let the people out for a night in the West long after they were already downing the free beers handed out by West Berlin pubs. The Berlin Wall had been breached by the slip of a weary politician's tongue. 'I made a lot of mistakes in my political career over the years,' says Schabowski, 'but this is the only one I can be proud of.'

The demolition of the Wall had not been planned by the Politburo, which still clung to the notion that issuing travel visas would appease the population's dissatisfaction. Throughout the night of 9 November and the following day, however, the people took the matter into their own hands by starting to dismantle it themselves, chipping away at the construction Honecker had said would stand 'for a hundred years'. By now, in a divine reversal of state power, the leaders could do nothing other than follow the decisions of their subjects.

Even the politicians of West Germany were caught off-guard by the development. They had issued ritual demands for the border to be opened for so long that they were unable to believe it when it happened. Chancellor Kohl, who was in Warsaw at the time, jetted back for a walkabout, but found himself surrounded by West Berlin radicals who drowned out the delegation's attempt to sing the national anthem with boos and catcalls.

On the evening of 10 November bulldozers and lifting equipment were moved in to the Eberswalderstrasse crossing in the north of the city and, to the cheers of the crowd, the first chunk of concrete was carried high in the air, like a giant decayed tooth. The residents of the street, divided for twenty-eight years by ideology and concrete, reached across the Wall to shake hands with their estranged neighbours, and toasts of vodka were clinked with chunks of Wall in the glasses. One by one, the sections were lifted out. Dust and concrete flew everywhere, including into my left eye, dislodging a contact lens. I watched the rest of the evening through an uneven blur and later filed an expenses claim to *The Times* reading, 'Replacement contact lens: old one lost due to falling Berlin Wall'.

In the week that followed I made excursions to the west with East German acquaintances who wanted to see everything, the most expensive shop, the wildest disco and – modest dream of the East – eat a real McDonalds hamburger. It seemed impossible to be sitting with these people in Kreuzberg cafés explaining unfamiliar menus. One friend reminded me that several years ago, standing at a bus stop in Erfurt, he had looked forward to the day when we could wait together for a London bus. 'When we're pensioners, maybe it will be possible,' he had said. Throughout the city the longest queues were outside the banks, where people queued for hours for their 'welcome money' of 100 Deutschmarks, and outside the sex shops, which profited throughout this period from the insatiable curiosity of people previously sentenced to state-sanctioned prudery.

That 9 November was the happiest day in the country's history. It was also its death-knell. There had long been theoretical dispute over whether the second Germany would ever be strong enough to survive with its borders open. But the manner of the opening, in haste and desperation, made it clear that the state had lost its authority. The next weeks were taken up with belated Party reforms, largely unnoticed by the people. The demonstrations continued, but now the cry resounding from the streets was no longer 'We are the people', but 'We are one people'.

So deeply entrenched was the distrust of Krenz that he received little credit for his decision to open the Wall, and when Hans Modrow took over from Willi Stoph as prime minister, the nation turned to him, largely ignoring the fact that Krenz was still leader. Modrow was also Moscow's man, whom Gorbachev hoped would take on the challenge of saving East Germany from extinction by establishing a confederation of the two German states. The idea also found favour with many left-wing intellectuals in West Germany, such as Günter Grass, who famously if eccentrically remarked that Auschwitz had forever denied Germany the right to be unified. This would have enabled the Soviet Union to allow the now inevitable convergence of the two Germanies, while protecting its security interests.

But the people did not want confederation: they wanted unity. They wanted it, not out of a deep attachment to the ideal of a unified German state, a dream which had faded on both sides of the border in the previous four decades, but because they sensed that the East German state had outlived its *raison d'être*. They had simply taken to heart the official line, explained earlier in the year by Otto Reinhold, the chief ideologist at the Central Committee's institute for social research: 'What justification has the GDR, separate from but alongside the Federal Republic, apart from its adherence to a socialist society? None, of course.' With its socialism in shreds, there was nothing left for East Germany to live for.

At the extraordinary Party Congress of 16 December, Krenz was voted out of office and replaced by Gregor Gysi, a lawyer with a sound record in defending human rights activists and who was acceptable to the opposition. He had represented the dissidents who had been packed off to England in 1988, and secured their return. The party changed its name to the Socialist Unity Party of Germany – Party of Democratic Socialism (SED-PDS). The unmanageability of the title reflected the party's cluelessness about how to deal with its past and determine its future. Gysi's role was defined as leader of the Party; the old title and role of General Secretary and the cornerstone of the Party's power, the Politburo, disappeared. The Party relinquished its leading role and real power passed to Modrow.

The new Party did at least remain true to one old communist dictum, however: when in trouble, purge. Krenz, together with Schabowski and all those who had served in the Politburo under Honecker, were stripped of their Party membership. Like naughty schoolboys, the erstwhile mighty had to wait outside while the decision was taken. Krenz sat for three hours on a wooden bench in a draughty corridor and was devastated when the news came. 'The Party has been my life,' he said, and walked off alone into the night without a friend or comrade to ease his passage into oblivion.

At the end of November Kohl addressed the Bundestag with a speech entitled 'Overcoming the Division of Germany'. He suggested a ten-point route to unification via economic co-operation, confederation and federation of the two states. It was a tentative document reflecting the gradualist approach to unity which West Germany had taken for the last twenty years. It also had 'made in Bonn' stamped all over it, failing utterly to take account of the speed of change and mood in the east.

On 19 December Kohl visited Dresden to meet Modrow, and spoke from the ruins of the Frauenkirche, destroyed in the bombing raids of the last war. His words were drowned out by chants of 'Unity, unity' and 'Helmut, rescue us'. The Brandenburg Gate, symbol of German strength and latterly of German division, was ceremoniously reopened by Chancellor Kohl and Hans Modrow on 22 December. Unification, it now seemed, was being effected by symbolism, with the politicians of East and West panting breathlessly in pursuit of the inevitable. Kohl, after his Dresden experience, was the first to realize quite how quickly things were moving.

The uninspiring ten-point plan was abandoned as the Chancellor harnessed the wave of enthusiasm for unification in the East. He seized his chance to follow Bismarck into the history books as the chancellor who united Germany, doubtless with the great leader's words ringing to inspire him. In 1871, on the occasion of the first unification of Germany, Bismarck announced that he had simply waited until he heard the steps of God resounding through events, and leapt forward to grasp a corner of his mantle.

On 1 February 1990, Hans Modrow called a press conference and announced that the government would no longer adhere to the principle of two German states and would agree to unification in four stages. The proposal bore the title *Deutschland einig Vaterland* (Germany, united fatherland). The cry from the streets of Leipzig and Dresden had been elevated into official policy.

Bonn was caught off-guard by the proposal. Modrow, whose prime concern was Soviet interests, had discussed the plan with President Gorbachev and secured his approval, but he had neglected to inform Chancellor Kohl. Relations between the two men had been poor since Modrow had visited Bonn in December to ask for economic aid for the East. Kohl had refused, saying that he was 'not prepared to throw good money at a bad system' and pursued his own plan for unification. Both Germanies were agreed on the fact that they wanted to be one, but the two leaders were far from united. Modrow's ideal united Germany was a neutral one, a suggestion which met with neither the approval of Bonn nor the rest of the Western Alliance.

In January 1990 the opposition was invited into the Modrow government to prepare for elections, which were held on 18 March, the first free vote in the East since the communists took power in 1949. At the polling station on Pankow's Mayakowsky Ring, the traditional haunt of the old élite, the former mighty emerged grudgingly to exercise the franchise they had denied to their people. Lotte Ulbricht, Walter's ninety-year-old widow, gazed stonily ahead as she marched to collect her voting papers, and a look of confusion spread across her features when she surveyed the choice of candidates from over sixty parties and groups.

Elsewhere, the public was more cheerful, queuing from the early hours in its enthusiasm to enjoy the novelty of a vote, and revelling in the new secrecy, which was taken so seriously by many East Germans that they refused to divulge their voting intentions even to families and friends.

The result was a sweeping victory for the conservative Christian Democrats, led by a viola-playing human rights lawyer, Lothar de Maizière. It was a vote not so much for the party itself, which had a rather dishonourable past in the east as a 'joke party' in the service of the ruling communists (and de Maizière was a little known figure), but for the western Christian Democrats and their promise of a monetary and state merger as quickly as possible.

For the human rights activists who had started the gentle revolution of 1989 the result was a bitter disappointment. While the people felt a debt of gratitude to their dissidents, they sought refuge from the country's economic plight and crisis of identity in the established parties of the West. The coalition representing New Forum and other protest groups received a mere 3 per cent of the vote. 'That night I felt very downcast,' recalls the Forum's Jens Reich. 'But then I reminded myself that we had free elections, freedom of travel and freedom from the old repressive apparatus which had dominated all our lives for so long. Actually we had achieved what we wanted.'

There is nevertheless a residual bitterness among dissidents, who look enviously at Poland and Czechoslovakia where the protestors 'of the first hour' eventually ended up in power. Ultimately, East Germany's opposition paid for its early timidity and lack of a clear alternative to communism by being marginalized from power. They regret that their society rushed through its renewal process into the arms of the West and the haven of the Deutschmark, and feel that an enforced loss of identity – one that had been forged in opposition to the regime – was the price demanded for monetary and state merger. They also bemoan West Germany's domination of the country's first free elections, where strategies were mapped out on the computers of Bonn and the main parties dispensed Coca-Cola and bananas at the hustings to woo the voters.

As early as late 1989, East Germans who wanted to reform rather than abolish their state had sensed that their cause was doomed. On New Year's Eve, as several hundred thousand Berliners swamped the Brandenburg Gate in a frantic orgy of togetherness, I celebrated with friends I had known since the difficult days of the mid-eighties, friends who had stayed in the East in the hope of changing the system while preserving an alternative to the West. For all the party paint and sparkling wine, the mood was one of apprehension tinged with nostalgia. At midnight we clambered on to the tenement roof to look down on the crowds hurrying towards the Gate from both sides. Gazing across the roofs at the fireworks flashing across the sky and at the jubilant masses cheering below, we all knew that this was the end of an era, that next New year things would be very different.

Today one still hear the angry cry, 'This isn't what we went on to the streets for, our aims were higher than this.' That is true, but it is what the majority of East Germans – too scared or unmotivated to go on to the streets – sat at home and desired. For the opposition, the previous months had been reminiscent of the epilogue of Brecht's *Caucasian Chalk Circle* called 'A short, golden time – almost of justice'. Now their time too had passed. The people had rejected both communist repression and utopian prescriptions of how they should live after it. They had rediscovered their right to choose what they wanted: even if it was the right to bananas.

By now East Germany's sovereignty was dissolving by the day. Even the National People's Army, the jewel in the crown of the Warsaw Pact and previously as strict a disciplinarian force as its Prussian forebear, was beginning to look ragged. It was perhaps little wonder. The newly-elected Defence Minister, Rainer Eppelmann, was a pacifist church minister who had formerly been imprisoned for his refusal to do military service and as such, was not a figure to inspire much enthusiasm within the armed forces.

On a visit to the show-piece First Artillery Regiment in Lehnitz, I expected to find East German pride intact at least among the military. The captain in charge of training was gloomy. 'The first question the recruits ask is, "Why is there still an East German army when everything else is collapsing here?" The second is, "Who are we supposed to think is the enemy now?"'

The new recruits, slouching back after their swearing-in ceremony (motto: 'We defend the gains of the glorious Soviet revolution'), looked unwilling to defend the revolution, or anything else for that matter, but they were at least relieved by the liberalizations. Previously, conscripts had had to wear uniform even off-duty, a ruling which made East Germany look as if it were constantly under occupation by its own troops.

The new government admitted for the first time East Germany's joint historical responsibility for the Third Reich's persecution of Jews, and apologized to the Jewish community for the anti-Semitism practised by communist East Germany as a result of its strong pro-Arab orientation. Within weeks of entering office it swept away the commitment to a command economy and removed the symbol of the hammer and compasses from official buildings.

The People's Chamber was no longer the old 'rubber-stamp palace', but it was unlike a Western parliament either. The bonds forged in opposition proved stronger than the newly-knotted party ties. Reform communists, Christian Democrats and former dissidents chatted easily together in the corridors and applauded each others' speeches. Asked about this strangely clubbable atmosphere by an uncomprehending Western reporter, the conservative Defence Minister Eppelmann replied, 'I was defended by Gregor Gysi (the communist leader) in court in the days when no one else would touch my case. How can I hurl abuse at him now and look as though I mean it?' That was the noble side of it: many also shared the bond of guilty secrets, recognizing or suspecting each other as former Stasi informers.

But the days of East Germany's cosy existence were numbered. Currency union with the Federal Republic and the end of all border controls was agreed for July and the whole country prepared for 'D-Mark Day', exploring the crevices of sofas and the backs of drawers for forgotten hoards of Ostmarks to be banked and converted into hard currency.

Before then came the hoarding – 'hamster-buying' as the German phrase has it – as thrifty housewives tried to stock up on products bought with Eastern currency. For weeks, there was no washing powder and bathroom cleaner to be had east of the Elbe. The tools of drudgery could be purchased perfectly well with the old currency, but for excitement and liberation, they wanted the new.

The arrival of the Deutschmark was a rushed affair, the timetable forced ahead by the continued exodus of East Germans to the prosperous West. Kohl hoped to stem the tide by giving easterners the much-coveted hard currency, but a year later the migration was continuing apace, with 15,000 people still moving west each month, lured by higher wages and better job prospects. Reading newspaper reports about the westward haemorrhage of the east's youngest, brightest and highest-skilled, it was often hard to tell summer 1990 from summer 1961, when the exodus had prompted the regime to erect the Wall.

Some 300,000 bleary-eyed *Pendler* (shuttlers) still travel up to ten hours every day back and forth across the old border to fill the poorly-paid manual jobs spurned by their western compatriots.

The Deutschmark was swapped for Ostmarks at the artificial rate of one-to-one up to a 4,000 Mark ceiling and thereafter two-to-one. This provided Easterners with an immediate windfall of hard currency. But this exchange rate was a blow to the struggling state enterprises, pushing their costs up to Western levels overnight and forcing them to compete on the same terms as their competitors in the Federal Republic. To Kohl's barely contained fury, the outgoing president of the Bundesbank, Karl Otto Pöhl, later described currency union as a 'disaster', saying that it had taken place at the wrong rate with too little preparation. Combined with the loss of the eastern European export market based on the soft rouble, the effects on industry were devastating. By October 1991 nearly a third of east Germans were unemployed or on government work schemes, while in the still flourishing west German economy only six per cent of the workforce had no jobs.

On the evening of 30 June the pubs overflowed with revellers downing their last cheap East German beers and the tills rattled for the last time to the tinny sound of Ostmarks. There was understandably little nostalgia for the currency itself. Nevertheless, for most people the real valediction of the state took place now rather than on unification day three months later, by which time it would be all over bar the speeches. Tipsy voices were raised for the last time in the East German national anthem 'Arisen From Ruins'.

Outside tiny banks in the suburbs, queues to withdraw the first Deutschmarks began well before midnight. Everyone had their dream that they wanted to turn into reality with the crisp new notes: holidays in Greece, washing machines and new cars were the favourites. Then there were the less expensive but equally hankered-after treats: real brand-name jeans to replace Cuban counterfeits, breakfast on the West Berlin Kurfürstendamm, colour films for the family camera. Purchases few Westerners would think twice about, but which the East's moribund economy had been unable to supply.

Nothing moves the modern German soul, east or west, to such flights of emotion as the Deutschmark, so it was only natural that the country should have taken leave of its collective senses that night. Television cameras barged into a hospital to film the first baby born into a hard-currency world. 'How do you feel?' asked the reporter. 'Just glad that it's there at last,' breathed the wan mother. She was talking about the Deutschmark, of course. Chancellor Kohl announced that the monetary merger 'would leave no one worse of and many better off': words which were to be thrown back at him mercilessly by the opposition and by many in the east when the side-effects of currency union – collapse of the eastern economy and spiralling unemployment – began to make themselves felt. It did not take long. Several East German factories were bankrupt the day after the union, many more in the following months.

With the population in the grip of an almighty economic hangover, the preparations for unification took place in a generally bad-tempered atmosphere. Lothar de Maizière, the mousy East German leader, was struggling to hold his querulous grand coalition together (the SPD finally voted to leave in August). He found Chancellor Kohl an increasingly difficult negotiating partner, and vice versa. De Maizière, true to the Huguenot stock from which he comes, is a sombre, rather stubborn man who, while prepared to embrace western democracy, was intent on preventing unification taking on the appearance of a corporate takeover. The view held by Chancellor Kohl and the vast majority of senior politicians in Bonn was that the East should be grateful for the economic salvation unity would bring and not dwell with too much nostalgia on what it was losing. The chasm of understanding between the politicians of Bonn and the newcomers from East Berlin represented the division of experience between the two Germanies.

Like most *Wessis* who had scarcely set foot in the country before November 1989, Bonn's politicians knew it only as a ghastly ragbag of images: the Berlin Wall, steroid-aided Olympic medallists, gerontobureaucratic leadership and crumbling houses. They could not imagine the East wanting anything other than to be rid of the old ways as fast as possible. Certainly they wanted no truck with the emotional hangover of the East German past.

De Maizière was an irritant to them from the moment he stood up in parliament to give his opening speech after the March victory. The speech bolstered his popularity at home as fast as it reduced it in Bonn, calling on the West to show more generosity and respect for the East's dignity and reminding Chancellor Kohl that the East was not dead yet. 'We have given our "yes" to unity. But we still have a decisive word to say about the road to it . . . unity must come as quickly as possible, but its conditions must be as good, as sensible as possible.'

His enthusiasm for establishing symbolic bridges between his country's past and future was touching, if sometimes a mite absurd. He approached Chancellor Kohl with a plan to adapt the German national anthem so that the first verse of the East German anthem could be set to the music of Handel's *Deutschlandlied.* An accomplished musician, he even wrote out the score of the new hybrid anthem and laid it on the negotiating table to prove that it worked (this was no accident: in 1949, Johannes R. Becher and Hanns Eisler had deliberately kept the metre of the Eastern anthem congruent with the western one, anticipating eventual unification albeit on socialist terms). This ill-fated musical interlude appears to have been the decisive breach between the two men. The Chancellor thought de Maizière eccentric and sentimental, and resented his pride and lack of gratitude. Wolfgang Schäuble, the interior minister who negotiated the unity treaty, recalls with some bite that he had to remind the East German leader that 'it was a matter of the GDR's accession to the Federal Republic and not the other way round'.

Within a short time, however, the economic effects of currency union had dangerously destabilized the East. The proud leader was forced to fly to the Chancellor's Austrian holiday home to request that unity be concluded as swiftly as possible to ward off social unrest. From then on he lost control of events, struggling, mainly in vain, to make his voice heard as the technocrats moved in to set the timetable for unification.

On the morning of 2 October 1990, less than eleven months after the fall of the Wall, the post-war era in Germany ended. The three Western Allies lowered their flags and ceded their status as occupying powers in West Berlin, relinquishing control of the city in a joint statement declaring, 'We three commandants will shortly leave Berlin and we shall carry with us a feeling of satisfaction that our collective efforts have been a success. The Berlin which we leave will be whole and free.' The Allies also took down their flags at the Dreilinden border post. After forty-five years of Allied control and division, the twin prices paid for the Second World War, Germany was to regain Berlin as its capital and claim its unity.

At the last session of the Volkskammer parliament de Maizière spoke of 'an atmosphere of satisfaction tinged with melancholy' and admitted that his 170 days in office, which had culminated in ungainly quarrels over the exact date and constitutional manner of unification, had not always been successful, 'We were not always on top of the task. There were times when the legacy of the past seemed almost too heavy to bear.' It was, he added, like a school-leaving party: 'A chapter is over and you find yourself remembering only the good bits.'

As midnight struck, a giant German flag was unfurled outside the Reichstag and the West German national anthem 'Einigkeit und Recht und Freiheit' ('Unity and Justice and Freedom') rang out. There were fireworks across Berlin, beery embraces and folk-songs as more than a million revellers converged again on the Brandenburg Gate, but the celebrations often bore a ritualistic feeling. Effective unification had occurred with the arrival of the Deutschmark, and the tribulations facing the new Germany were by now too close to be hidden behind Dionysian revelling.

De Maizière was not alone in his melancholy. On 3 October 1991, a country ceased to exist, and with it a large chunk of the identity of its citizens. Not the flag-waving, ideological fervour its self-deluding old élite had hoped for, but the bond of those who had suffered, laughed and finally revolted together. From today, the old certainties were gone, the cosy warmth of the antiquated provincialism which remained the domin- ant ethos of the East to its end, had evaporated. Konrad Weiss, a dissident of 1989 and a supporter of rapid unity, commented with some discomfiture that the reality was rather like having your country pulled from under your feet.

Many West Germans, too, watched the celebrations with unease, sensing that the easy days of ever-increasing growth and unassailed prosperity were at an end. While every village throughout the East celebrated at midnight, few cities in West Germany could raise even a cheer on the streets to mark the event. From now on, 16 million east Germans and 60 million west Germans, separated by opposing systems for more than four decades, were back under one roof. On this day they were a nation united. New divisions replacing the old would be felt in the months to come.

10

One Nation

In Our Newly Built Flat

People here saved for half a lifetime for a spluttering Trabant. Then along comes the smooth Mercedes society and makes our whole existence, our dreams and our identity, laughable. Never mind the patients, sometimes I feel lost and depressed.

> Hans Joachim Maaz, a psychotherapist, describing the trauma
> of a people coming to terms with life in the west

On May Day 1989, 800,000 people marched down East Berlin's Karl-Marx-Allee, past the platform where a tottering Erich Honecker raised a gracious hand to his citizens. They responded with hearty if tuneless renderings of their carefully prepared, spontaneous hymns of gratitude. Herr Honecker craned to hear the words, and suddenly a smile of pure delight broke through his habitual grimace as Group 23 passed by, under a giant banner of an urban skyline, intoning to an oompah-beat:

> How good it is to live in a newly built flat
> In Marzahn, in Marzahn
> The neighbours are so friendly, always time for a beer
> In Marzahn, in Marzahn.

Nowadays, outside the overfilled employment exchange amidst the tower blocks, the intercessors have concocted a new version:

> How good it is to queue in our newly-opened dole office
> In Marzahn, in Marzahn.

The estate, sprawling over thirty square kilometres, houses 170,000 east Berliners, of whom 60,000 are now looking for work in the wake of the economic collapse. Barely ten years old, the area already has the air of a triste tribute to the architectural ideal of the socialist past. The dole office has been hastily installed in a vacant apartment block – the invisible hands in East Berlin's planning department had catered for youth clubs, OAPs, single mothers and Vietnamese guest workers in Marzahn, but in the safe stagnation of the seventies a dole office was something, like bananas and VW Golfs, that only the West had.

Just up the road in Hohenschönhausen, the next clump of apartment blocks, a milestone in Herr Honecker's grand housing design was celebrated by a personal visit. You can still see the nail-holes from the plaque which read: 'Here, on 12 October 1988, in the presence of the General Secretary of the Central Committee of the Socialist Unity Party of Germany and President of the Council of State Erich Honecker, the three millionth apartment was given to the people within the framework of the housing programme, the heart of the Party's Social Policies instigated in 1971.'

The plaque is gone now and so is the Fischer family, the recipients of this particular largesse. They fled their historic home after becoming the targets of a hate-mail campaign and threats. 'Everyone thought we must have been in the Stasi because we were given that famous flat,' mutters a taciturn Herr Fischer. 'Actually it was because I am a roofer by trade like Honecker and it's been nothing but a damn curse from the day we got it.'

Newly-built flats for roofers were the symbol of success the regime prized above all others: concrete monuments to the state's care of its workers. But alongside the flesh-and-blood proletariat were installed the legions of trusty employees of the security police, border troops, army, and civil servants.

A flat here was the first lowly rung on the ladder of privilege extended to those the state needed most. Even now, the inhabitants still gossip about the possible Stasi affiliations of their neighbours. 'He must have been in the Firm. He had only been here for two weeks and they came to install a telephone,' they murmur. Everyone knows that ordinary mortals, outside the 'Firm's' protection, had to wait seven years for a line.

In Marzahn they have not been as quick to turn their backs on the old ways as elsewhere in the city. Gregor Gysi, head of the Party of Democratic Socialism which rose from the ashes of the old Communist Party, has the PDS's only direct mandate here in an area which, despite the incursion of video shops and amusement arcades, is still unmistakably East Germany with a capital E.

The soulless but modern apartments were the aspiration of many East German families contending with a shortage of living space and decades of neglect of the country's housing stock. The row upon row of identical blocks are distinguished only by bright murals around the doors: a practical orientation to help children find their way home. Its sheer scale sets it apart from similar housing projects in the West. And yet compared to a high-rise estate in West Germany or Britain, Marzahn is an oasis of civilization, the window-boxes neatly tended, patches of green hopefully dotted with saplings which it is not yet the custom of youth to destroy the day after planting.

The pride the old leaders felt in their housing programme has rubbed off on the residents, who staunchly defend the area. 'The worst thing,' says a resigned housewife, scooping up a stray paper from the front of her flat with a tut at the falling standards it symbolizes, 'is the inevitable decline in the next few years. Marzahn is fighting a losing battle for its dignity.'

The fate of Marzahn is a microcosm of that of the rest of the old East Germany as it makes the painful transition from socialism to capitalism, from the enforced warmth of the nanny state to the chillier freedoms of democracy. Unemployment, the once unthinkable evil, is now regarded as an endemic condition.

There is also the less tangible but equally bleak sense of living in the midst of an outdated monument to a beaten system. It is impossible to forget the old days here: a housing programme of the size and architectural complexity of Marzahn amidst the crumbling neglect of the rest of East Berlin was a sign of the government's obsession with grandiose symbolism. Now easterners are bored with symbolism, whether of the Erich Honecker or Helmut Kohl variety.

You may not have liked the Workers' and Peasants' State, says Dirk Barth, who lives in a new block in the Hohenschönhausen district, but at least you knew your place in the world. 'When I look back, I don't know what is stranger: the way we lived before or the way we live now. They seem so unconnected and yet we're still the same people in the same place . . .'

Behind their standard-issue doors each individual family has been adjusting to life in the unified Germany. People are uncomfortably aware of their dual identity: then as the losers of history, dodging round the shortages, inconveniences and repressions of life under communism; and now, unexpectedly, as the victors, charting their way through superabundance, swerving round the mirages of prosperity.

The rich bewilderment of choice and change has succeeded the cosy predictability of the niche-society, where most careers ran along similar tracks and jobs were for life in industry or in the state apparatus. Barth used to work as a warder in the notorious Rummelsburg jail, guarding prisoners whose felony had been *versuchte Republikflucht* (attempting to flee the republic). Most had also been charged with *Grenzverletzung* (injuring the border). 'The word always struck me as absurd: how could you injure a wall and barbed wire?' he asks.

But he did not question the nature of his own former employment and says that he could not understand why people wanted to leave the East. After unification, he was accepted for retraining and is now working in the Tegel prison of west Berlin. He admits that learning to deal with the new legal system is a struggle. 'All the laws have different numbers from our old ones and half of the old crimes don't even exist in the west.'

His flat is appointed with the cheap exotica of an outsize palm-tree and an aquarium. 'When the currency union came I said right, that's it. Out with all this old furniture. It was a new start. I didn't want to stay living in a flat where everything from the wallpaper to the light-fittings reminded me of the old East Germany.' His wife, resplendent in a T-shirt with the slogan 'New Lifestyle', is delighted with the changes. Their two children are already at home with the assorted west German brand names, and squabble happily about the desirability of various makes of racing bikes.

Her husband has little time for nostalgia. One of nature's Schweik-like survivors, the collapse of his country has cost him little personal anguish. 'What is the point in examining your own navel? Human beings are infinitely adaptable. I don't deny that I believed in our society then, but now I see things differently. That's just the way things turned out.' It is a common cry from the legions of Party faithful who have adapted enthusiastically to the new order.

He left the Party in November 1989. 'I had to be in it for my job but I never really grasped what all that Marxism-Leninism was about.' Talking to Dirk Barth provides an amusing reminder of the days when the state tried to drill the precepts of dialectical materialism into every worker, regardless of their interest in ideology or capacity for understanding. Sometimes even the state cheated a little, as Barth recalls,

I wanted to train as an officer. I passed all the tests with flying colours but got a 5 (an E grade) in Marxism-Leninism. So they said 'all right, we'll ignore that if you do reasonably well in your Russian.' I sat up for two nights trying to remember what I'd learned in Russian at school and still got another 5 in the exam. So they said to me, 'Comrade Barth, if you want to take the path of an officer in the German Democratic Republic, you can be bad at political philosophy or Russian, but not both.' I thought 'stuff it', and stayed at the prison. No one cared how much you understood communism there as long as you could deal with the prisoners.

For every east German as immune to the gremlin of introspection as the Barths, there is a Jana and Dieter Schultz who cannot merely shrug of the caesura in their existence. They are the Barth's next-door neigh-bours and yet they inhabit different worlds, unable and unwilling to shake off their old beliefs, to change mid-life.

Previously they worked for the Agency of Commercial Co-ordination, known to the few who were aware of its existence as KoKo, the clan-destine hard-currency branch of the foreign trade ministry responsible for earning the Deutschmarks needed to keep the moribund economy from collapse. They are still proud of their efforts, despite the triumph of the inevitable. Schultz recounts with a grin:

We were some of the best businessmen in Europe. In the West, my job would have been quite normal. Here we had to work in the middle of a chaotic economy, in conditions of absolute secrecy, and still come up with the goods. You can't just leave your convictions and sacrifices behind. I still believe in our aims, despite the collapse. I wake up in the night thinking, 'Why couldn't we have done it better? Given our socialism more of a chance?' It didn't need to end the way it did, but the stupidity of those in power finished it off for us.

Asked about KoKo's dubious reputation – it administered a secret arms export firm and quietly sold off priceless art from the country's national collections to favoured western buyers – he employs one of the argu-ments which featured with increasing frequency in the communists' arsenal as their economic exigency replaced ideological strictness by Arthur Daly ruses: 'We helped sustain socialism with capitalist means, that's all.'

The need for secret outfits like KoKo was, he admits, a symptom of the gradual deformation of the socialist idea. 'Our jobs were part of that deformation – but I cannot imagine that capitalism is all we were made for. It seems a low expectation to have of humanity.' He is currently unemployed and critical of the efficiency of the privatization drive, which led to wholesale closures of eastern enterprises. 'I resent being treated like a child just because I lived on this side of the Wall,' he says. 'People are so keen to emulate the West that they forget their own capabilities and achievements. As a country, we have sold ourselves short because we were so keen to emulate the West.'

The street names on the estate long bore testament to the already half-forgotten representatives of Schultz's ideals. One could drive up Ho-Chi-Minh Strasse into the Street of Liberation and the Alley of the Cosmonauts for a quick history lesson. The Karl Maron Strasse, commemorating the first interior minister, intersected neatly with Heinrich Rau Strasse (instigator of the socialist planned economy). But this litany of socialist heroes is being wiped off the city's street maps as the names and symbols of the old state are discarded by a society intent on a ritual cleansing and renewal. The process verges on the obsessional. After a local whip-round raised the cash to topple the statue of Lenin from the square bearing his name (to be rechristened Square of the United Nations), many Berliners began to question whether – in the troubled new Germany – there were not worthier causes for public charity.

Sooner or later, says the Berlin Senate, the names will all have to go, but as a resigned spokesman explained, westerners have enough trouble finding their way around the housing estates as it is, and altering them too fast would simply create a giant maze.

For the uninitiated, Marzahn is quite enough of a maze already. Lothar Viebig, a policeman from the west, has been on loan to the district for the last year to help build up a force strong enough to cope with rising crime. He listens to the blur of instructions on his walkie-talkie and calls to his eastern colleague Lothar Schaal for clarification: 'Otto-something-or-other-Street. Why did you lot have so many Ottos?' Down at the station, the duo are dubbed Lothar-east and Lothar-west for simplicity's sake.

Lothar-east was a Vopo (*Volkspolizist*, or people's policeman) for twenty-four years and knows every corner of the estate – an advantage in the pursuit of petty criminals who take to the narrow connecting alleyways to escape the pursuing patrol cars. He is touchingly proud of his smart new uniform with its leather jacket, but points wistfully at his bare epaulette. 'I used to have three stars – a sergeant,' he says. Eastern police, no matter how senior, are back in the role of trainees, stripped of their rank to be retrained in the ways of western law enforcement. They earn half the salary of their new colleagues.

The signs of degeneration are already there. Corpses of cars lie abandoned on every second street corner, plundered by DIY mechanics. The wheels and engine have been removed overnight. Shoplifting is rife. The cornucopia of Kaisers' supermarket, which moved into the premises of the state buying hall in 1990, attracts daily pilfering. Alcohol and coffee are the raiders' favoured spoils although, as the manager explains, 'Until recently it was bananas.' Once the symbol of western luxury, the humble banana was the single item most hankered for in the near fruit-free zone of the GDR. I had friends in Leipzig who, asked if they would like anything brought from West Berlin, desired only bananas, which they were convinced were necessary to the healthy development of their children's digestion. Nowadays, the banana is just another fruit. No one talks about its miraculous properties. Like unification, it is no longer a cherished dream but a fact of life.

At night, however, in the shadows of the blocks, violent crime is beginning to scar the estate. Muggings are common and impoverished housewives have turned to discreet prostitution to supplement their family's waning incomes. A special police commando unit has been brought in from the west to cruise the streets here, with riot gear and truncheons at the ready. Friday nights are eventful. The youth clubs are already divided into rival camps of left-wing punks and right-wing skinheads itching to re-enact the street battles of the twenties.

Marzahn has one small victory to its name, however, having sent the first tentative drug barons packing without clients. Money is too tight and the drilled lessons about the horrors of drugs, emphasized by the regime as the 'vice of capitalism', have acted as – so far – a deterrent.

The row of tinies seated obediently on their standard-issue potties at the 24th Child Care Facility will be the heirs to whatever becomes of Marzahn. For now, they enjoy state-provided child care in conditions western families would envy, a fringe benefit of state socialism which will be more sorely missed than all its other dubious achievements put together.

It is still possible to tell by a glance at each child's clothes something of the parents' stage of leave-taking from the old ways. Gone are the days of cosy uniformity. Half the toddlers – indistinguishable from their brethren in working-class west Germany – wear the luminous colours of street fashion, their hair cropped into the current vogue with a pointless straggle of a few strands like a hamster's tail at the back.

The rest romp stubbornly in their old garb, courtesy of the now defunct People's Own Childrenswear Collective, the girls touchingly old-fashioned with peasant scarves and outsize bows in their hair, reminiscent of tiny Soviet gymnasts, the boys in woollen hats despite the bright sunshine. (As in the rest of the Eastern bloc, toddlers were trussed up against the cold more assiduously than their peers in the West.)

Next door in the kindergarten, the older children have seen the familiar world change around them. 'They were a bit puzzled when the picture of Erich Honecker disappeared from the wall,' says Iris Walzel, who runs the kindergarten. The state's return on free child care was an early training in collective living and political education at Peter and Jane level, including incongruous attempts to familiarize the children with the characterless state leadership. 'There will be no pictures of any politicians on my walls any more,' she says briskly. Her thirteen staff (for 110 children) were left with the task of explaining the collapse of the state to the under-sixes. 'It is very hard to tell children that someone who was a good man last week is a bad man this week,' she says. 'Some just said that Erich Honecker was ill, others were more honest and said that he had got some things wrong and that new uncles were going to take over and make our state better.'

The vocabulary is comically reminiscent of a parent attempting to explain a painful divorce, which on reflection it is – a decree nisi between the state and its citizens. Now she battles to explain unemployment. 'In the west it is a fact of life, for us it is still a trauma. The children pick up their parents' anxiety that the current situation will not get better.'

She admits that she regrets the loss of the security the old system offered. Like many middle-aged east Germans, her view of unity is a blend of relief and resentment, punctuated by the familiar *cri de cœur*: 'Surely not everything we lived for was in vain . . .'

'Whatever the detractors say, we had social security here. It was a safer society for children to grow up in. Why couldn't the west take over our good ideas? Why does everything have to be destroyed just because it was the way things were before?' The hankering for old certainties was a theme which often arose in conversations with east Germans in the year after unity. The realization that a nanny-state, guiding the individual through life from cradle to grave, was incompatible with other freedoms they desired has been slow to dawn.

The strict timetable has been abandoned, the tiny desks no longer arranged in rows. In the old days, even the babies in the crèche were put to bed at a nationally stated time. But east German child care remains stricter and more old-fashioned than its western counterpart, with the emphasis on group activity, including that unmistakable feature of eastern street life, the 'six-pack pram' in which half-a-dozen toddlers are still pushed around, to the double-takes of astounded west German businessmen.

Dr Spock stopped at the Wall. 'The parents don't want the do-what-you-like attitudes of west Berlin,' says Walzel scathingly. 'Children should learn to listen to other people and subdue their wants for the good of the group. That's not exaggerated collectivism, it is a basic rule of social tolerance.'

But tolerance is still in short supply in the everyday world of the unified Germany, and easterners' envy and resentment of their compatriots is exacerbated by westerners' arrogant dismissiveness towards their neighbours now that the first flush of fervour for the union is over. Neither side is yet at home in their new Germany.

It was always too much to expect that the mighty Federal Republic would turn to its puny neighbour for advice on how to live. The relationship of greater and lesser Germany, the success and failure of post-war years, was too entrenched for that. And yet the east knows the uses of adversity, how to make window-boxes out of concrete, humour out of hardship, the painfully garnered experiences of a generation, as valuable now as then.

The celebrated flats of Marzahn will remain a part of the Berlin skyline long after the regime that conceived them has faded into the depths of memory. They bear testimony to the fact that it is easier to dissolve a state than pull down its monuments, simpler to eradicate a system than erase the marks it leaves on the people who lived inside it.

Divided in Unity

The end of the division of Germany cannot be allowed to mean that the history of East Germany and its memory are simply wiped out. For the people between the Elbe and the Oder, the existence of the GDR will not become a mere footnote in world history. To have lived here will always remain an indelible part of our biographies. The combination of the daily tussle with the system in all of its negative aspects and the modest happiness which we strove for and often achieved inside it has given us a feeling of belonging together, a separate identity. One has to leave a city behind before it is possible to appreciate how high its towers stood over one.

Lothar de Maizière, last East German Prime Minister,
interview with the author, 1991

Ossi to *Wessi*: We are one people.
Wessi to *Ossi*: So are we.

Post-unification joke

Sometimes the Arnold Zweig Strasse in Pankow looks much as it did when in autumn 1989 I first clapped eyes on it and shuddered: grey low-rise concrete blocks blending into the drizzling Berlin sky. Opposite, the Ethiopian embassy still stands on an untended patch of scrubland, to the chagrin of the ambassador, who has been relegated to the status of consulate and receives few visitors.

This was the home appointed to me as a correspondent by the ministry of foreign affairs' 'Office for the Provision of Services'. It turned out not to provide many, apart from a handyman to attend to the loud and erratic plumbing, a standard feature of East German housing, and a cockroach-killing service. The plumbing is as unreliable as ever, while the cockroaches seem to have drawn fresh vitality from unification.

Outside, there is still a straggling queue for the single public telephone in the vicinity. The model was dubbed the 'glasnost telephone' because it was simply mounted on to the outside of buildings with no cabins or casing, so that the contents of every call were broadcast to passers-by. The waiting-list for private phones is still depressingly long.

On other days I stand at the window and marvel at the tiny changes mirroring the greater ones. I am the only flat-holder not to have bothered to saw off the flag-pole holder protruding from the balcony. For the other residents it was clearly a matter of priority. They preferred not to be reminded of the days when they were cajoled and bullied into hanging out flags. The 'buying hall' has become a supermarket and there are soft-porn magazines at the check-out where the piles of *Neues Deutschland* used to stand. The baker round the corner offers eight kinds of coffee, and countless varieties of mass-produced strawberry and kiwi cakes instead of the old-fashioned macaroons and foot-size slabs of apple cake from his own back kitchen.

Where Trabant cars once lined up in an eccentric rainbow of baby blue, chewing-gum fawn and mustard yellow, there are bright red VW Golfs and the odd lustrous green or silver Mercedes. It takes four times as long to drive home from the centre of town. The traffic jams are unrelenting. Suddenly, everyone seems to be driving, all the time, easterners heading west for work, westerners heading east for investment. The radio drones that there is heavy congestion on the road south to Leipzig, north to Rostock, west to Hanover and east to Poland. Berliners are on the move, although whether anyone is getting anywhere with less than a ten-hour delay is open to doubt.

Time to resort to the number 46 tram, which still wends its sluggish way, like a giant orange caterpillar, from Pankow, through the crumbling Wilhelminian terraces of Prenzlauer Berg, once the haunt of East Berlin's opposition, into the centre. 'You must be mad,' says a neighbour. 'There are fights and muggings every night on that line now. It's not like the old days, remember.'

Berlin is a real city again: as capital of the united Germany it has swiftly acquired both the grandeur and the brutality that its new status entails. The Bundestag voted with all the grousing and soul-searching one would expect of the German parliament to move here, although the Bonn lobby's subsequent delaying tactics could delay the transfer until the end of the century.

On the first anniversary of unification the evening TV schedules were full of politicians, authors and pundits dissecting the fate of the new Germany one year on. The week before there had been a spate of brutish racial attacks throughout the east. The economic recovery is more reluctant to appear than was hoped. There is a proliferation of new, tart jokes in which the *Ossis* emerge as dumb naifs, the *Wessis* as arrogant know-alls. East German publishing houses, institutions and theatres are threatened with closure. Friends, many highly qualified, telephone asking if I know anyone who needs a secretary or a cleaner. Often there is a catch of desperation in their voices. Rents, although still well below western levels, have tripled. The work-force is paid, on average, half the standard wage for the same job in the west.

Chancellor Kohl admits that the economic problems are more serious than he thought. A middle-aged man on the number 46 tram tells anyone who will listen that he never thought that unity would be like this. Both are victims of their own self-deception. It has become a pub truism that the Wall may be gone, but it still stands in the minds of east and west Germans. The error was in the wishful thinking of both sides, predicated on the assumption that because they belonged together as a nation they would get along together without effort.

The Chancellor profited from the 'gratitude vote' from unification in the general election held in December 1990, with a landslide victory for his Christian Democrat party in the east. The following spring, he was unable to set foot over the former border without being met by a hail of eggs and accusations of breaking his promise that monetary union would leave no one worse off. His star raced across the political firmament in 1990, but plummeted to earth like a meteor in 1991. The party will have to struggle to regain its electability before polling day comes around again in 1994. Its main hope appears to be that the opposition Social Democrats look equally over-awed and uneasy at the thought of shouldering the burden of government.

Many critics at home and abroad have accused Kohl of rushing into unity. This is unfair, given the narrow window of opportunity to squeeze the deal out of the Soviet Union and the pressure from the streets of the East. Currency union should probably have been carried out at a different, less generous exchange rate to ward off the total collapse of the East's industry, but even that is not the salient point.

His mistake was not the timing or manner of unity, but the way in which he has dealt – or avoided dealing – with its aftermath. He chose to lull the peoples of east and west with assurances that there would be no major jolts on the road to prosperity and, most specifically, no increase in taxes. There were. He implied that unification could be achieved by virtue of goodwill and neglected to mention the many sacrifices it would demand. Most seriously, Kohl failed to explain to west Germans why unity was a necessary and desirable step, leaving the impression that it had been imposed on them merely for the benefit of the Chancellor and the people of Leipzig and East Berlin. He has found himself left with a population of churlish westerners and disillusioned easterners. The west is only gradually developing a sense of mission in rebuilding the east and belatedly coming to accept that the country which is emerging about them will be fundamentally different in character and aspirations from the old, cosy Federal Republic. Post-unity, Kohl has slumped back into familiar ways, parroting used slogans and avoiding uncomfortably close contact with awkward questions. It is as if his own sense of the historic significance of events expired at the end of unification year.

The merger of East and West Germany has created a unique scenario: it is the first time a socialist economy has been transformed overnight into a capitalist one. The Treuhand agency, responsible for the privatization of the east's old state companies, is the dominant force in the process. Over 8,000 companies have passed through its books, making it the largest enterprise in the world. It is still too early to draw a balance of its successes and failures, but its role in setting the foundations of the east's economic future is undisputed.

The symbolic importance of the Treuhand was appreciated early by the anonymous assassins of the terrorist Red Army Faction, who gunned down its first president, Detlev Rohwedder, in his home on Easter Monday in 1991. It was a murder calculated to strike at the heart of the united Germany and its renewal. In fact, the project backfired by gaining the agency a sympathy it had previously lacked in the east. Rohwedder's successor, Birgit Breuel, keeps as strong a rein as possible on an organization whose vast size makes corruption and error inevitable. She admits that her success will ultimately be judged by how quickly eastern companies can be sold off and set to work again. 'My greatest triumph will be the day the Treuhand is no longer necessary: the day the east's economy runs like any other.' But even she admits that day is a long way off.

Western managers and administrators are being encouraged to come east with their skills. Despite the pioneer spirit of many, forsaking familiar comforts for the unpredictable ways of emerging capitalism, there is still a hesitation about heading east to work, yet more to living there.

My own western acquaintances cannot believe that I have stayed in the east 'now that it is all over', as if I had installed myself here to watch an experiment which is long concluded. 'We really must get you somewhere proper to live,' says one, opening the bathroom door to find that the movement automatically switches off the light inside. 'Somewhere proper' is defined as west Berlin, half a mile down the road.

Eastern friends pop in to indulge in the latest litany of grumbles about insults, real or imaginary, meted out to them by *Wessis*. Much of it is self-preservation mechanism, protecting inferiority complexes which are never far away. Some have modelled themselves faithfully on the West German original. There is a depressing proliferation of aubergine linen jackets and outsize leather sofas. Others have fled into stubborn east-Germanness. On the outside of a crumbling block in Prenzlauer Berg someone has smeared in large letters '*DDR: Trotzalledem*' (GDR: in spite of everything). Cato taken to extremes, obstinacy elevated to absurdity.

It is not always possible to guess correctly who will have jumped which way when we meet again. The evening gatherings around hearty dishes of noodles and meatballs and washed down with Berliner Pilsner are growing fewer. Turning up on one invitation in the expectation of finding the old crowd in jeans and home-knitted jumpers, I was greeted by the hostess in a mini-dress and the host in a tie. There was asparagus and trout. My turn for culture shock.

For most of 1990 Katharina was desperately worried about her future working for the state Interflug airline, rightly, as it turned out: it closed in summer 1991. She was delighted to find a job with Lufthansa in west Berlin. Long discussions followed about what one should wear to work in the west so as not to stand out as the newcomer. After a few weeks she turned up fuming at the condescension of her colleagues, who referred to her as 'the one from the east' and ventured that it must be hard for her to cope with the pace of life in a western office. She informed them tartly that they should try plotting flight routes on an out-of-date computer, with telephone lines which worked only when they felt like it and a management whose qualifications for the job were those of the correct ideology rather than aptitude.

Many west Germans still hold the view that because the east German

Useful character for NR.

economy did not work, neither did most of the people in it. They are unwilling to believe that a political system as moribund as this could throw up the odd university department worth maintaining, an academy of arts or sciences of high standing, computer research worth funding further. If 'unification' was the word of the year in 1990, 'winding-up' was the slogan of 1991. The general rule has been that whatever there were two of before, there should be one of now, and that the eastern variant should be the one to go. After following this policy assiduously, and leaving many affected employees with the impression that they and their futures were being gradually 'wound up' too, the government admitted that closer examination of many of the country's research institutes had revealed that they might well be worth keeping after all. Battle has been joined for reprieve, with only the few assured of success.

East Germany was both politically and economically a highly unsatisfactory model. But the view of it as a total and utter failure in every regard is exaggerated and primarily useful to those in west Germany who enjoy preening themselves on their reputation as models of efficiency. This is broadly true in industry, as its awesome record confirms. In the service sector, it is a bad joke. A west German office is a place where the chairs are ergonomically adjusted, the colour scheme is perfectly matched and the coffee machine gurgles smugly in the background. On the approach of anything so troublesome as a customer, the perfectly turned-out secretary will languidly conclude her telephone conversation with a friend announcing, 'Have to go. It's totally hectic in here today.'

Katharina's experience with her western colleagues is not an isolated example. Their behaviour, too, is rooted in insecurity. Unification has robbed many west Germans of the certainty that came of knowing that the alternative to their society was ghastly. As long as the bedraggled country existed next door, they could feel good about their democracy, economy and culture – in short about themselves. East Germany was a mirror into which West Germans could glance now and then, certain that it would confirm the impression that they were the fairest of them all.

The totality of East Germany's collapse, from proud, stubborn communist state in October 1989 to the willing object of a takeover bid by West Germany one year later, has made it difficult for its people to retain their pride. To their frustration, many of their former leaders have been swift to admit the disasters unleashed by the communist gospel they preached for decades. Günter Schabowski, the former Berlin Party chief who announced the fall of the Berlin Wall, now draws a sober balance from his own part in the experiment:

The inexcusable thing is that we committed injustices against our own people in order to prove that our view of the world was right. These forty years have been a painful but – forgive me if it sounds cynical – perhaps a necessary lesson. If nothing else, they should have taught mankind that it should never attempt such arrogance again – for whatever ideology.

Many exegeses on the subject of East German identity have been forwarded in the aftermath of unity. Most stress the solidarity and cosiness of the disappeared world behind the Wall, what the dissident Jens Reich has called 'the crowded warmth of the cow-shed'. A feeling of being in the same boat together, the equality of the have-nots rather than the haves, the camaraderie of the little people sticking out a tongue when the mighty turned their backs. These were all components of the phenomenon.

They tend, however, to err on the positive side, ignoring the fact that these virtues were the product of necessity. There is a lot of talk about the primacy of human contact, of more intense personal relationships in the east. Westerners who came to live here often found a depth of friendship, an open-heartedness missing in our own societies. It was tempting to romanticize it. But with the benefit of hindsight and colder dissection of the circumstances, one can also recognize how intricately interwoven were the strands of true friendship and useful contacts. A free and functioning economy is one in which you do not have to win the local garage mechanic as a bosom friend to get your sparkplugs fixed.

Needing one another to get by is different from needing one another. People had, on average, more friends in the East than in the West as a form of spiritual and practical support network. The 'coldness' and 'lack of solidarity' of which many complain now is little more than a normalization of personal relationships outside the context of shortage and constraint.

Nevertheless, it has been sad to watch close friendships falling apart, to see people united by their dislike of the communists discover that they are political foes now and ill-able to cope with the shift in the parameters of their world. The regime was a superstructure to which everyone from the functionary to the dissident related as a central point in their existence. Now that it is gone, frustrations are scattered at other targets. East German society has become more pluralist and diverse. Many of its people are discovering interests, weaknesses and ambitions they never knew they had. The similarities, even among like-minded people, are fewer. Painfully often, I have seen one partner in a relationship left behind, physically or emotionally, as the other took a new and hitherto undreamt-of direction.

An alternative, less flattering view of identity is presented by one of the best new commentators to emerge from the east, the journalist Christoph Dieckmann. He sees it as tethered to the old order, and thus shattered by its fall:

This state was not capable of change. Neither were we. The collective psyche of the GDR and its entire organism stood and fell with the old system. Our small, humdrum lives were like this: we belonged to it, it belonged to us. Even a topsy-turvy world is home when everyone lives there. The system held only as long as it lied. When it confessed, it was lost.

On Dieckmann's theory, the bottom has simply fallen out of the east German world, leaving its inhabitants to plummet into nothingness. It is a pessimistic representation of what has happened. But the sharp rise in suicides, the growing waiting-lists for psychological help, the marital breakdowns – doubled in a year – would indicate that he has a point. This is a society whose past identity is obsolete and which has not yet found a new one.

The days of euphoria, when people believed that unity would turn them overnight from impoverished, browbeaten siblings into prosperous, confident fellow-citizens, from ugly ducklings to swans, are over. The old opposition bemoans the passing of ideals in the new society. How many of their fellow-countrymen ever really cherished the ideal of polite anarchy to which they aspired is dubious. But in a perverse way, east Germans *have* lost an ideal in the last year and are suffering from withdrawal symptoms. The dream of the west as a secular paradise has been snatched from them. No matter how bad things were 'over here', one could always dream of the alternative 'over there'. Now that over there is over here, it looks a lot less appealing. It looks like hard work.

East Germany these days is an unpredictable society with an edge of disconcerting neurosis to it. Few want to go back to the old days (although many more than would publicly admit it), but many fear the future. The generation between forty and sixty carries the greatest burden of unification. Unlike the over-sixties, they are too young to have the emotional attachment to the memory of a unified Germany to comfort them; unlike the under-forties, they are too old to profit materially from the change. Many will not work again until retirement.

It is also a harsher place in which to live. The appalling attacks on foreigners in October 1991 drew attention to something that many had worried about for some time: an increasingly overt racism only belatedly taken seriously by the federal government. This is not a problem limited to the new *Länder* – west Germany also has its share of incidents, fuelled by an indecisive asylum policy, but the problems in the east are specific, extreme and conditioned by the past.

Several thousand guest workers, predominantly from Vietnam, Angola, Cuba and Mozambique, lived here. They were not encouraged to integrate into the community but installed instead in barrack-like hostels on housing estates. Hostility to foreigners is nothing new. A violent skinhead movement had been established in the main cities since the early eighties. It was, however, a forbidden topic for the media and never mentioned in the speeches of politicians, who preferred to parrot slogans about solidarity with the oppressed and leave it at that. One sensed racial prejudice everywhere. Usually, it took the form of completely ignoring the problem, though sometimes the real sentiments would slip out unguarded. 'Poor you,' announced one of my neighbours in the university hostel when he found out I was sharing with three Polish students, 'If there are two lots of people I cannot stand, it's Poles and Jews.'

The breakdown of the strict policing system and the authority of the state at the end of 1989 unleashed a wave of violence against foreigners. Many who had merely been cheap labour for the regime were sent back home when their contracts ran out. At Schönefeld airport I happened upon forty Vietnamese navvies, each trying to steer six bicycles into the freight room. They were leaving with the spoils of their stay. Although badly paid by East German standards, they had flocked to the country for a two-year stint, lured by the contractual promise of half a dozen bicycles at the end of the stint. These, I was told, were highly valued at home and would fetch two years' wages.

Only one had learned German in his time here. 'What was the point?' he said. 'They didn't want to talk to us, they just wanted us to dig the railway for them. We were not people here, we were just labour.' He was pleased to be going back. In the last months the hostel had been attacked three times and they were scared to go out after dark. He seemed to be taking nothing back that he would treasure from his once-in-a-lifetime trip outside Vietnam – except his bicycle.

A year after unification, it was hard to avoid the conclusion that the lucky ones were those who got out in time. Not a weekend passes now without the report of an assault on an asylum-seekers' home. In Hoyerswerda in the autumn of 1991 a rabble of neo-Nazis succeeded in forcing the evacuation of a foreigners' hostel by persistently attacking it.

The residents had to leave under police guard, shielding their faces from the mob. The young skinheads who threw missiles and jeered at those they had expelled were not alone that night. Safely back from the action, but close enough to witness it and offer support and applause, stood groups of ordinary people, from their twenties to their seventies. They were law-abiding, quiet family men and women, the sort who shun street altercations with the law, but they had turned out to show their approval for the drumming-out of foreigners from their estate.

The litany of justification was depressingly familiar. 'They have no place here', 'They are taking our jobs', 'Germany for the Germans'. Behind the prejudice, one sensed the fear of these people, afraid of unemployment, rent-rises and debt, afraid of falling to the bottom of the pile in the new society. An easily-defined enemy was a welcome diversion.

It is a mistake to lay the blame for these events at the door of the official extreme-right movements, to whom far too much media attention is given in Germany and beyond. Whether in the form of Franz Schönhuber's Republican Party, which gained a seven per cent share of the vote in the 1989 European elections, or the German People's Union (DVP), which crossed the five per cent hurdle in the Bremen city election of October 1991, they are a perennial blip on the political screen. But as soon as they show signs of success, then a mixed guilt and panic factor comes into play which tends to ensure that their advance is short-lived. More alarming are the non-aligned, local movements springing up throughout the east and based on the old underground networks of skinheads and the generally aimless with a penchant for Friday night violence. No remote control was needed to organize the terror of Hoyerswerda: it was a home-grown, grass-roots outpouring of hatred.

Only late in the day did the government and in particular the then interior minister Wolfgang Schäuble come to realize that the policy of simply blaming organized neo-nazi groups for racism is inadequate. The social vacuum created in the east by the collapse of communism, coupled with the economic pressure of unification is a breeding ground for both violent and quiet extremism. It is no accident that the worst attacks have taken place in Dresden-Neustadt, Halle and Hoyerswerda. These were blighted areas under the communists and they are blighted still. They will be the last to feel the benefits of recovery, if they ever do. They are in danger of becoming Germany's new ghettos, ignored by the planners and deserted by all who have the economic means to leave.

A west German talk-show invited one young Dresden skinhead called Marco on to the panel to talk about the attacks. He might as well have just landed from another planet for all the common ground between him and his fellow-guests. Predictably and painstakingly liberal, they delivered their affidavits of outrage before dishing out sociology textbook theories of how to deal with Marco's feelings of alienation. One almost began to feel sorry for the lad, trapped in a web of cloying '*Wessi*' understanding. At one point, asked to define what he had against foreigners, he responded in the broadest Dresden accent heard outside cabaret parody, 'They don't even speak proper German'. The dialect was so thick and alien to the ears of the western audience that his statement had to be translated into High German by the interviewer.

In many areas of society the gap between the two Germanies still seems to be widening rather than closing. It is as if the speed with which state unification was achieved is being compensated for by the slowness with which true, inner unity is being established.

A junior-school teacher acquaintance set her class an essay on the differences between *Ossis* and *Wessis*. Most of the children concentrated on the experience of their parents, producing percipient observations on easterners lacking confidence and looking more scared when crossing a busy street. One boy wrote, 'An *Ossi* is sometimes unemployed, a *Wessi* never is.' The award for the most concise judgement must go to the child who wrote, 'A *Wessi* talks louder'.

What will it take to bring the Germans back together again? The pragmatists such as the Job-like Social Democratic Oskar Lafontaine pin true unity to economic equality. It is true that one can ill-imagine a society at ease with itself in which a nurse in Hanover earns almost twice the salary of a nurse in Halle. But the dangers of rapid pay-rises racing ahead of productivity are well known, and Germany is a country with an historically-conditioned fear of inflation. Estimates of how long it will take until the two parts of the country share the same living standard range from ten to twenty-five years.

Even that is not enough. The politicians of Bonn, seconded by the Bundesbank, have in common with the failed Marxists of yesteryear a tendency to reduce the task of national reconstruction to an economic affair. Yet it is depressingly easy to imagine a Germany in which the coarser inequalities have been evened out and which still remains split by envy, condescension and mistrust.

It is easy to forget that west Germans, too, are passing through a period of unsettling upheaval. The accession of the east has changed the axis of Germany. Hamburg and Berlin are booming, while North-Rhine Westfalia and Bavaria are concerned about their future. The old Federal Republic was conceived on the Rhine and baptized in its Roman Catholic waters. With Berlin as capital and the Lutheran territories of Saxony and

Thuringia in tow, the country to emerge from unification will exhibit far stronger Protestant elements and will inevitably undergo a shift of geographic and historical sensibilities.

Many Germans west of the Elbe have come to feel closer to their Dutch, French and Italian neighbours than to their countrymen east of the river. Now they too will have to become accustomed to a stronger eastern-orientation, adumbrated in the closer ties forged with the former Soviet Union. The Polish border is just 50 miles from Berlin and Polish commentators have a particularly sharp eye for Germany's contortions. One of them, Andrzej Szczypiorski, tells the following story about his neighbours. He was sitting with a German friend, drinking wine on a terrace in Baden-Baden. The Badeners, said the man, were not really German. They liked good wine and beautiful women and only the Rhine separated them from France. They belonged to French culture and their only link with Germany was their language. Szczypiorski travelled on to Hamburg and fell into conversation with a landlord, resplendent in tweed jacket, sailing cap and pipe: the modern embodiment of Hanseatic lore. 'Up here,' said the publican, 'We are not really German. Scandanavia and Great Britain are our influences. We look to the sea. We are individualists, we need our freedom. We are not like the Germans.' Szczypiorski scratched his head and told the man of his conversation a few days earlier in Baden-Baden. 'Where shall I go to find the real Germans?' he asked. 'Go to the GDR,' came the reply, 'There you will find the real Germans.'

The anecdote strikes me as a curiously apposite response to the despondent question many east Germans often ask: 'What have we to bring to a unity in which the other party is so obviously dominant?' For it may well be that the east can help return to Germany its historical essence, perverted by Hitler, stranded by division.

For all its efforts to be a model Soviet satellite, East Germany remained a bastion of Prussian social conservatism. It never lost the whiff of the nineteenth century. Its codes of conduct were rigid, its children strictly disciplined, respect for elders was so deeply ingrained that it was one of the major factors in impeding political change. Manners were more formal, unspoken rules more binding than in the west. These are not traits which can be thrown off quickly. A whole generation will pass before they fade, much longer before they disappear completely. Even when they are gone, their legacy will still be felt.

The restoration of Frederick the Great's bones to Potsdam in summer 1991 closed a circle which remained incomplete as long as there was a border drawn through Germany. The return of a dead king who embodied both the negative and the positive in the Prussian tradition, gave back to Germany a part of its history of which it had been deprived, the price extracted for the Second World War.

The old Federal Republic consciously played down many of the instinctive German elements in political life, seeking consensus rather than passion in its domestic politics, inoffensiveness rather than determination in its foreign policy. Its priorities were reconciliation with France and Britain, its democratic model was America. It was in many ways a negation of Bismarck's vision of a mighty, self-sufficient and influential nation state. It was based on a paradox – seeking to free itself from guilt by binding itself into the Western Alliance both strategically and spiritually. The determining precepts were those of innocuousness and reconciliation. This could never be other than a temporary state of affairs, although the Cold War lent it the appearance of permanence.

The Germany which came into being on 3 October 1990 is whole, free and sovereign. It is also a country in the midst of a more radical and deep-reaching change of role than many of its own people and its neighbours realize. As a demographic giant of 80 million people in the heart of a still evolving Europe, it is faced with the balancing act of establishing its confidence and sovereignty without alarming its neighbours.

Sometimes, the trickiness of the exercise leads to giddying swerves of direction and emphasis. During 1990, we feasted weekly on pledges from Chancellor Kohl and Hans-Dietrich Genscher that the outcome of unification would not be a German Europe but a European Germany. The image projected was that of the united Germany as political pygmy, burying itself deep within the European Community. At times the language took on a comically fetishist overtone: tether us quickly into a European superstructure, Bonn seemed to be crying, otherwise we might be tempted to become too mighty for our own good. Save us from ourselves.

That phase was succeeded by febrile activity, with Germany anxious to establish itself as the architect of reconstruction in eastern Europe, the Balkans and the Soviet Union. Genscher's critics warned of galloping *Aktionismus* which can be roughly described as the desire to do something swiftly in every situation, regardless of the fact that it might well be better to do nothing for a while.

The war in Yugoslavia became the first concrete test of the united Germany's self-confidence. Its historical sympathies with the Hapsburg empire and the occidental Catholic nations of Croatia and Slovenia were strengthened by the pro-Serb federal army's aggression against the breakaway republics. Germany led the campaign for recognition for the two republics by the EC: a move which reawakened disquieting memories of German-Croatian liaison during the Second World War. The new Germany chose to place modern and, from its perspective, moral concerns above traditional considerations of war-guilt in its scale of priorities. Despite pressure from its European partners to hold back, it pressed ahead, dragging the reluctant British and French in its wake. It was a statement of defiant normality: the right to go it alone, the right to take a risk.

The step did nothing to quell the fears among European partners that the united country would take on a dominant diplomatic and economic role. At home, it unleashed a heated argument about the new pursuit of *Machtpolitik*, or power politics, a phrase loaded in modern German with strong negative connotations. The Yugoslavia chapter was useful in that it forced everyone to think more carefully about the country's future impact and to face up to the consequences of its return as a major player on the world stage after forty-five years in the wings. The task of constructing a strong and stable foreign policy in a country whose geographical position between east and west forces it to nod both ways, will be one of the most complex of the next few years.

Will a united Germany prove economically dominant? As far as the reconstruction of eastern Europe goes, its importance is without doubt and it is difficult for Britain, France and America to object, given their own lack of commitment to the region. It may well be that Germany will gain with investments and exports in the east the domination that it failed to achieve with all its cannons in two world wars.

In terms of western Europe, the Deutschmark is unlikely to lose its status as the strongest currency, despite signs of recession and overstrain in 1992. The question exercising both Germany and its neighbours is whether the new power can balance its economic might with political restraint.

By 1994, all 380,000 Soviet troops should have left east German soil and the forces of the Western Allies will have abandoned all but their NATO posts. East and West Germany, which for four decades have sought to establish post-fascist identities by imitating their respective superpowers, must now turn their attention towards each other. A common national identity, late discovered, mutilated by Nazism and suppressed by division, is no longer easy to define. It may well be that it has ceased to exist and that the task of the years ahead is not to rediscover but to recreate it.

The inheritance of forty years of Soviet-style communism and the imprint of its ill-fitting ideological saddle are unmistakable in eastern Germany, in the architecture of its cities, its polluted swathes of countryside, in the uncertainty and self-doubt of its people. The vestiges of mistrust and alienation, of recent history spent in opposing camps, divided not only by stone and wire but by experience and horizons, also bring less visible but still considerable difficulties for the people of western Germany in the post-unification period.

The new Germany will have to recast itself out of the stuff of east and west, out of their disparate traditions and orientations. It cannot be other than an exhausting and exhilarating process. The pessimists of 1949–1989 were wrong. Uniting Germany was the easy part. The real challenge is to unite the Germans.

Chronology 1945–1992

8 May 1945 Unconditional surrender of the German Wehrmacht. Founding of the Communist Party of Germany (KPD) in Berlin.

17 August–2 September 1945 Potsdam conference divides Germany into four zones. Territories east of the Oder and Neisse are handed over to Poland.

5 March 1946 Churchill refers to an 'Iron Curtain' in Europe in his Fulton speech.

20 April 1946 Merger of Social Democrats and Communists in the Soviet Zone into one Socialist Unity Party (SED).

5 June 1946 America announces a reconstruction plan for western Germany – the Marshall Plan.

June 1948 Currency reform in Western zones and West Berlin is followed by the Soviet blockade of West Berlin. Allied airlift lasts 11 months.

23 May 1949 Constitution of the Federal Republic of Germany enacted.

12 September 1949 Theodor Heuss is elected first president of Federal Republic.

15 September 1949 Konrad Adenauer is elected Chancellor.

7 October 1949 Foundation of the German Democratic Republic with Walter Ulbricht as leader.

6 August 1950 East Germany signs the Görlitz Treaty accepting the Oder-Neisse line as its state boundary with Poland.

19 March 1952   Stalin proposes a neutral, unified Germany which the Allies and Chancellor Adenauer reject.

17 June 1953   Uprising in East Berlin and unrest in other cities crushed by Soviet tanks and internal security forces.

19 October 1957   First implementation of the Hallstein Doctrine – the Federal Republic breaks off relations with Yugoslavia after the latter recognizes the German Democratic Republic.

27 November 1958   Kruschev issues an ultimatum calling on the Western allies to leave West Berlin and threatening to hand over access routes to the East German government.

13–15 November 1959   Social Democrats abandon class-based socialism for consensual path at the Bad Godesberg conference.

13 August 1961   Building of the Berlin Wall begins.

17 October 1963   Adenauer resigns, succeeded by Ludwig Erhard.

1 December 1966   Grand Coalition in West Germany between the Christian Democrats/Christian Socialists and the Social Democrats.

31 January 1968   Hallstein Doctrine modified. Bonn re-recognizes Yugoslavia.

21 October 1969   Willy Brandt is elected Chancellor. New coalition of Social Democrats and Free Democrats.

19 March 1970   First meeting of heads of government of the two German states between Chancellor Brandt and Prime Minister Stoph in Erfurt followed by return visit in Kassel.

3 May 1971   Erich Honecker succeeds Walter Ulbricht as leader of East Germany.

17 December 1971   Transit agreement reached between East and West Germany.

21 December 1972   Signing of the Basic Treaty on relations between East and West Germany.

6 May 1974   Willy Brandt resigns as Chancellor after the discovery of Günter Guillaume, an East German spy, in his office.

15 May 1974   Helmut Schmidt (SPD) becomes Chancellor.

1 October 1982   Free Democrats change their coalition allegiance to the Christian Democrats. Helmut Kohl succeeds Helmut Schmidt as West German Chancellor.

6 March 1983   Christian Democrats win the West German election. Coalition with the Free Democrats follows.

19 June 1983   The West German government agrees to guarantee a loan of 1 billion Marks to East Germany.

June/July 1984   The West German representation in East Berlin is forced to close for five weeks after occupation by East Germans demanding political asylum.

4 September 1984   Honecker cancels planned visit to West Germany under Soviet pressure.

7–11 September 1987   Honecker makes first visit of an East German leader to Bonn.

17 January 1988   Arrest of prominent dissidents at Rosa Luxemburg Day demonstration. Vera Wollenberger, Werner Fischer and Bärbel Bohley leave for England and a compulsory half-year stay outside the GDR.

2 May 1989   Hungarians begin dismantling border fences with Austria.

July/August 1989   East Germans begin to seek asylum in West German embassies. Bonn closes missions in East Berlin, Budapest and Prague due to overcrowding. Several thousands travel to Hungary, attempting to leave the GDR.

11 September 1989   Hungary opens its borders allowing East Germans to leave for West Germany via Austria. Mass exodus via Hungary and Austria begins.

30 September 1989   Hans-Dietrich Genscher announces that East Berlin will allow 5,500 East Germans in the FRG's Prague embassy and a further 800 in Warsaw to travel to West Germany on special trains.

4 October 1989   Riots in Dresden railway station as demonstrators try to spring aboard train to West Germany.

7/8 October 1989   Celebrations marking the 40th anniversary of the founding of the German Democratic Republic. Mikhail Gorbachev delivers speech encouraging reforms. Tens of thousands of protestors join anti-regime demonstration which is quelled by the police and security services.

18 October 1989   After a swell of protests, notably the Monday Demonstrations in Leipzig, the Politburo votes to replace Erich Honecker, leader for eighteen years, by Egon Krenz.

23 October 1989   300,000 people demonstrate against Krenz's government in Leipzig.

4 November 1989   One million East Germans demonstrate for reforms in East Berlin: the largest protest of the revolution.

7 November 1989   Government and prime minister Willi Stoph resign.

8 November 1989   Politburo resigns.

9 November 1989   Egon Krenz orders the opening of the Berlin Wall, announced by Günter Schabowski.

13 November 1989   Reform communist Hans Modrow becomes prime minister.

1 December 1989   The Volkskammer strikes the leading role of the Communist Party from the constitution. Investigations begin into corruption and abuse of power by Erich Honecker and other former politicians.

6 December 1989   Krenz resigns his post as Chairman of the Council of State.

7 December 1989   'Round Table' forum for dialogue between all parties and new opposition groups convenes for the first time.

8/9–16/17 December 1989   Extraordinary SED Party Conference elects reform communist Gregor Gysi as leader. Party renames itself SED–PDS (Socialist Unity Party of Germany-Party of Democratic Socialism). Later reduced to PDS.

19 December 1989   Hans Modrow meets Helmut Kohl in Dresden to discuss a treaty of extended co-operation between the two Germanies. Thousands of demonstrators greet the Chancellor with cries of 'Germany One Fatherland'.

22 December 1989   Brandenburg Gate opened by Helmut Kohl and Hans Modrow.

21 January 1990   Egon Krenz, Günter Schabowski and other former leading officials are stripped of Party membership.

30 January 1990   At a secret meeting between Hans Modrow and Mikhail Gorbachev in Moscow, the Soviet president agrees to the unification of the two German states.

1 February 1990   Hans Modrow proposes a three-stage plan for German unity under the title 'Germany One Fatherland'.

5 February 1990   Eight opposition members enter government as ministers without portfolio.

18 March 1990   First free elections in East Germany won by the eastern Christian Democratic Union, led by Lothar de Maizière.

1 July 1990   Currency union. The Deutschmark becomes the sole German currency.

3 October 1990   Unification of East and West Germany.

2 December 1990   The first all-German general election results in a win for the Christian Democrats led by Helmut Kohl.

13 March 1991   Erich Honecker flees Germany for Moscow.

1 April 1991   Assassination of Detlev Rohwedder, President of Treuhandanstalt responsible for the privatization of east German industry.

6 September 1991   Lothar de Maizière resigns after allegations of links to the Stasi security service.

October 1991   Neo-Nazi attacks on asylum-seekers' hostels in east and west Germany reach their peak.

20 January 1992   A former East German border guard is jailed for three and a half years in the first trial for the killing of a would-be escapee.

10 February 1992   Former minister of state security Erich Mielke is placed on trial for the 1931 murders of two policemen.

East Germany: Dramatis Personae

Johannes R. Becher 1891–1958 Poet and founder member of the Communist Party of Germany (KPD) in 1918. Emigrant in Soviet Union. He was Minister of Culture 1954–58.

Wolf Biermann 1936– Poet and songwriter. Son of Jewish communist murdered in Auschwitz. Moved to East Germany as student in 1953. Assistant director of Berliner Ensemble Theatre. From 1962 he was a prominent critic of the regime in verse and song. He was stripped of citizenship 1976, causing exodus of writers and artists and protest against the regime's cultural policies.

Bärbel Bohley 1945– She founded the opposition group 'Women for Peace' in 1982. Was arrested in January 1988 for participation in illegal Rosa Luxemburg demonstration. Founder member of New Forum opposition movement, September 1989.

Willy Brandt 1913– West German Social Democrat. Emigration in Scandanavia, correspondent in the Spanish Civil War, he was active in international resistance work to the National Socialist regime. In 1957 he was elected ruling mayor of West Berlin, post held until 1966. Chancellor 1969–74. Father of *Ostpolitik* and the diplomatic recognition of East Germany. President of SPD 1964–87. He now holds the party's honorary presidency.

Bertolt Brecht 1898–1956 Dramatist and poet whose best-known plays include *The Caucasian Chalk Circle*, *The Threepenny Opera* and *Mother Courage*. Emigrant in various states, he returned to East Germany in 1949 to set up the Berliner Ensemble Theatre together with his wife Helene Weigel. Brecht's literary estate is now handled principally by his daughter, Barbara Brecht-Schall.

Otto Grotewohl 1894–1964 Chairman of Braunschweig Social Democrats and member of the Reichstag until 1933. In 1945 he became chairman of the SPD in the Soviet zone and promoted the unification of the Social Democrats with the Communists in 1946. He remained in leadership of the merged Party until his death.

Gregor Gysi 1948– Human rights lawyer, reform communist, who replaced Egon Krenz as the leader of the renamed Communist Party (PDS) December 1989. An MP in the first all-German parliament.

Erich Honecker 1912– The son of a coalminer in the Saarland, Honecker was a communist activist as a young man. In 1935 he was arrested for illegal political activity and imprisoned in Brandenburg jail. He was first head of the Free German Youth movement (FDJ) and in 1958 entered Walter Ulbricht's Politburo, responsible for security questions and planning the erection of the Berlin Wall. He succeeded Ulbricht as Party leader in 1971, and was deposed October 1989, fleeing to the Soviet Union in March 1991 and seeking refuge in the Chilean embassy after the coup.

Walter Janka 1914– Publisher and Spanish Civil War veteran. In exile in Mexico he founded the communist newspaper *El Libro Libre*. General director of DEFA film studios 1948–51. Director of the publishing house Aufbau 1952–56, Janka published Thomas Mann, Bertolt Brecht, Ernst Bloch and Georg Lukács. He was arrested on charges of counter-revolutionary conspiracy against Walter Ulbricht and sentenced in a show trial to five years' imprisonment. He was rehabilitated in 1989.

Egon Krenz 1937– Succeeded Erich Honecker as head of Free German Youth until 1983, when he became a full member of the Politburo with responsibility for security questions and youth affairs. Succeeded Honecker as General Secretary in October 1989 and held power for forty-four days, ordering the opening of the Berlin Wall. He resigned in December 1989.

Jürgen Kuczynski 1904– Economic historian and commentator. Exile in London, leading function in Communist Party of Germany in Britain. Author of the forty-volume *History of the Working Classes in Germany*. Work for Strategic Bombing Survey in America. He assisted Ruth Werner, his sister, in intelligence work for the Soviet Union. From 1950 to 1958, he was a member of the East German parliament. Former director of the East Berlin Economic Institute.

Lothar de Maizière 1949–   East Berlin lawyer, known for his defence of church activists. Became Prime Minister after first free elections in March 1990. After unification, deputy chairman of all-German Christian Democrats and minister with east German portfolio in cabinet of Chancellor Kohl. In September 1991 he resigned all office after allegations of earlier co-operation with the ministry of state security.

Erich Mielke 1907–   A member of the KPD since 1926, Mielke worked in the Party's secret military wing. He fought in the International Brigades in the Spanish Civil War and was active in purges of non-communist republicans. He worked in the Soviet Union 1940–45 and helped establish political police in the Soviet zone. Minister for State security 1957–89. Placed on trial in Berlin, February 1992, for the murder of two policemen in 1931.

Hans Modrow 1928–   First Secretary of East Berlin Free German Youth 1953–61 followed by various Party posts in Berlin. Was Dresden Party chief 1973–89. Prime Minister from November 1989 to March 1990, presiding over transition to multi-party system.

Wilhelm Pieck 1876–1960   A carpenter who joined the Social Democrats in 1895, in 1918 was a founder member of the Communist Party of Germany (KPD) and held a seat in the Reichstag 1928–33. Emigration in France and Soviet Union. Leader of KPD in exile after 1933. He was President of East Germany 1949–60.

Jens Reich 1939–   Professor of Microbiology and dissident, was a founder member of New Forum in September 1989. Member of first freely elected East German parliament and of the post-unity all-German parliament.

Günter Schabowski 1929–   Editor-in-Chief of *Neues Deutschland* 1978–85. Berlin Party chief 1985–89. Prominent member of the Politburo of Egon Krenz responsible for media. Announced the fall of the Berlin Wall at a press conference on 9 November 1989.

Karl Eduard von Schnitzler 1918–   Communist from aristocratic background. PoW in Britain and trained as a journalist at the BBC. Installed by British authorities as head of North German Radio 1945–46 but defected to the Soviet zone. Chief commentator of East German radio and television.

Willi Stoph 1914–   Longest serving Politburo member 1953–89. Head of East German government 1964–89.

Ernst Thälmann 1886–1944   Leader of Communist Party of Germany 1924–33. He was arrested in the Nazi purge of communists after the Reichstag fire, succeeded as leader by Wilhelm Pieck. Died in Buchenwald concentration camp in 1944.

Walter Ulbricht 1893–1973   Joined SPD in 1912 and the Communist Party in 1918. A communist member of the Reichstag 1928–33. Emigration in Paris and Soviet Union. In 1945 he returned to Germany as head of the 'Ulbricht Group', responsible for building up administration in the Soviet Zone of Germany. In 1946 he became Deputy Chairman of the Socialist Unity Party. He was First Secretary and the country's leader 1953–71, succeeded by Erich Honecker.

Ruth Werner 1905–   Communist Party member since 1924. GRU intelligence officer in China, Switzerland, Poland and Great Britain under the code-name 'Sonya'. She passed Klaus Fuchs' atom bomb blueprint to Moscow. She returned to East Germany in 1950 and had a brief career there as a functionary, later as an author.

Christa Wolf 1929–   East Germany's best-known author, whose works include *The Divided Heavens* (1963), *Reflections on Christa T.* (1968) and *Cassandra* (1983). She won the Georg Büchner Prize for German Literature in 1980. Focus of bitter post-unification debate about the role of writers in the East.

Markus Wolf 1923–   Son of the dramatist Friedrich Wolf. He passed his childhood and youth in the Soviet Union and returned to Germany in 1945. Worked as a journalist at the Nuremburg trials. He was head of East Germany's espionage service from 1956, also Deputy Minister for State Security. He left office in 1987 to begin a new career as an author. In October 1990 he fled to the Soviet Union. He was arrested on treason charges on his return to Germany in 1991, later released pending investigations.

Political party abbreviations:
KPD   (Communist Party of Germany) Founded 1919, merged with Social Democrats 1946.
PDS   (Party of Democratic Socialism) Reform-communist party, successor to SED after the 1989 collapse. Represented in first all-German parliament.
SED   (Socialist Unity Party) Communist-dominated party resulting from the merger of KPD and Social Democrats (SPD) in East Germany.

Select Bibliography

Andert, Reinhold and Herzberg, Wolfgang *Der Sturz: Erich Honecker im Kreuzverhör*, Aufbau, Berlin, 1990

Bentley, Erich *The Brecht Memoir*, Carcanet, Manchester, 1989

Benz, Wolfgang *Die Geschichte der Bundesrepublik Deutschland*, Fischer, Frankfurt am Main, 1989

Brandt, Willy *Memoirs*, Hamish Hamilton, London, 1992

Brecht, Bertolt *Letters 1913–1956* Ed. John Willett, Methuen, London, 1990

Childs, David *The GDR: Moscow's German Ally*, Unwin, London, 1988

Fricke, Karl E. *Die Staatsicherheit*, Verlag Wissenschaft und Politik, Cologne, 1989

Gniffke, Erich W. *Jahre mit Ulbricht*, Verlag Wissenschaft und Politik, Cologne, 1966

Honecker, E. *From My Life*, Pergamon, Oxford, 1981

Janka, W. *Schwierigkeiten mit der Wahrheit*, Rowohlt, Hamburg, 1989

Kuczynski, Jürgen *Dialog mit meinem Urenkel*, Aufbau, East Berlin, 1988

Leonhard, Wolfgang *Die Revolution entlässt ihre Kinder*, Kippenheuer und Witsch, Cologne, 1955

Mayer, Hans *Der Turm von Babel: Erinnerung an eine Deutsche Demokratische Republik*, Suhrkamp, Frankfurt, 1991

Mittenzwei, Werner *Das Leben des Bertolt Brecht*, Aufbau, East Berlin, 1986

Przybylski, Peter   *Tatort Politburo*, Rowohlt, Berlin, 1991

Reich-Ranicki, Marcel   *Ohne Rabatt: Uber Literatur aus der DDR* Deutsche Verlags-Anstalt, Stuttgart, 1991

Schabowski, Gunter   *Der Absturz*, Rowohlt, Berlin, 1991

Schnitzler, Karl Eduard von   *Meine Schlösser oder Wie Ich Mein Vaterland Fand*, Verlag Neues Leben, East Berlin, 1989

Spittmann, E. and Fricke K.   *17 June 1953* 2 Edition Deutschland Archiv, Cologne, 1982

Staritz, Dietrich   *Geschichte der DDR 1949–1985*, Suhrkamp, Frankfurt, 1985

Stern, Carola   *Ulbricht*, Ullstein, Frankfurt, 1964

Werner, Ruth   *Sonya's Rapport*, Chatto and Windus, London, 1991

Weber, Hermann   *Geschichte der DDR*, DTV, Munich, 1985

Wolf, Markus   *Die Troika*, Claasen, Dusseldorf, 1990
— *Im Eigenen Auftrag*, Schneekluth, Munich, 1991

Index

Bräunig, Werner 150
Brecht, Bertolt: attitude to GDR 142–6;
  Caucasian Chalk Circle 213; death 144;
  executors 137; *Galileo* 39; GDR cultural
  policies 64–5; 1953 uprising 48, 141–4; on
  Becher 66; reputation 135–6, 139–40, 148;
  'To Those Born Later' 63; Ulbricht's
  attitude 43, 140–1; women 144–5
Brecht, Stefan 137
Brecht-Schall, Barbara 137–9
Bredel, Willi 9, 67–8
Brest-Litovsk, Treaty of 4
Breuel, Birgit 230
Brezhnev, Leonid 81–2, 84
Brinkman, Peter 206
Britain-GDR Society 185
Buchenwald camp 22–3, 147
Bukharin, Nikolai 34, 44

Cairncross, John 28
'Carlos' 96
Catherine the Great 4
Ceausescu, Nicolae 60, 72, 173
Ceausescu, Nicu 177
censorship 22, 153–6
child care 225–6
Christian Democrats (CDU): formation 14;
  FRG 83–4, 86–7; GDR foundation 1;
  intimidation 22; land reform 15; 1990
  elections 212, 229; support 20, 22
Church, role of 127, 169, 193–4, 238
Churchill, Winston 21, 32, 43, 45
Clara Zetkin old people's home, Berlin 26
College for Juridical Affairs 96
Comecon 119
Cominform 21
Comintern 9, 13, 21
  School 6–8, 9, 109
Communist Party of Germany (KPD):
  foundation 14–15, 44; Honecker 80;
  intellectuals 147, 153; Pieck 9; SPD
  merger 16–19, *see also* SED; Ulbricht
  9–10, 11, 23, 80; Werner joins 30
concentration camps 22–3, 98, 147
crime 225, 228
Cripps, Stafford 33
Culture Association 169
currency 23, 214–15, 229

Dahrendorf, Gustav 16
Day of Unity 57–8
DDR *see* German Democratic Republic
DEFA 57, 68, 150, 181
Demke, Christoph 126–8, 194
Deng Xiaoping 204
Dessau, Paul 136
Dieckel, Friedrich 132

Dieckmann, Christoph 234
Dircksen, Herbert von 179
dissidents 189–90, 212
dogs, guard 130–1
Dostoevsky, Fyodor 4
Dresden, 'freedom train' fighting 197
Dubček, Alexander 71
Dunker, Hermann 44–5

East Berlin Friendship Society 185
East Germany *see* German Democratic
  Republic
Eisenhower, Dwight D. 119
Eisler, Hanns 2, 64, 136, 216
elections: 1946 19–20, 22; 1949 24; 1989
  194–5, 204; 1990 20, 61, 211–12
Eleventh Party Plenum 150
Engels, Friedrich 18
Eppelman, Rainer 194, 213, 214
Erhard, Ludwig 147
European Community 239–40

Fechner, Max 17
Fechter, Peter 122
Federal Republic of Germany (FRG):
  character 238–9; foundation 1, 2–3, 20;
  GDR relations 83–6, 163–5, 192; writers
  148
Feist, Margot *see* Honecker
Feliks Dzierzynski regiment 96
Festival of Political Song 188
Fichte, Johann Gottlieb 136
Fischer family 220
Fischer, Werner 192–3
Fleischer, Wolfgang 165
Fodorova, Sarah 78
Foote, Alan 34, 35
Frankfurter Allgemeine Zeitung 86, 89
Fraser, Lindley 179
Frederick the Great 238
Free Democrats 83, 86
Free German Youth (FDJ): Brecht 135, 141;
  formation 41; Honecker 77, 80, 141; role
  1, 80, 100, 167, 186; Ulbricht 49
Freiligrath, Ferdinand 21
Fuchs, Klaus 29, 33, 36, 42, 43
Führer, Christian 193, 202
Fürnberg, Louis 136, 167

Gaedecke, Herbert 59
Galbraith, Kenneth 42
Galileo 39
Gandert, Gero 181–2
Gauck, Joachim 105, 194
Gaudian, Christian 132
Gehler, Matthias 194
Genscher, Hans-Dietrich 75, 239